Jan van Ruusbroec,
Mystical Theologian of the Trinity

Studies in Spirituality and Theology

Lawrence Cunningham, Bernard McGinn, and David Tracy

SERIES EDITORS

Jan van Ruusbroec,
Mystical Theologian
of the Trinity

RIK VAN NIEUWENHOVE

UNIVERSITY OF NOTRE DAME PRESS
Notre Dame, Indiana

Copyright © 2003 by University of Notre Dame
Notre Dame, Indiana 46556
All Rights Reserved
http://www.undpress.nd.edu

Published in the United States of America

Library of Congress Cataloging-in-Publication Data
Van Nieuwenhove, Rik, 1967–
Jan van Ruusbroec, mystical theologian of the Trinity / Rik Van Nieuwenhove.
   p.   cm.— (Studies in spirituality and theology)
      ISBN 0-268-03261-0 (cloth : alk. paper)
      ISBN 0-268-03262-9 (pbk. : alk. paper)
   1. Ruusbroec, Jan van, 1293–1381.   2. Mysticism—History—
      Middle Ages, 600–1500.
         I. Title.   II. Series.
      BV5095.J3 V36   2003
         248.2′2′092—dc21
            2002151531

In memoriam,
Nele Van Nieuwenhove
(1962 – 1995)

CONTENTS

Acknowledgments xi

Introduction 1

Chapter 1. Life and Works 7
Life and Context
Ruusbroec's Oeuvre

Chapter 2. Apophatic Theologian or "Phenomenologist 29
of the Mystical Experience"?
Experience, Consciousness, and Transformation
Ruusbroec and Mystical Theology
　Ruusbroec's Trinitarian Theology
　Jamesian Experience or Apophaticism?
　Exemplarism and Transcendence
　A Single Intention and the Enjoyment of God
　Self-Transcendence in Vanden Blinkenden Steen
　Ruusbroec and the Brethren of the Free Spirit
Observations

Chapter 3. "A flowing, ebbing sea": Trinitarian Doctrine and *Regiratio* 77

Regiratio
   Albert the Great
   Aquinas
   Meister Eckhart
   Ruusbroec's Trinitarian Theology and Regiratio
The Relation between the Divine Being, Nature, and Persons
   The Modelessness of the Divine Being
   Nature and Being
   The Role of the Fatherly Nature in the Generation of the Son
   The Procession of the Spirit
   The Persons
Observations

Chapter 4. "Made to the Image": Ruusbroec's Anthropology 101

In the Image of the Trinity
"The Natural Way"
Sin, Image, and Likeness
The Originality of Ruusbroec's Teaching on the Soul as Image
Observations

Chapter 5. "He, remaining God, became man for man to become God": Ruusbroec's Christology 121

Nothingness and the Nature of Evil
The Person of Christ
   A Theory of Physical Redemption?
   Enhypostasization
   Christ, Source of Grace
Trinitarian Love and Christ's Redemptive Work
   Love as do ut des
   The Eucharist as Spiritual Nourishment
   Sacrificial Offering and the Theory of Satisfaction
Participation in Christ's Redeeming Activity
Observations

Chapter 6. The Common Life: Deification according   157
to Ruusbroec

The Justification of the Sinner
The Goal of Deification: The Common Life
  A Brief Overview
  The Contemplative Life and the Union with God beyond Distinction
  Participating in God's Love and Knowledge
  A Theocentric Focus, or Being "Intent" on God
  Separation and Union: Epektasis
  Anthropology, Epektasis, *and the Common Life*
  Anthropology, Christology, and the Common Life
  Summary
The Process of Deification in the Active and Inner Lives
  The Active Life
  The Inner or God-yearning Life
Observations

Conclusion   193

Notes   197
Bibliography   233
Index   245

ACKNOWLEDGMENTS

I have incurred a great number of debts during the writing of this book.

Werner Jeanrond, University of Lund, and Jos Decorte, Catholic University of Leuven, first introduced me to medieval thought and spirituality. Jos Decorte, one of the finest medievalists of the Low Countries, tragically died some time ago. I would like to think that this book is a modest tribute to his legacy by one of his former students.

I would like to thank Lewis Ayres, currently at Candler School of Theology, Emory University, for supervising my initial research on Ruusbroec. I found in Lewis a sympathetic and able reader. His perceptive comments and advice greatly enhanced this text.

I am grateful to all my colleagues in the School of Hebrew, Biblical and Theological Studies, Trinity College Dublin, for creating an intellectual climate so conducive to research. I am especially indebted to my most immediate colleague in the theological area, Maureen Junker-Kenny, for her kindness and support.

A very special word of thanks for Bernard McGinn, the Naomi Shenstone Donnelly Professor in the Divinity School of the University of Chicago, who devoted considerable time and effort to reading earlier versions of the manuscript and who made many incisive comments that greatly contributed to the quality of this book. I am grateful and humbled that a scholar of his standing and reputation was willing to do this. Lawrence Cunningham, Professor of Theology at the University of Notre Dame, also went to great lengths to read and comment on this work, leaving me very much indebted.

I am grateful to the staff of the University of Notre Dame Press, especially Barbara Hanrahan, Director, and Rebecca DeBoer, Managing Editor, for their professionalism and expertise, and to Sheila Berg, for editing this book.

Guido De Baere, editor in chief of Ruusbroec's *Opera Omnia*, kindly allowed me to refer to the magnificent critical edition and make use of the English translation. I am greatly appreciative for this.

My friends in Flanders, Dirk Vander Schueren, Koen Steenackers, and Frank and Wim Van Breusegem, were always happy to provide accommodation for me during my visits to libraries in Belgium. My parents have encouraged my research for many years, and I am glad I now have the opportunity to express my gratitude for their support.

Finally, a word of heartfelt thanks to my wife, Rose Cunningham, who succeeds so well in creating a loving and warm environment in which our two daughters, Anna and Muireann, and I can flourish. Without her love and friendship, none of this would have been possible, or even attempted.

I would like to dedicate this book to the memory of my sister Nele, who passed away soon after I began my research on Ruusbroec. All those who had the privilege to know her are aware of the pain of having to live life without her.

INTRODUCTION

Jan van Ruusbroec (1293–1381) must rank as one of the finest mystical theologians of the late medieval period. Engaging with his works is a worthwhile exercise for a number of reasons. First, Ruusbroec is undoubtedly one of the most radical trinitarian thinkers in Western theology. Second, he stands at the end of a rich tradition of theology and spirituality, from which he drew many insights that he incorporated into a balanced theological and spiritual synthesis very much his own. In his writings we find remote echoes of Augustine, Pseudo-Dionysius, Gregory the Great, Bernard of Clairvaux and the Cistercian School, the Victorines, Bonaventure (through Hughes Ripelin of Strasbourg), Meister Eckhart and the Dominican School, and beguine spirituality. Third, Ruusbroec stands at the dawn of the modern age, in which the nature of "mystical theology" drastically changed in nature, and his works therefore witness to both the legacy of the past and the concerns of the new era. Unfortunately, his works remain relatively unknown outside the Dutch-speaking world and no major study on his theology exists. This study hopes to further the knowledge and interest in Ruusbroec's oeuvre outside the circle of traditional Ruusbroec studies (usually conducted by Flemish and Dutch scholars in Antwerp).

The title of this study implies a certain perspective on the nature of mystical theology, about which I say more in the following chapters. Indeed, calling Ruusbroec a "mystical theologian" makes a claim that must be substantiated throughout this book. After all, Ruusbroec is usually characterized as a "mystic" or even a "phenomenologist of the mystical experience" whose main relevance lies in his descriptions of a direct, unmediated mystical union between God and the soul. My claim that Ruusbroec is writing in a specific tradition of mystical theology that contains the resources for a critique of our modern (mis)-understanding of the nature of mystical union in terms of an immediate experience of God is a controversial aspect of this study.[1] This is not to deny that Ruusbroec offers some exciting descriptions of the transformation of the human person in response to God's grace—and if one wants to call these descriptions "phenomenological" I do not object, although the term is somewhat vague. However, I take issue with interpreting Ruusbroec's descriptions of union between God and the soul in terms of an unmediated, direct experience of God. Scholars who advocate this Jamesian reading even go so far as to compare Ruusbroec's descriptions of "mystical experiences" with those of "similar" descriptions in rather different traditions, such as Buddhism.[2] This focus on "mystical experience" (so typical of a Western culture in which religion has increasingly become a privatized source of consumerist consolation and "spiritual" self-gratification) has contributed, in my view, to a lack of engagement with Ruusbroec's theology in recent decades. No major study on Ruusbroec's theology has appeared, in any language, during the last fifty years. In what follows I hope to demonstrate that Ruusbroec has an exciting theology worth investigating, and this is another, more important contribution I would like to make. In fact, given the originality of Ruusbroec's trinitarian thought, his theology has acquired a new relevance, given the present revival of trinitarian theology.[3]

Focusing on Ruusbroec's trinitarian theology also allows us to corroborate the recent refutation of popular misunderstandings in relation to the nature of Western trinitarian theology in general. The notion that the founding father of Western theology, St. Augustine, recognizes the ontological primacy of essential unity over personal diversity in God (God is essentially one, except in the divine persons, who are defined in terms of relations) while Eastern theology (at least in the Patristic period) reveals a tendency to give a certain preeminence to the personal diversity over essential unity (God is identically monad and triad) has been convincingly refuted in recent years.[4] This important rereading of the Latin theological tradition allows us to situate in their proper context theologians such as Bonaventure or Ruusbroec who put the dogma of the Trinity at the heart of their theological vision. Whereas the interpretation originating from T. de Régnon's work represents a distorted version of the history of doctrine, its continued and unquestioned use indicates that major texts from the history of trinitarian theology have not been the subject of detailed scholarly consideration for many years.

That Ruusbroec's theology has been almost completely overlooked in recent scholarship was a main impetus for me to examine his distinctive contribution in this area. However, I soon realized that recent Ruusbroecian scholarship was not only one-sided, but its basic assumptions were *obstructing* a proper understanding of Ruusbroec's message. Ruusbroec needs to be seen as a representative of mystical theology—a tradition that finds its origins in the writings of Pseudo-Dionysius—which is a specific discourse aimed at subverting any creaturely notions we might have of God and which involves a radical transformation of our ways of relating to God, the world, and ourselves. As I show throughout this work, this discourse implies a *critique* of any claims of direct "experience" of God. An irony of recent scholarship is that Ruusbroec himself was quite aware of a growing "modern" or "experiential" misunderstanding and was at pains to distinguish his own project from that of those who understood the goal of Christian life in psychological or experiential terms, as were some other mystical theologians, such as the author of *The Cloud of Unknowing*, to mention but one example. However, as the Neoplatonic origins of this theology became more and more remote at the end of the Middle Ages, their efforts were to be of no avail. It is only in recent decades, as our understanding of Neoplatonic dialectics has grown, that we have been in a position to understand their work in its proper context.

The last major study to appear on Ruusbroec's theology was written (in Dutch) by Father A. Ampe almost half a century ago.[5] An introductory German study by B. Fraling, published in 1967, was greatly indebted to Ampe's work, without innovating in any significant degree.[6]

Ampe's work is an easy target of criticism. He wanted to explain Ruusbroec's work without any reference to the wider tradition, which is, of course, a debatable methodological limitation. When Ampe occasionally does refer to other authors to shed light on Ruusbroec's theology, he usually makes reference only to the writings of Thomas Aquinas, although a reference to the Franciscan tradition might have been more appropriate.[7] Finally, Ampe is quite unclear about the exact status of Ruusbroec's descriptions of the union between God and the soul and is not free from an experiential reading as he, quite excusably at that time, did not fully grasp the dialectical nature of the Neoplatonic tradition in which Ruusbroec was writing. Other criticisms are raised throughout this study. However, the fact that I need to go back to a study written in the middle of the previous century is both revealing of the present state of Ruusbroec's studies and a tribute to the last great Ruusbroec scholar. With the exception of L. Moereels who wrote a commendable introduction to Ruusbroec's thought, albeit with a limited audience in mind and a very specific focus,[8] later scholars (for example, J. Alaerts, A. Deblaere, T. Mertens, G. De Baere, P. Mommaers, and F. Willaert) have failed to engage seriously with Ruusbroec's theology. However, they should be credited with the continuing work on the critical edition of Ruusbroec's oeuvre—an enormous task for which they deserve our utmost admiration. So far, six of the projected ten volumes have appeared.

In the first chapter I introduce Ruusbroec and his world and discuss his main works. The second chapter deals in an introductory manner with the status of Ruusbroec: is he a negative theologian, or is it justifiable to read him in light of Jamesian presuppositions? The third chapter outlines Ruusbroec's trinitarian doctrine with particular attention to the notion of *regiratio* (the return of the divine Persons into their shared unity), which gives Ruusbroec's concept of God its remarkably dynamic character. Chapter 4 then explores how we are made in the Image of the Trinity. This will bear out the relevance of Ruusbroec's negative theology: our created being is one with and indistinct from God's Image (who reflects the Principle of the triune God) and is therefore already naturally attuned to participating in the life of the Trinity. However, this participation is only possible through Christ. Ruusbroec's christology, the subject of chapter 5, contains some fascinating points that need to be understood in light of the trinitarian love as mutual self-gift. Chapter 6 concludes this exposition of Ruusbroec's theology with a discussion of the transformation of the human person in response to God's grace. In it, I return to some of the issues raised in earlier chapters. I argue that Ruusbroec does indeed describe the effects of divine grace on the human person but that we should refrain from construing this in terms of an unmediated, direct "mystical" experience of God. Ruusbroec is concerned with the transformation of the human person who acquires a selfless, theocentric focus in whatever she does. By being "intent" on God in whatever we do, we "rest" in God. Thus we will lead the "common" life, a life (in imitation of Christ) in which contemplation and virtuous activity are perfectly integrated in a perfect reflection of the "common" nature of the Trinity, which is both activity in the Persons and "enjoyable rest" in the perichoretic unity.

CHAPTER I

Life and Works

Life and Context

Jan van Ruusbroec was born just south of Brussels, in the little village of Ruisbroek, in 1293. He died in winter 1381, at the age of eighty-eight, and was beatified in 1909. We know relatively little about his life. Two biographies of Ruusbroec have been preserved, one written during his lifetime by Brother Gerard (Geraert van Saintes), a Carthusian from Herne[1] and friend of Ruusbroec, and the other by Henricus Pomerius (Hendrik Utenbogaerde) (1382–1469), an Augustinian from Groenendaal.[2] Gerard's biography is actually a prologue to a manuscript in which he compiled five of Ruusbroec's works—hence the Middle Dutch title, *Die Prologe van her Gerardus*. Gerard's "prologue" is a good biographical resource. Written while Ruusbroec was still alive, probably around 1363, it is devoid of the usual extravagances typical of hagiography. From Gerard's account we learn that Ruusbroec was first a chaplain at St. Gudula (St. Goedele) in Brussels. With Frank van Coudenberg, a "pious man of means," Ruusbroec withdrew in 1343 to a dwelling in the Zonien Forest, in the Groenendaal valley, to pursue a more secluded life. Coudenberg welcomed both laypeople and monks into the retreat. Gerard notes that although Ruusbroec would have preferred to stay away from these gatherings, he did not object, because he knew that Coudenberg wanted to increase the piety of these people and—significantly—because he "knew, as he teaches in his writings, that he could be active 'in earthly matters and simultaneously rest in God.'" (I will have a lot more to say about this harmony between activity and "resting in God" throughout this book.) Gerard mentions that the members of the community (numbering ten in total) adopted the Rule of St. Augustine in 1350. Gerard claims this happened under God's guidance and in order to secure the community's permanence, although the community also may have been subject to external pressures (and the growing general hostility towards people living together without taking proper vows). Interestingly, Gerard highlights some of the background to the origin of *Boecsken der Verclaringhe* (The Little Book of Clarification). Gerard and his fellow Carthusians were a bit puzzled if not disturbed by what Ruusbroec wrote on the gift of counsel in his first book, *Het Rijcke der Ghelieven* (The Realm of Lovers), and they invited him to clarify the matter. Ruusbroec told them that he had not been aware that the work had been copied, but he declined the offer to see it returned and explained that he would write another work to dispel any misunderstandings that might have arisen from it.[3]

Pomerius was born in 1382 in Brussels, studied at university, and became a *Magister Artium*. At the age of thirty he joined the Augustinian canons in Groenendaal. He wrote *De Origine Monasterii Viridis Vallis* (On the Origins of the Groendendaal Monastery) between 1414 and 1420. This work relies on a number of sources, including a (lost) biography of Ruusbroec written by Jan Van Schoonhoven (d.1432) and oral testimonies of those who had known Ruusbroec personally. Pomerius's account of Ruusbroec's life and the foundation of Groenendaal is quite different in nature from Gerard's: it is more concerned with presenting his fellow monks with an inspiring and commendable example than with historical accuracy. We learn that to the astonishment of his nanny, Ruusbroec, only seven days old, stood up in the bathtub, that later in life Ruusbroec was writing underneath a tree surrounded by a mysterious circle of light—and many other exciting stories involving battles with demons, apparitions after his death, and so forth. Taking liberties with historical accuracy also involved the claim that Gerson, after initial reservations about some of Ruusbroec's works (especially Book III of *Die Geestelike Brulocht* [The Spiritual Espousals]), later changed his mind and felt Ruusbroec's works were beyond suspicion. There is not a trace of historical evidence for this claim. Nevertheless, despite some stereotypes inspired by the *Life of St. Benedict,* Pomerius offers some interesting material. He mentions, for instance, the visit of Geert Grote to Groendendaal—an event that is more likely than not to have taken place, given Grote's admiration for Ruusbroec's works, some of which he translated into Latin.

It is intriguing that Ruusbroec's father is not mentioned by any of his biographers. Pomerius briefly mentions Ruusbroec's mother (whom Ruusbroec left when he was eleven years old, after which she joined a beguinage) and his uncle, Jan Hinckaert, canon at St. Gudula in Brussels, who took care of the young Ruusbroec and provided for his education. The absence of Ruusbroec's father from the two biographies has been a source of puzzlement to scholars and has led to some interesting speculation, for example, that Jan Hinckaert may have been more than just Ruusbroec's uncle. But in *Van den Geesteliken Tabernakel* (The Spiritual Tabernacle), Ruusbroec lashes out at those religious who live from the goods of the Holy Church and who ought to be pure in body and soul but "support their children in their own house, openly and unblushingly, as proud as if they had them from a legitimate spouse."[4] Is it conceivable that Ruusbroec would have written this if he himself was what German scholars call "eines Pfafenkind" (i.e., the child of a priest)?[5]

Traditionally, scholars have divided Ruusbroec's life into two parts: the period in which Ruusbroec was a priest in Brussels and the Groenendaal period (from 1343 onwards). However, G. Warnar has argued that we should divide Ruusbroec's career into three parts: the period of priesthood in Brussels (1317–43), the period of priesthood in Groenendaal (1343–50), and the time he spent as prior in the Groenendaal Monastery, after the community had adopted the Rule of St. Augustine (1350–81).[6] The issue is not without relevance, as it impinges on the dating of some of Ruusbroec's works. One of the major Groenendaal manuscripts says about Ruusbroec's most voluminous work, *Van den Geesteliken Tabernakel:* "This book has been written for a large part *(pro magna parte)* by Jan van Ruusbroec when

Life and Works 9

he was still a secular priest, while the remainder has been completed after his entry into the religious life *(post ingressum religionis)*."[7] Scholars had traditionally taken *post ingressum religionis* to mean the move from Brussels to Groenendaal. This then led to the conclusion that in the Brussels period Ruusbroec wrote *Dat Rijcke der Ghelieven, Die Geestelike Brulocht, Vanden Blinkenden Steen* (The Sparkling Stone), and a major part of *Van den Geestelijken Tabernakel*. If, however, we understand *post ingressum religionis* to refer to the time after the community adopted the Rule of St. Augustine, the volume of Ruusbroec's output becomes more evenly distributed: it is now accepted that Ruusbroec probably only started writing the *Van den Geestelijken Tabernakel* after 1343 (while he was a priest at Groenendaal) and that he must have finished it some time after 1350 (when he became prior). It is a matter of debate whether he wrote *Vanden Kerstenen Ghelove* (The Christian Faith) in Brussels or in Groenendaal (before his profession in 1350). What seems certain is that he wrote the following works after he became prior at Groendendaal: the remainder of *Van den Geestelijken Tabernakel, Vanden Seven Sloten* (The Seven Enclosures), *Een Spieghel der Eeuwigher Salicheit* (The Mirror of Eternal Blessedness) (1359), *Van Seven Trappen* (The Seven Rungs), *Boecksen der Verclaringhe*, and *Vanden XII Beghinen* (The Twelve Beguines). This new chronology allows us to see a closer connection between the character of Ruusbroec's writings and his new status from 1350 onwards: in the works written after 1350 (e.g., *Vanden Seven Sloten, Spieghel der Eeuwigher Salicheit, Vanden Seven Trappen,* and *Van XII Beghinen*), Ruusbroec addresses a specific audience (usually nuns and beguines), whereas before this date his works were written for a more general audience.[8]

During his lifetime, Ruusbroec witnessed major political, economic, cultural, and religious changes, which are important for a proper understanding of his thought. In 1300 Brabant roughly contained the present-day province of Brabant (the area around Brussels, Mechelen, and Leuven), part of the present-day province of Antwerp, all the way to the Rhine in the Netherlands (including Breda and Den Bosch). Although Brabant was not part of Flanders, its linguistic and cultural ties lay firmly with Flanders (containing Aalst [Alost], Brugge [Bruges], Gent [Ghent], Kortrijk [Courtrai], Doornik [Tournai], Rijsel [Lille], Bouvines). Despite its economic dominance, the political influence of Flanders was waning, mainly as a result of French influence and the divisions within the major cities (such as Brugge, Kortrijk, and Gent) between patricians and guilds. These two factors were connected: the nobility and patricians sought the support of the French king against his vassal, the Count of Flanders, who had to take into account the well-being of the major guilds. As the major Flemish towns were dependent on England for the import of wool, the count had to resist French influence as much as he could. Not all Flemish counts were sympathetic to the needs of the Flemish towns, and the fourteenth century saw major rebellions, especially in Gent in 1338 and 1379. After the peace treaty between Philip IV and Edward I in 1299, France invaded Flanders and imprisoned the Count of Flanders, Gwijde van Dampierre. The major Flemish towns rose against the French occupants, which resulted in the Battle of Golden Spurs in Kortrijk (Courtrai), on 11 July 1302, in which the French army was crushed by the town guilds, thereby safeguarding the autonomy of Flanders for the time being.

There were important cities in Brabant too, but here the relations between the major towns and its ruler, the Duke of Brabant, were usually more harmonious than in Flanders (where the count often sided with the French king against the ascending towns) and were generally less affected by external political events. The Charters of 1312 ("Kortenberg") and 1356 illustrate this policy. They guaranteed certain privileges to the towns of Brabant. In 1312 Duke Jan II realized that after his death a regent would be necessary until his son, Jan III (1312–55), came of age. To secure the loyalty of towns and nobility and to avoid abuse of power of the regent, he issued the Charter of Kortenberg. Even more significant was the charter known as the "Happy Entry" (Blijde Inkomst), issued after the death of Jan III (who did not have any male successors) in 1355 by his daughter Johanna and her husband, Wenceslas of Luxemburg, stipulating that Brabant would remain indivisible and that the consent of the towns would be required before the duke engaged in warfare. The sentiment of autonomy within each of the major towns contributed in part to Brabant, Flanders, and Holland remaining separate political entities for the time being. This was to change with the arrival of the Burgundian dynasty, which would lead to a major cultural and political flowering of the Low Countries at the end of the Middle Ages.

The details of this political development are beyond the scope of this book. However, given the major cultural achievements of Flanders (especially in the world of religious painting), a few words are not out of place. Philip the Bold (who held Burgundy in apanage from his father) married Margareta van Male in 1369 at the instigation of his brother Charles V, aiming to restore order in France's troublesome northern neighbor. Margareta's father, Lodewijk (Louis) van Male, Count of Flanders, used the power of his son-in-law to deal with revolts in Flanders in the period 1379–85. This was especially true in Gent, where unemployed textile laborers blamed the francophile politics of the count for the economic malaise. Eventually Philip the Bold assisted his father-in-law, thereby safeguarding his own inheritance. In 1385 a daughter and a son of Philip married two children of Albrecht van Holland. These marriages eventually led to the unification of Burgundy and Holland (the lands owned by the Wittelsbach dynasty). Meanwhile, Johanna of Brabant and Wenceslas remained childless. Johanna wanted to leave Brabant to Margareta and Philip, but local resistance forced a deal: Brabant agreed to accept Philip's second son, Anton, as duke only on the condition that Mechelen (Malines) and Antwerp were returned to Brabant and the other Burgundian lands were inherited by Philip's other son, John the Fearless. After his murder in 1419, Philip the Good reigned in Flanders (1419–67) and within eleven years owned Brabant and Holland. Ironically, while in 1363 King Charles V of France believed he had solved the problems of France along its northern border by arranging a marriage between his brother Philip the Bold and Margareta van Male, Countess of Flanders, by 1433 Philip the Bold and his descendants had gradually built a state that nearly surrounded the French royal domain with a belt of territory extending from Flanders, Brabant, and Holland in the north to the Duchy of Burgundy in the southeast.

Flanders (and to a lesser extent Brabant) had known unprecedented wealth during the thirteenth century and became, with northern Italy, the major economic region in Europe. The effects of the Hundred Years' War (1337–1453) were, however, to have a negative impact on the textile industry. More important, overpopulation, famine, and the scourge of the Black Death were to have a devastating effect on the Low Countries (as elsewhere in western Europe). The height of the plague is usually considered to be the years 1348–49. However, Jan Boendale, a Flemish chronicler, claimed that in 1316 a third of the population perished after bad harvests and the plague.[9] There were plagues in 1349, 1358, 1361, 1368–69 (especially virulent in the Low

Countries), and 1374–75. Economic depression led to peasant revolts in Flanders in the period 1323–28, which took on a radical egalitarian character (similar to the French Jacquerie), as well as the urban rebellions in Gent.

Although Ruusbroec lived in a time of great political, cultural, sociological, and religious turmoil, his works appear to have been unaffected by most of these changes, with one notable exception: the religious climate. During his lifetime, he witnessed the decline of the mendicant orders due to internal rivalry between Dominicans and Franciscans, the crisis of the papacy (between 1309 and 1378 there was what Petrarch called the "Babylonian captivity," followed by the western schism between 1378 and 1417), the rise of extra-ecclesial religious movements such as the rather extravagant flagellants, the beguines, and the Brethren of the Free Spirit, and so forth. Although Ruusbroec wrote after the Council of Vienne (1311–12), where the beguines had been condemned, his attitude towards them was anything but negative, albeit some of them may have been in need of spiritual guidance. Given that Ruusbroec was in close contact with beguines and that he was almost certainly familiar with some of their writings, it is important to discuss the beguine movement in the Low Countries. This movement has to be seen in light of the high level of urbanization in the Low Countries (due to intense trading activities), as well as other factors of a more general nature but closely related to urbanization, such as a new "secularism," better and more widespread education (mainly due to town schools), which led to increasing literacy among the laity, and the rise of vernacular writings, especially by women.[10] A new positive emphasis was put on "living in the world." This new "worldliness" implied that it was now no longer necessary to withdraw from the world to lead a fully spiritual life. Although Ruusbroec's life may seem to suggest that he is a representative of the older ways—after all, he withdrew into the forest to pursue a life of contemplation—a more in-depth examination reveals a different picture: Ruusbroec clearly taught that laypeople too can attain the same spiritual heights as monks or nuns. For instance, his letter to Mechtild, widow of Johannes van Culemborg (sometime after 1350), who lived in the world, deals in some detail with the contemplative life. Similarly, the addressee of Letter 2, Catherina van Leuven, seems to have been living in the world. Several of his other letters (4, 5, 6) seem to be addressed to wealthy ladies living in the world, although they are less speculative in nature than Letter 2.[11] This new secularism found expression, not just in original religious movements of the day (such as the beguines and the Brethren of the Common Life), but also, slightly later, in the world of art (religious painting in particular, such as the works of Jan Van Eyck and the Flemish Primitives).[12]

Throughout the thirteenth century we find a remarkable harvest of works written by women in the vernacular. Most of the women writing mystical treatises in the vernacular were either beguines or Cistercian nuns. The beguine movement has attracted extensive attention in recent years, not in the least from feminists. Women who decided to live a religious life outside the convent without taking vows—thereby defying the medieval notion that a woman was either married or in convent—are bound to inspire admiration in the modern commentator. However, demographic factors may have played a role in the origin of the movement. With urbanization, women moved from rural to urban areas. It could probably be argued that both the explosion in numbers of women joining Cistercian houses at the beginning of the thirteenth century and the phenomenon of the beguine movement were responses to "die Frauenfrage"—the surplus of (marriageable) women during the thirteenth century and beyond.[13] Of course, socioeconomic circumstances do not explain the specific religious nature of the response they elicit. The fact that initially many of the *mulieres religiosae* (an umbrella title covering nuns, recluses, and women living a religious life at home or in small groups) were Cistercian is significant, for it helps to explain the christocentric nature of the mysticism of many of these women. The close ties between the Cistercian movement and the beguines—some Cistercian nuns (including Beatrice of Nazareth [d.1268], whose work Ruusbroec may have known) were previously beguines or had close contacts with them—probably go some way in accounting for the christocentric mysticism of the beguines in general.[14] Ruusbroec (whose mother entered a beguinage) must have been fairly supportive of the beguines, judging by the nature and the tone of the poem that precedes the prose text of his last work, *Vanden XII Beghinen*. However, he always insisted on the need to remain faithful to the Church and its sacraments. It has been suggested that *Vanden XII Beghinen*, which had been completed at the beginning of the 1370s, is probably a response to heretical ideas that had taken root in the Rhineland and, to a lesser extent, in northern France and Brabant.¹⁵ In this work, Ruusbroec contrasts a healthy spirituality with a number of heresies, but he does not suggest that all beguines are guilty of these heresies. In fact, Ruusbroec shows himself to be at least as critical of the Church of his day as of popular spiritual movements. Indeed, he became increasingly vocal in criticizing the state of affairs in the Church. In *Van den Geesteliken Tabernakel* he gives this colorful description of the dignitaries of the Church: "In the early Church, the apostles and holy bishops walked across the world and converted people from unbelief. But now it's a different story. When a bishop or an abbot visits his people, he will arrive with 40 horses, extended family and at great expense. But he himself does not have to pay for it. The change (*correctie:* conversion) for the better is in his purse but not in his soul."¹⁶

In his last work the tone is no less cutting:

> Thus the holy Church is now divided into two groups, the wicked and the good. But it seems that Satan has more disciples than Christ. The religion that Christ and his disciples have founded from the beginning, Satan and his followers are destroying. Christ and his disciples were poor in earthly goods, and rich in heavenly virtues. The prelates and the priests, who now rule the Church are rich in goods and poor in virtues[;] . . . the disciples of Judas who now reign over and rule the holy Church are greedy, envious, and miserly; and they all have spiritual goods for sale. If it were possible and if they had the power, they would sell Christ, his grace and eternal life to the sinners for money. For they are like their master, who sold Christ's life to the sinful Jews for money, and hanged himself in eternal torments of hell. . . . And although they sell to sinners holy absolution, [even from] excommunication, and everything that is temporal, they cannot sell what is eternal: the grace of God and the manifold gifts hidden in the holy sacraments, which one can neither buy nor sell, which Christ gives to those who are worthy of it.¹⁷

The last sentence suggests why Ruusbroec can freely criticize the Church and yet demand allegiance to it from his readers: because its salvific power is derived solely from Christ, "the holy Church cannot err, nor can the innocent be deceived by the wickedness of priests."[18] He also distinguishes between sin and sinner: "The clergy has become blind and wanders from the straight way of truth. We must not judge anyone, or criticize or despise them in our heart; for that belongs to God alone. It is especially forbidden to us [to judge] those who are above us and who rule us on God's part in the holy Church. But we may well criticize sin and praise virtue; that is the rule of our Lord Jesus Christ and his saints from the beginning."[19] Interestingly, Ruusbroec claims that as soon as Christianity became a state religion ("when the emperors and kings were baptized"), the moral decline set in as a result of the privileges bestowed on the Church, and, Ruusbroec continues, "many good people were asked by God to leave the world and flee to the desert" to serve God unhindered.[20] This may reveal something of Ruusbroec's own partiality for the contemplative lifestyle.

Ruusbroec's Oeuvre

Some scholars distinguish two kinds of writings in Ruusbroec's oeuvre, namely, the early mystical-speculative works *(Rijcke, Brulocht, Steen)* and those written later in which he offers spiritual guidance to the soul.[21] However, I believe we should not exaggerate the significance of this distinction. *Spieghel,* for instance, fits well in both categories, whereas *Tabernakel* does not really fit into the second category. Similarly, Ruusbroec's last work, *Vanden XII Beghinen,* contains subtreatises that fit neatly into the first category. At any rate, it is important to note that Ruusbroec did write some major mystical-speculative works (e.g., *Rijcke, Brulocht*) in the Brussels period, although the intended audience may not be as clearly delineated as in some of the later works.

Dat Rijcke der Ghelieven is Ruusbroec's first work and was written long before he withdrew to Groenendaal, probably in the period 1335–40. After it was finished, Ruusbroec expressed some reservations about further copying of the work, for reasons that are not entirely clear. Although he had forbidden his secretary to distribute it, it was given to the Carthusians in Herinnes who copied it. As pointed out earlier, when Ruusbroec visited the Carthusians, they offered to return the copies—an offer Ruusbroec declined. He indicated, however, that he would write another book to clarify some of the main issues. This would be his *Boecsken der Verclaringhe*.

Whatever the nature of the reservations Ruusbroec may have harbored about his first book, it is undoubtedly a masterpiece, containing some of the most beautiful expositions of his trinitarian theology and anthropology. It also has an extremely intricate structure; it describes the mystical progress by weaving together many different aspects, such as the seven gifts of the Spirit, the choirs of the angels, the beatitudes, and analogies with the heavens and Christ's humanity, divinity, and the Trinity. As the work has never been translated into English and contains some of the main aspects and characteristics of Ruusbroec's thought, I present the following summary as a first introduction to his thought.

The work is divided into five parts, structured along the following antiphon inspired by Eccl 10:10: "The Lord—has led—the just person—along straight roads—and has shown him the Kingdom of God." In Part I Ruusbroec deals with the Lord, his mercy, power, justice, and wisdom. Part II explains how we have been "brought back" through God's action (the seven sacraments are dealt with in summary fashion) from the exile of sin. Part III, dealing with the just person in merely one page, is followed by a description of the ways along which God brings us back. Ruusbroec discusses an external, sensuous way *(een lijflijc sinlijc wech)*, a natural way, and a supernatural or divine way. The first way refers to the four elements and the heavens— that is, they can function as an external sign or vestige pointing to God. The natural way refers to the way of natural virtues and is divided into two parts: first, Ruusbroec discusses the four lower powers, namely, the irascible power (to be adorned with the cardinal virtue of prudence), the concupiscible power (to be adorned with temperance), and the two powers typical of the human being, the reasonable power (to be adorned with justice) and free will (to be adorned with fortitude). This connection between the four parts of the lower soul and the four cardinal virtues seems original to Ruusbroec. Second, he goes on to discuss the three higher faculties of the soul, memory (or mind), intellect, and will. Ruusbroec's description of this natural way is highly interesting and will be the subject of further examination. He draws a fascinating parallel between the structure and operation of the three faculties and the three Persons within the Trinity. This suggests

Ruusbroec's positive evaluation of our creatureliness: as we have been created in the image of the Trinity, we display a natural rhythm analogous to that of God. It also suggests that the natural way is the foundation of the supernatural transformation; that is, for Ruusbroec too "grace perfects nature and does not abolish it."

The supernatural way is Ruusbroec's main concern in his first work, and his discussion comprises the bulk of it. Through faith, hope, and charity we receive the Spirit and his seven gifts. The first gift is fear of the Lord, resulting in humility, obedience, and self-abnegation. It makes us resemble the poor in spirit (Mt 5:3), the angels of the lowest choir, and Christ as God and man (the very fact that the Son assumed a human nature is sufficient evidence of God's humility). The next gift is, in Latin, *pietas,* but Ruusbroec calls it *goedertierenheyt* or *ghenadicheyt,* mercifulness or benevolence, resulting in charity, compassion, and patience. The people who receive this gift are the meek of the beatitudes (Mt 5:7) and are likened to the archangels. (Ruusbroec gives the example of Gabriel who actively served God and brought Mary a message of mercy and compassion.) They resemble Christ in his divinity (e.g., God's mercifulness) and humanity. The gift of knowledge allows us to attain a proper discernment of situations and people, including ourselves. This proper sense of self-knowledge explains why Ruusbroec compares people who have received this gift to those who mourn (Mt 5:5) and the angels of the third choir, that is, Virtues or the Powers (*doechde ofte crachte;* Latin: *Virtutes*). Given their discernment, they perfect the two lower ranks of the angels as Virtues, while as Powers they command the two lower ranks. Again, Ruusbroec draws a parallel with the human and divine knowledge and discernment of Christ. He then briefly returns to the hierarchy of the lower soul, pointing out that the irascible power is adorned with fear and humility, the concupiscible power with meekness and benevolence, and the reasonable power with knowledge and discernment.[22] This completes the perfection of the active life or the life of virtue. The next three ranks deal with the inner or God-yearning life.

Given that the angelic hierarchy consists of nine ranks while there are only seven gifts of the Spirit, Ruusbroec introduces a lower and a higher form of strength and counsel respectively. Spiritual strength raises the soul above temporal things and makes it free from every inordinate creaturely attachment. Not surprisingly, the soul is compared to the Powers *(Potestate)* always desiring to be intent on God. Here the soul is likened to those who thirst for justice (Mt 5:6), because justice is nothing else but "to be empty and unconcerned with creatures and to be always . . . intent on God."[23] Because of this intent on God, this person resembles Christ in his divinity (in the life of the Trinity there is a continuous desire to flow back into the divine unity and to generate the Persons of the Trinity) and in his humanity (Christ always desired, and was intent on, God). The higher form of strength results in spiritual compassion and sorrow over the sinfulness and misery of people. The same beatitude applies to them as in the lower form of strength. Ruusbroec likens these people to the Principalities *(Princen):* they are intent on God, like the Powers, but they are also oriented towards his creatures in compassion. Interestingly, Ruusbroec draws a parallel between the gift of strength and the in-going and out-going movement of the divine nature. Similarly, the humanity of Christ was always turned towards God and was continually intent on God with desire, and yet he was also constantly concerned with sinful people, displaying compassion and mercy towards them.[24] When discussing the lower gift of counsel, Ruusbroec develops further this trinitarian dimension. He pays particular attention to the parallel between the generation of the Son within the Trinity and the divine touch *(gerinen)* in the soul. (I discuss this in greater detail in chapter 6.) Ruusbroec applies Mt 5:7 to the merciful because they have been transformed by God's mercy, and he compares them to the Dominions *(Dominaciones)* because they are raised higher than the five previous ranks of angels, without elaborating on these (somewhat strained) comparisons. He develops the similarity with Christ's divinity and humanity in some detail. More specifically, he draws a parallel between the fecundity of the divine nature and the *gerinen* in the soul. They also resemble Christ's divinity on three levels: on a natural level (the foundation of natural mysticism, discussed in chapter 4), a supernatural level (the transformation through grace), and the level of beatitude in the afterlife. Nevertheless, Ruusbroec is at pains to point out that all of this is mere analogy: we are similar to the divine unity and activity, but we do not become this unity: "This is not one [and the same] unity but everyone, in grace or in glory, has his own unity and activity according to the nobility (of his soul)." [25]

Ruusbroec's discussion of the higher form of the gift of counsel leads to a treatment of the third life, usually called the contemplative life. In his first work, however, he seems to subdivide the third life into a fruitive dimension (mirroring the fruition of the paternal unity), a contemplative dimension (mirroring the generation of the Word), and the common life (mirroring the Spirit). Those who have received the gift of counsel (who still resemble the merciful of Mt 5:7) bear a likeness to the divine *regiratio:* "all rational creatures, angels and human beings, whom God made in his likeness in grace or glory, flow back because of this very likeness into the unity of their mind *(in eenicheyden hare ghedachten)* and have a natural inclination towards, and an enjoyable immersion with recollected faculties in, God's supra-being, as in their own ground."[26] The exact meaning of this convoluted sentence will become clearer in the next chapters. What we see at this stage is that Ruusbroec makes a close connection between the processions and return of Son and Spirit and the (re-)creation of the human soul. He also closely links the being of God and the being of creatures: "all beings are suspended without intermediary into the divine being *(alle wesene hanghen sonder middle in dat godlijcke wesen)*."[27] Ruusbroec compares the people at the first stages of this third life to the Thrones, the lower rank in the third and final angelic hierarchy, for reasons that are, again, somewhat artificial: they possess God and God possesses them "as his own throne and rest, for they are one in single enjoyment [fruition] with the [divine] being without difference."[28] If these statements are puzzling to us today, we should bear in mind that Ruusbroec's contemporaries were equally at a loss, and Ruusbroec wrote his *Boecksen der Verclaringhe* to explain the meaning of the phrase "without difference." Again Ruusbroec illustrates his meaning by referring to the humanity and divinity of Christ: Christ's soul was overflowing with fruition, just like the divine Persons enjoy the divine unity in modelessness.

The sixth gift of the Spirit is understanding *(verstandicheyt)*. It allows us to acquire an even greater likeness *(ghelijc)* to God. As suggested earlier, here Ruusbroec focuses on the generation of the Word or Image from the Father to highlight the contemplative dimension of our union with God. Here we are compared to Cherubim (illuminated by Wisdom), Christ as Image and as human contemplator, and to the pure in heart who shall see God (Mt 5:8) and who remain undistracted *(onverbeeldet)* by earthly things, contemplating the modelessness of the divine supra-being.[29] That Ruusbroec contrasts contemplation of God with distraction by creaturely beings reveals, as I hope to show, what he means by contemplation.

Finally, there is the gift of wisdom bestowed in the topmost aspect of the mind *(dat overste der inghekeerder ghedachten;* Latin: *apex mentis):*

> Because the eternal Father has beautified the inner mind with fruition in union, and with capturing and being captured in self-loss so that the mind becomes a throne and haven for God; and because the Son, God's Wisdom, has beautified the inner intellect with is own Clarity to contemplate the face of fruition; and because the Holy Spirit now wants to beautify the inner will and the unity in which the faculties are suspended, to allow the soul to taste, to know and to savor how good God is, [for all these reasons] this taste is so great, that it appears to the soul as if heaven and earth and their inhabitants would melt away and become annihilated in this bottomless taste.[30]

Each of the three final stages is associated with one of the Persons of the Trinity and one of the faculties in the soul: the fruitive dimension was associated with the Father and the memory or mind; the Son enlightens our intellect (contemplative dimension); and the Spirit inflames our will and introduces us to the common life, a life in which there is both fruition and activity, mirroring the out-flowing and in-flowing of divine love.[31] We now resemble the peacemakers (Mt 5:9), for we have made peace with God and all his creatures. We are also similar to the Seraphim who know, love, and enjoy God (*Rijcke,* 86: *inden Seraphynnen es ondersceet in claerheyden, ende in minnen, ende in ghebrukelijcheyden*). Again the trinitarian dimension of the highest stage of the mystical union is emphasized. They are the most "common" of all angels, in Ruusbroec's sense of the word: because they supremely love, know, and enjoy God, they are also more intent on the happiness of his people.[32] Similarly, we resemble Christ's humanity, the most supreme contemplative, lover, and enjoyer *(die hoochste scouwere ende minnaere ende ghebrukere),* and the most "common" *(ghemeyne),* available to all who desire him.

After having explained the pinnacle of the mystical union—the common life—Ruusbroec finishes his work by examining in part V "the Kingdom of God." He briefly discusses the external Kingdom of God—the four elements and the three heavens—describing in some detail how they will be transformed at the end of times (these five pages contain some traditional eschatological views, a topic that Ruusbroec will not develop in any of his later works). This is followed by a discussion of the natural world and the Holy Scriptures as pointers to God. Finally, he examines the Realm of God in grace and glory and in God himself. It is interesting that Ruusbroec outlines the main characteristics of this Realm by describing the "fruits of virtue" in the active, God-yearning, and common life. In other words, he describes the Realm of God by describing the transformation of the human person in response to God's grace. The fruits in the active life are obedience and compassionate kindness that have become part of one's inner self. In the God-yearning life we are characterized by love that permeates our body and soul and which makes us intent on God, stirring us to work virtues and to attain union with God. Finally, we are given the fruits of illumination by receiving an infinite clarity (in the intellect) and an incomprehensible love (permeating the whole soul), which leads to utter enjoyment: "thus the common person will reside in the topmost of his mind between being and faculties, between fruition and activity."[33]

From this brief overview we can make a number of interesting observations. First, Ruusbroec's mystical theology is deeply trinitarian. This trinitarian theology is highly original and extremely dynamic, containing moments of activity, return, and fruition or rest. Second, like many other medieval authors, Ruusbroec seems to have a fondness for intricately structured treatises: in his first work the gifts of the Spirit, the beatitudes, Christ's humanity and divinity, the angelic hierarchies, and the constellation of the planets and the heavens (a topic that was not discussed in my summary) are all woven into a highly complex pattern. It has also become clear that we should not take these intricacies too seriously: they are often strained, and Ruusbroec himself does not shy away from reduplicating some of the gifts of the Spirit in order to fit the other elements within his scheme. Another characteristic feature is that Ruusbroec freely transforms the tradition from which he draws. Relating the angelic hierarchies to the transformation of the human person in response to grace is reminiscent of the work of Pseudo-Dionysius, as appropriated in a more interiorized manner by Bonaventure,[34] although in this case (as distinct from Ruusbroec's presentation in *Van Seven Trappen*) the actual hierarchy of the angels seems indebted to Gregory the Great's hierarchy, which differs from the presentations of both Dionysius and Bonaventure.[35] Most of the main elements of Ruusbroec's later teaching are already present in his first work, such as the trinitarian dimension, the division of spiritual growth into three "lives,"[36] the link between the divine processions and the (re-)creation of the human person, including his theology of the Image, and his view that our mystical transformation has a natural foundation (which, if severed from grace, can act as the basis for "natural mysticism").

Ruusbroec's second work, *Die Geestelike Brulocht* (The Spiritual Espousals), is now widely regarded as his most important. He himself valued the work highly, if Brother Gerard's testimony is to be believed.[37] The work exists in part or in its entirety in almost forty Middle Dutch manuscripts, was known in the Rhineland in 1350, and was translated into Latin by Willem Jordaens in 1360 and by Geert Grote in 1375. It is likely to have been written around 1335.[38] The *Brulocht* is divided into three books or parts. The first part deals with the active life or the life of virtue, the second with the god-yearning life, and the third with the contemplative life. Each book in turn is divided along the verse from Mt 25:6: "See—the Bridegroom comes—go out—to meet him." Thus each time, Ruusbroec deals with the conditions of "seeing" God before describing the "coming" of Christ in the soul. He then continues to describe the way we should respond to Christ's coming ("go out"), and finally he sketches the union of God and soul ("meeting"). The contents of this work are examined in greater detail throughout this book.

Vanden Blinkenden Steen (The Sparkling Stone) is a highly attractive little treatise, written immediately after *Die Brulocht,* if the sequence of Ruusbroec's works as listed by Pomerius is to be trusted (and we have no reasons to doubt it). The title of the work is inspired by Rv 2:7. The "sparkling stone" refers to Christ himself who will be given "to anyone who transcends himself and all things."[39] Brother Gerard mentions that the work was written at the request of a hermit who had discussed the contemplative life with Ruusbroec and who wanted a written account of the main issues. Some traces of the conversation are still discernible in the treatise.[40] In this work, Ruusbroec, after having examined the nature of the contemplative life, deals with a number of objections that had been raised against his work, such as the obfuscation of the distinction between God and soul (*Steen*, 641ff.) and between the union with God in this life and the beatific union (*Steen*, 753ff.) and the need for active knowledge and love in our union with God (*Steen*, 629).[41] A brief summary and a short exposition of the common life conclude this work.

After some more short treatises (*Vanden Vier Becoringhen* and *Vanden Kerstenen Ghelove*), Pomerius mentions *Van den Geesteliken Tabernakel* as the sixth work. This major work was also the most popular, judging by the number of extant manuscripts. It too was translated into Latin by Jordaens. It is bound to strike the modern reader as somewhat strange. It is an original reinterpretation of the Tabernacle built by Moses in the desert as an allegory of the transformation of the soul. Ruusbroec attributes striking meanings to every element of the Tabernacle by seeing them as rich symbols of the transformation of the Christian believer in response to the grace of Christ (see Ex 24–31, 40). Because of the detailed and elaborate nature of the allegorical interpretations, a summary of the work would be both tedious and superfluous. Nevertheless, the book contains some interesting passages on the way Noah and Moses prefigure Christ (*Tabernakel*, 3–9), the significance of self-abnegation (*Tabernakel*, 13–15, 231–33), the effects of God's grace (*Tabernakel*, 32–37, 87–89, 119–20, 195–96), and the transformation of our three faculties and the role of humility in this (*Tabernakel*, 54–59, 107–9). There are also some important christological passages (*Tabernakel*, 40–44, 69–71, 110–16, 135–38, 154, 174–75) and, as suggested earlier, scathing criticism of the Church of his day. This was a source of concern to Brother Gerard, who omitted some of the more trenchant passages when copying the manuscript.[42]

After his profession in 1350 Ruusbroec wrote the remainder of his works, usually with a female audience in mind. First, there was *Vanden Seven Sloten* (The Seven Enclosures), probably written around 1350, dedicated and addressed to Margareta van Meerbeke, a Clare nun from Brussels whom Ruusbroec visited (as we learn from Ruusbroec's first letter, also addressed to her). The highly attractive work *Een Spieghel der Eeuwigher Salicheit* (The Mirror of Eternal Blessedness) was written in 1359 with the same Clare nun in mind. It focuses on the role of the eucharist in the spiritual life.[43] This work contains some of Ruusbroec's most renowned passages on his theology of the Image. The "Mirror" refers in the first place to the Son who reflects ("images") the paternal nature and who is the exemplary cause of all created beings, and, second, to the soul in which God impresses his Image. Ruusbroec can then describe the union of the soul with God's Image in a highly striking metaphor: "There is eye to eye, mirror to mirror, image to image."[44] The exact status of the work is not entirely clear: perhaps it is as much a letter as a treatise in the proper sense, and therefore it does not have the intricate structure of most of the other major works of Ruusbroec. *Van Seven Trappen* (The Seven Rungs) was in all likelihood also addressed to Margareta. It is a beautiful treatise, sketching the seven rungs of the transformation of the human person. Again, Jordaens and Grote made a Latin translation. Grote expressed some concern about Ruusbroec's treatment of the hierarchy of the angels. As in his first work, Ruusbroec used the hierarchy of the angels to describe the gradual transformation of the soul. However, here he presents the angels in an order different from those of Gregory the Great and Dionysius. After this, Pomerius lists *Boecsken der Verclaringhe* (The Little Book of Clarification), written at the request of Brother Gerard who had raised some questions about a number of passages from *Rijcke*. *Boecsken* was therefore written sometime after 1360. As the context surrounding its origin suggests, the book is an apology or a defense of his main doctrine, written in a clear and concise manner. Ruusbroec's last work is *Vanden XII Beghinen* (The Twelve Beguines). The title is inspired by a large poem that precedes the main text, describing the attitudes of different beguines to Christ. In his first work Ruusbroec had already turned to poetry to summarize or elucidate his teachings. His poetry usually has a naive, sometimes somewhat robust or even primitive character, although occasionally it becomes genuinely beautiful, as in the following passage from *Vanden XII Beghinen,* in which a beguine complains of her religious desolation:

> Die neghende sprac:
> 'Her Jhesus mine hevet mi ghelaten;
> ic volghe hem na in vremden straten,

Aldus leve ic in dolen.
Haddic voren yet, nu en hebbic niet,
Daarom lidic swaer verdriet:
Hy hevet mijne herte ghestolen.'

(The ninth said:
"The Lord Jesus' love has deserted me.
I follow after him in foreign streets.
And so I live in wandering.
If I had something before, I have nothing now.
This is why I suffer heavy grief:
He has stolen my heart.")

The prose text that follows is somewhat lacking in structure. Surius attributes this lack of focus, somewhat euphemistically, to the inspiration of the Holy Spirit.[45] Some repetition may be attributable to the fact that the work as we know it may be a compilation of at least three or four separate works.[46] The editors of the recent critical edition divide the work into two parts, the second of which is in turn divided into three parts. Part I includes the introductory poem, followed by a treatise on the nature of contemplation (*Vanden XII Beghinen,* 1, 1–867). The first section of Part II extends to 2a 690 and mainly deals with true faith, as contrasted with heresies against the Father, Son, and Spirit, and the appropriate response to God's grace in love. The following section (2b 1–2653) is the largest in the book and deals with the planets as symbols of God and the spiritual life, although it also contains some important christological excursions. The third section of Part II is more explicitly christological in character, using the office hours of the Church as a framework to comment on the Passion of Christ (2c 1–1440).[47]

Finally, eight letters have been preserved, one of which was discovered by K. Schepers in a manuscript held in Cambridge as recently as 1999. Most of these letters have only been preserved partly or completely in Latin.

That Ruusbroec wrote in the vernacular probably goes some way to explain why his writings have not been studied in great detail outside the Dutch-speaking world in recent years. Nevertheless, their original language did not stand in the way of the transmission of his teachings in the centuries after his death. Even during his lifetime his main works were translated into German and Latin by Jordaens (d. 1372) and Grote, founder of the *Devotio Moderna* (d. 1384). After his death, translations appeared in English (fifteenth and sixteenth centuries), Italian (1565), French (1606), Spanish (1696), and so forth. Surius's Latin translation (first printed in 1552) was of paramount importance in the dissemination of Ruusbroec's influence throughout Europe.[48]

CHAPTER 2

Apophatic Theologian or "Phenomenologist of the Mystical Experience"?

Experience, Consciousness, and Transformation

The notion of "experience" in relation to mystical theology would require a full study in itself. However, to clarify the general presuppositions that underlie this study, some brief comments are necessary. I have two major reservations about the notion of "experience." First, as has been widely observed by many scholars in the field of mysticism, the notion is extremely vague and ill defined.[1] It therefore has to be qualified. The phrase "experiencing God" is too vague and lacks in content, if only because "God" is part of the equation (i.e., because God cannot be objectified, speaking of "experiencing God" is fairly problematic, as I explain forthwith). We therefore need to qualify the phrase "experiencing God" in a number of ways, such as a "cosmological," "anthropological," "historical," or "aesthetic" experience of

God.² A cosmological experience of God, then, refers to perceiving something of God's mystery in the created world and in nature (e.g., on a mountain walk). The anthropological experience can cover more diverse meanings and can refer to the quest for meaning, human relations, boundary experiences, and experiences of suffering, overwhelming joy, finitude, and so forth. A historical experience is probably more overtly social in character and could refer, for instance, to the experience that God is with his people throughout history. The aesthetic experience of a great piece of art can also evoke religious meaning. The observant reader will notice that all these "experiences" are mediated, for instance, in nature, existence, history, or art. This brings me to the second and more important concern.

Is it meaningful to speak of an immediate, unmediated experience of God? Undoubtedly, until quite recently this was one of the unquestioned presuppositions governing the popular perception of "mysticism" as well as a number of scholarly studies in the Jamesian tradition dealing with mysticism. It is still the dominant approach in Ruusbroec studies, as recent publications illustrate.³ William James's influential study *The Varieties of Religious Experience* both chronicles and furthers the modern understanding of mysticism in terms of an immediate, unmediated experience of God. James collected an impressive amount of material describing the mystical states of consciousness in terms of ineffability, noetic quality (or illumination), transiency, and passivity.⁴ The following account from *The Varieties* captures the modern understanding of mysticism adequately.

> [A]ll at once I experienced a feeling of being raised above myself, I felt the presence of God—I tell of the thing just as I was conscious of it—as if his goodness and his power were penetrating me altogether.... Then, slowly, the ecstasy left my heart; that is, I felt that God had withdrawn the communion which he had granted.... I think it well to add that in this ecstasy of mine God had neither form, color, odor nor taste; moreover, that the feeling of his presence was accompanied by no determinate localization.... But the more I seek to express this intimate intercourse, the more I feel the impossibility of describing the thing by any of our usual images. At bottom the expression most apt to render what I felt is this: God was present, though invisible; he fell under no one of my senses, yet my consciousness perceived him.⁵

My main worry with James's account, and the understanding of mysticism it presupposes, is that it seems to imply that God can be turned into an object of experience and can thus be "captured" or "appropriated." This critique may at first seem counterintuitive. After all, it could be argued that not all experiences necessarily imply a manipulative, objectifying attitude towards that which is being "experienced." We can think of experiences in which the "object" becomes "subject" and the experiencing "subject" becomes "object." For instance, when confronted with a major piece of art, it could be said, the subject is the one who is being overwhelmed and affected; for example, listening to Bruckner's Adagio from his Symphony no. 9, *we* are being "captured" or appropriated, rather than the other way around. Therefore, talk of "unmediated experience of God" would not necessarily imply an "objectifying" or instrumentalizing attitude towards God. However, if one looks into the matter in greater depth, it immediately transpires that this view is highly questionable. Pursuing the musical analogy: even when the listener passively experiences the valedictory beauty of Bruckner's swan song, she will only be able to do so after she has become familiar with Bruckner's (somewhat long-winded) mode of expression, his unusual musical texture, his layered melody building, and so forth. If she does not, she will not be susceptible to the expression of sorrow and hope, consolation and acceptance the music conveys but will conclude (with E. Hanslick) that Bruckner's symphonies are "gigantic snakes." Clearly, even the aesthetic experience entails a moment of "appropriation." This being the case, can we really maintain that God can be experienced in an immediate manner?

In a world where participating in the life of the Church has become unattractive and some of the main tenets of Christian doctrine seem to have become implausible or even outlandish, the notion that we can "experience" God in an immediate manner is bound to have some obvious appeal. It also meets the religious needs of people living in an increasingly individualized society. These general observations also go some way to explain why people can now "practice" mysticism outside the context of the Christian faith and the life of the Church. As we will see, Ruusbroec identified this practice of what he calls "the natural way." What he has to say about it acquires added significance in the light of our contemporary situation and the popular attraction of "mysticism." However, the preoccupation with mystical experience does not end here.

In respected academic circles some have seized on the supposed mystical experience of God to give some intellectual credence to belief in God. The work of W. Alston is a case in point.[6] Drawing on the description of the religious experiences reported by James, he characterizes mystical experiences in the following terms: (a) it is experiential, as contrasted with thinking of God or reasoning about God; (b) the experience is direct—it seems to the subject that she is immediately aware of God; (c) the experience is usually lacking in sensory content—it is a nonsensory presentation of God; (d) it is a focal experience, one in which the awareness of God attracts one's attention so strongly as to blot out everything else. Alston then addresses whether these experiences are actually experiences of *God.* He first argues that there is a prima facie justification to accept the reliability of our experiences—unless there are strong enough reasons to the contrary. Beliefs formed on the basis of experience possess an initial credibility by virtue of their origin, especially if they are shared by many individuals: "any socially established belief-forming practice is to be accepted as a source of (generally) true beliefs unless there are sufficient reasons against its reliability."[7] If the criticism that there are no effective intersubjective tests for accuracy is leveled, Alston makes the point that the critic of mystical experiences is guilty of epistemic imperialism, subjecting the outputs of one belief-forming practice to the requirements of another. While the critic argues that a mystical perception cannot lay claim to putting its subject in effective touch with objective reality (because she cannot validate this status in the way she can with sense perceptions), Alston points out that there are other, unquestioned sources of belief that work quite differently from sense perception (such as introspection) and that they are nevertheless given credence. It would be absurd to reject introspection as a source of knowledge because of the unavailability of tests to ascertain whether the sadness somebody experiences has objective reality.

Whatever philosophical merit this argument has—although the assumption that belief in God does not have any prima facie evidence against it seems somewhat naïve—I suspect that mystical theologians such as Eckhart, John of the Cross, and Ruusbroec would be profoundly uneasy with such a line of reasoning, insofar as it seems to instrumentalize our relation with God and appears to "objectify" God—to turn God into an object of experience. I suspect they would question the meaningfulness of the expression "immediately experiencing God" in light of their unrelenting emphasis on the transcendence of God. Given that God radically transcends our spatiotemporal categories, is talk of immediately experiencing God not as inadequate as talk of measuring a point? Using the supposed experience of God as ammunition to strengthen belief in his existence is, I feel, strangely inattentive to traditional religious sensibilities and is evidence of the sort of extreme "experientialism" that has been questioned in recent years by a number of authors. One of the more interesting contributions in this field is undoubtedly that of D. Turner.[8]

In his engaging study *The Darkness of God,* Turner argues that descriptions of union between God and soul should not be read in "experiential" terms but in light of a Neoplatonic discourse that contains the resources for an implicit critique of an interpretation of mystical union in experiential terms. Below I discuss how Turner's interpretation impinges on the doctrine of Ruusbroec (whose writings have been studied almost exclusively from a Jamesian perspective). For now my main concern is to deal with Turner's argument in general.

Turner argues that the hierarchical worldview of Neoplatonism (and the underlying ideas of degrees of reality and of a scale of proximity to the primary cause), on the one hand, and the Christian idea of creation out of nothing, on the other, resulted in a specific discourse in which it is not inconsistent to argue that creatures may be nearer to or farther from God ontologically, but there cannot be any degree of proximity in which God stands to creatures. Some created things— for example, human beings—are ontologically "nearer" to God than others (e.g., rocks), but God is not ontologically "nearer" to either of them, as God's relation to creatures is not mediated by distance. In short, the relation of distance between God and creatures is asymmetrical: creatures may be more or less like God, but there cannot be any respect at all in which God is "like" any creature.[9] This view is evident in Dionysius's distinction between similar and dissimilar similarities, which also needs to be seen in light of the Neoplatonic acknowledgment of a hierarchy of being. As is well known, Dionysius argued that dissimilar similarities are less tempting than the similar similarities that might lead us to believe that they capture the divine reality in a more adequate way. The same perspective is found in the view according to which some "names" can be more similar to God than others, given the hierarchy of being, and yet the more "similar" ones are equally inadequate in capturing the divine reality, given God's transcendence in relation to his creatures.[10] Given these general views on the fusion of Neoplatonic ontology and the Christian doctrine of *creatio ex nihilo*, Turner goes on to examine in great detail the repercussions of this fusion for our speech about God. It is here that his most original contribution lies, namely, in the way he understands the traditional distinction between cataphatic and apophatic theology.

Whereas most scholars understood Bernard of Clairvaux and Julian of Norwich to be positive or cataphatic theologians because they describe the union with God in positive terms, and Eckhart and John of the Cross negative or apophatic theologians because they describe God in "negative" terms, such as "darkness" or "desert," Turner argues that the truly apophatic level is situated elsewhere. He describes the cataphatic as the "verbose" element, drawing on metaphors of all kinds to describe God: in its cataphatic mode, theology is "a kind of verbal riot, an anarchy of discourse in which anything goes."[11] Given that God created the world, all created things provide a potential source of imagery for the description of God. However, because nothing creaturely describes God adequately, all of this imagery has to be negated too. This brings us to the apophatic level. Here we use clashing metaphors to negate the imagery itself. Turner makes the crucial point that negative language about God is no more apophatic in itself than is affirmative language, for "the apophatic is the linguistic strategy of somehow showing by means of language that which lies beyond language."[12] In short, Turner draws our attention to an important distinction: between the strategy of negative propositions and the strategy of negating the propositional; between that of the negative image and that of the negation of the imagery.[13] Only metaphors ("God is Light") can negate other metaphors ("God is Darkness"). To convey something of the failure of both metaphors to reveal what God is, the two metaphors are simultaneously affirmed: "God is a Brilliant Darkness." Here, according to Turner, we meet the genuinely apophatic level: "by the juxtaposition of affirmative and negative images is achieved the negation, in the sense of the transcendence, of the imagery itself."[14]

Bernard McGinn has pointed out a number of weaknesses in Turner's account.[15] First, Turner overstates his case. He mistakenly assumes that one branch of apophaticism is representative of the whole medieval mystical tradition in general. It is indeed to be regretted that Turner does not discuss Bernard of Clairvaux's mystical theology, or that of the Cistercians in general. Second, McGinn points out that even the authors Turner discusses (Augustine, Pseudo-Dionysius, Bonaventure, Eckhart, John of the Cross, etc.) had a more complex attitude towards experience than Turner allows. Similarly, "experience" too could function on a first-order level: as the dialectic between the cataphatic and the apophatic cannot be dissolved, it can be argued that the experiential might continue to play an important role in the dialectic of apophaticism. Because Turner somewhat artificially separates the first-order from the second-order or apophatic level, while in reality they are more fused than his analysis suggests, McGinn's observation in relation to the continuing significance of "experience" seems to gain weight. Before I examine McGinn's views I would like to add some thoughts of my own.

I fully share Turner's reservations about an "experiential" reading of medieval apophatic texts—*especially* if "experience" is construed in terms of immediacy, unmediatedness, and passivity. Turner also seems correct in affirming that the fusion of Neoplatonism and the Christian doctrine of creation out of nothing has repercussions for the language in which we describe the relationship between God and creation (including the human soul). My main reservation with Turner's approach is that he seems to reduce apophaticism to talk about (the limitations of) God-talk. In Turner's interpretation, apophaticism becomes talk about God-talk, not talk about God. But mystical theology, even when apophatic, is more than a linguistic device aimed at subverting our views on the relation between God and soul and bringing to light the inherent limitations of our cataphatic God-talk. According to Turner, apophaticism is a second-order description of the logic of negation itself.[16] This becomes especially evident in his discussion of Pseudo-Dionysius. According to Turner, when Pseudo-Dionysius denies of God both "similarity" and "difference," he is not referring to properties of God (or his relation to the world) but to "properties of language."[17] Similarly, he writes: "Since we have no language in which to describe the deficit between our metaphors and the reality they reach out to, we are in a position only negatively *to express the deficiency*."[18] Again, it seems odd to suggest that the primary aim of major mystical theologians was nothing else but to reveal something of the inadequacy of our God-talk. Thus, Turner's interpretation seems to open up a reductionism of its own: mystical theology ends up revealing something about the limitations of our language, rather than revealing something of God and his relation to the world.

Nevertheless, even if one can raise questions about the somewhat general scope of Turner's argument and his characterization of apophaticism, his reservations about the use of the word "experience" to describe the nature of mystical theology remain relevant—especially, as I suggested earlier, when "experience" is understood in the Jamesian sense of an immediate, unmediated experience of God. McGinn too, although less hostile towards the concept and happy enough to use it,[19] raises concerns, arguing that the term "experience" is often too vague and too ambiguous to prove very useful. Also, it tends to place the emphasis on special altered states (visions, raptures, locutions) that are only incidental to the core of mystical theology. For this reason he espouses the term "consciousness," which, he feels, is a more precise and fruitful category than experience. Mystical theology, then, revolves around "an immediate consciousness of the presence of God."[20]

Although McGinn, quite rightly, points out that mystical theology should not be understood in isolation from the wider religion of which it is part and that it is a process or way of life, I am not entirely at ease with the category "consciousness." It has a definite psychologizing ring to it—at odds with the wider perspective McGinn advocates—and, also, the critique leveled earlier (at the preposterous nature of the claim that we can have an unmediated experience of God) applies equally to the claim that we can have a consciousness of the immediate or direct presence of God. In fairness to McGinn, his brief introduction to the first volume of *The Presence of God* is nothing but a heuristic sketch, which will be fleshed out as his project develops, with all relevant issues examined in greater detail in the last volume. Similarly, his concluding remarks on Bernard Lonergan's notion of "mediated immediacy" (p. xx) seem to suggest that more is to be said on the "immediacy" of the consciousness of God.

What can we learn from all of this? First, we should keep in mind that discussions about the nature of "apophaticism" only have secondary importance. It is a scholarly debate about the nature of mystical theology and its central categories. It therefore operates on a meta-level; the mystical theologians themselves only occasionally concern themselves with these issues.[21] Second, we should be reluctant to attempt to characterize the multifaceted tradition of mystical theology by using one or two categories, especially if these were not widely used by the authors themselves. Both "experience" and "consciousness" have a fairly meager record in this regard. Undoubtedly, Bernard of Clairvaux used the expression "the book of our experience" *(in libro experientiae)* in *Sermon 3,1* on the Song of Songs and elsewhere, but the context suggests that it is doubtful he meant much more than what we mean when we say that one has to draw on the "experience" of a living faith to discuss spirituality. Even if one concedes that Bernard understands "experiential" in terms of "experience of God," as some of his writings suggest, this experience is always mediated and shaped by the Christian faith and would be unthinkable outside this context. Despite his emphasis on experience, Bernard emphasized the chasm that separates God and soul[22] and would have found it difficult to make sense of an immediate, unmediated experience with God. The link with the modern, Jamesian understanding is therefore tenuous, to put it mildly. Similarly, the notion of consciousness was not widely used by either patristic or medieval authors.

Different authors use different metaphors, and even when they use similar metaphors, such as the "Birth of the Son in the soul," they often mean different things (as is the case with Eckhart and Ruusbroec). This is why general discussions about categories such as "experience" or "consciousness" only have limited value. However, since we have to make texts that have been written centuries ago intelligible in language that is meaningful to us, let us have a final look at the notion of experience.

Is Turner correct in claiming that an experiential understanding is at odds with the central beliefs of the some of the major figures of apophatic theology? A nuanced answer to this question is only to be obtained by looking at some specific texts in some detail. In my view, the idea of an immediate, unmediated experience—or consciousness—of God would have been unacceptable to a number of major mystical theologians, including Gregory of Nyssa, a founding father of mystical theology. I want to briefly discuss Gregory's views for three reasons. First, he exerted a considerable influence on Pseudo-Dionysius, who is a pivotal figure in the history of Western mysticism (and whose influence stretched as far as Ruusbroec and beyond). Second, engaging with Gregory's work allows us to see how a major mystical theologian can safeguard God's transcendence and mystery and simultaneously hold the view that we can dwell in the "presence" of God. Thus, his work is relevant to us today because he thematizes the problem of divine presence and absence in a fairly explicit manner, by examining how God can be both unknowable and knowable. Third (and closely related to the previous point), Gregory develops a dialectic of yearning and fulfillment that we will encounter again in Ruusbroec's writings.

Gregory of Nyssa (335–95), one of the Cappadocian Fathers whose significance for trinitarian theology cannot be overemphasized, makes some extraordinary innovations that have to be seen in light of the theological controversies of his time, especially the debate surrounding Arius and his followers. Gregory stressed the infinite and incomprehensible nature of God. He does not argue that God is incomprehensible because of the weakness of the human mind (a theological commonplace); he argues that God's nature in itself is infinite and inexhaustible as such. This was a major innovation quite abhorrent to the Greek mind.[23] This innovation has to be understood against the Neo-Arian teaching of Eunomius, who argued that God is not divided or subject to change, or split from one *ousia* into a threefold *hypostasis*, for he is always and absolutely one, remaining uniformly and unchangeably God. Thus, Eunomius argues that there can be only one Supreme and Absolute One—not a second or third, which come after the one and are therefore derivative and inferior. Gregory accepted that God is unchangeable and indivisible. In fact, seeing that God is infinite, it makes sense to say that a plurality or hierarchy of separated beings is impossible. In other words, there may be "three subjects," Gregory argued, but their infinity means that they are not three separate beings or substances. There cannot be degrees of infinity or being within God's infinite being. Because Father, Son, and Spirit are infinite, they cannot be treated as three separate things. You cannot separate one infinity from another. They can be distinguished, however, by their mutual relations. In the *Life of Moses* Gregory examines the implications of the idea of the divine infinity and unknowability to argue that we cannot fully grasp God's nature.[24] In this work Gregory describes how the inexhaustibility of the nature of the divinity leads to a dialectic of yearning for God that will never be satisfied, or rather, it will be satisfied in remaining unsatisfied. This is what scholars call *epektasis*.

The treatise *The Life of Moses or Concerning Perfection in Virtue* is divided into two parts. After a brief exposition of Moses' life (inspired by Exodus) Gregory goes on to give an allegorical interpretation of the same text. Interestingly, this second part is called "*Contemplation* on the Life of Moses." In summary, Moses meets God on three occasions:

A) The encounter with the *burning bush* (*Life* II, 19–30; cf. Ex 3:1–14). This is the first revelation of God to Moses. It is the first stage in Moses' spiritual journey. It results in conversion and purification (*apatheia* or serenity).

B) The *Cloud* (*Life* II, 162–66; cf. Ex 20:21: "Then the people stood at a distance, while Moses drew near to the thick darkness where God was"). Gregory suggests that the further the mind advances and the more it becomes focused on God, the more it becomes aware of the divine incomprehensibility. The Cloud illustrates that God is above all knowledge and comprehension.[25]

C) Seeing *the back of God* (*Life* II, 219–55). Moses asks to see God face-to-face. God replies that Moses is allowed to see God's back but not his face (Ex 33:23). Whereas Moses desired an immediate vision of God, God does not fully grant this wish but allows Moses to see his back. Obviously, seeing that God is not bodily,[26] we cannot interpret this in a literal fashion, and therefore Gregory puts forward a beautiful allegorical interpretation. Moses desires to meet God in an immediate fashion; this wish is denied (or it is granted insofar as it is denied) because if God were to fulfill it, it would bring our desire for God to an end, for "the true sight of God consists in this, that the one who looks up to God never ceases in that desire."[27] Given the infinite nature of God, Moses' wish cannot be fulfilled.[28] Gregory makes a case for the infinity of God by developing a reductio ad absurdum: if God were not infinite, he would have been "bounded" or circumscribed by something that is not God/Good, and this is unacceptable.[29] Having thus shown that God is infinite, it follows that our desire for God can never be fully satisfied but must expand and grow the more we become focused on God: "This truly is the vision of God: never to be satisfied in the desire to see him."[30]

So what does "to see God" mean for Gregory? Gregory answers this question in greater detail in no. 240ff by referring to the "back of God." Moses is allowed to see the back of God; that is, he will see God when he follows him. Appealing to Lk 9:23 and 18:22, Gregory states: "He who follows sees the back. So Moses, who eagerly seeks to behold God, is now taught how he can behold him: to follow God wherever he might lead is to behold God."[31] There is therefore a strong emphasis on virtue rather than on mystical experience.[32] To see God means to follow Christ in a life of virtue.

Gregory's emphasis on God's unknowability leads to a problem. After all, the beatitude "Blessed are the pure of heart, for they shall see God" clearly states that at least some of us will see God. In his commentary on the beatitudes, Gregory asks how this is to be reconciled with other biblical statements that affirm that "No man has ever seen God" (in Jn 1:18; also 1 Tm 6:16 and Ex 33:20). To deal with this issue, Gregory explains that "seeing God" can be understood in a twofold sense: first, as knowing God in an immediate fashion, and this he rules out; second, as being united to God through purity of life, and this is the right way to understand the meaning of the beatitude. Interestingly, Gregory argues that a virtuous person can "see" God by looking at his own purity and goodness, which reflects the divine Goodness: "Hence, if a man who is pure of heart sees himself, he sees in himself what he desires; and thus he becomes blessed, because when he looks at his own purity, he sees the archetype in the image."[33] Thus, even though we cannot see God we can see reflections of God in this world (and in human persons) through God's creative and sanctifying activity in the world. Gregory compares seeing God to attaining health: it is not very beneficial to know something about good health; it is more beneficial to possess it. Similarly: "The Lord does not say it is blessed to know something about God, but to have God within oneself.... I do not think that if the eye of one's soul has been purified, he is promised a direct vision of God; but perhaps this marvelous saying may suggest what the Word expresses more clearly when he says to others, *The Kingdom of God is within you*."[34] In short, according to Gregory, we cannot have an immediate knowledge of God, but we can be transformed, become deified, and only in this sense can we be said to "know" God. Gregory's ideal is one of transformation/deification, not experience. There is, in other words, a dialectic of knowing and unknowing present in Gregory's work that is probably not very different from the dialectic of absence and presence we find in the writings of other mystical theologians. McGinn too emphasizes that consciousness of the "presence" of God does not do full justice to the texts of mystical theologians, and he suggests that we should also be attentive to the notion of divine "absence." This dialectic of presence and absence has to be understood in light of what Gregory has to say on our inability to immediately know God. God is present insofar as we are transformed, become deified; but this transformation takes place against a backdrop of a God who remains utterly unknowable in himself—and who is, in that respect, absent.

In my view Ruusbroec gives us a similar picture. Ruusbroec points out that while some people might think that they experience God, they experience nothing but themselves (a sentiment later echoed by John of the Cross). As he puts it in his last work, *Vanden XII Beghinen:*

> We find several wrong and misled people, who have neither a contemplative nor an active life. Nevertheless, they consider that they are the wisest and the holiest in the whole world. These are the ones who are freed of images of all things, and who, in bare nature, without grace and without virtue, turn inwards above reason in their own being; there they find inactivity, rest and imageless bareness. That is the highest point to which nature, without grace, can come. But since they are not baptized in the Spirit of our Lord in true charity, they can neither see God nor find him or his glorious realm in their being. But they find their own essence: an imageless and becalmed inactivity; and there they imagine that they are eternally blessed.[35]

Nevertheless, being devoid of images is a crucial aspect of Ruusbroec's own ideal of the contemplative life. In *Vanden XII Beghinen,* 2a 658, he states that a contemplative life awaits all those "who can rid themselves of images *(ontbeelden),* and freely serve and love God alone in spirit." I hope to explain throughout this study how his own ideal differs from the psychological or experiential understanding he rejects in the passage quoted above. Further on in the same work Ruusbroec reiterates this message: "False emptiness has deceived you, so that you imagine that you are gazing upon God; nevertheless, you know little or nothing of God. For in your imageless turning-inward, above reason and without consideration and above all your soul's faculties, you find the bare essence of your soul free and empty by nature, just as God has created it; and then you imagine that it is the inactive essence of God, and that you see God, and that you yourself are the Wisdom of God, Christ, God and man."[36]

And yet Ruusbroec himself elsewhere describes the authentic mystical union in similar terms:

> Enlightened men have found within themselves an essential inward gazing above reason and without reason, and an enjoyable inclination surpassing all modes and all essence, sinking away from themselves into a modeless abyss of fathomless beatitude, where the Trinity of the divine Persons possess their nature in essential unity. See, here the beatitude is so simple so without mode that there is an essential gazing, inclination and distinction of creatures pass away. For all spirits thus raised up melt away and are annihilated by reason of enjoyment in God's essence which is the super-essence of all essences. There they fall away from themselves and are lost in a bottomless unknowing.[37]

The full implications of this quotation will become clear throughout this study. For now, in light of the previous discussion, two issues arise. First, it seems clear that Ruusbroec wants to convey more than talk about God-talk. He is attempting to say something about the relation between the soul and God rather than merely about language about God. Second, there is the issue of the exact status of union with God, described in the quotation just above, in light of the preceding quotation in which Ruusbroec challenges those who mistakenly believe that they experience God in their own essence.

The full answer to the latter problem is developed in later chapters. I attempt to show that Ruusbroec holds a middle course between the (implausible) claim that we have a direct, immediate experience of God, on the one hand, and the notion that God is totally unknowable to us, on the other. More specifically, I argue that Ruusbroec, fully aware of the relentlessly creaturely status of the human being and the transcendence of God, denies that we can have an immediate experience of God. But Ruusbroec does describe a union between God and soul in terms of love and knowledge, painting a detailed picture of the "transformation" (*ghetransformeert ende overformet* in *Brulocht* c 198–99 and numerous other places) of the soul in response to God's grace. This also implies that for Ruusbroec, union with God is always a participated and analogous affair. I will develop this theme by examining Ruusbroec's notion of *gelycke*, or similitude.

Before he describes the mystical union, Ruusbroec usually gives an account of his trinitarian doctrine in an almost scholastic manner. This feature, which may at first surprise the modern reader, has to be seen in light of his teaching on similitude (likeness) or analogy. What Ruusbroec has to say on this is essential if we are to correctly interpret his expositions on the nature of "the union without distinction" (or the contemplative life). As I show in chapter 4, Ruusbroec argues that the essence of the human person is a relatedness to God: "We are all one life in God in our eternal Image above our createdness."[38] However, we always remain other than God:

> We are other than God and cannot become one, but remain in otherness, that is: where we subsist in ourselves, each in his own person; there God has made us like to him in bare nature *(ende daer hevet ons god hem ghelijc ghemaect in bloeter natueren)*, after the mode of our higher faculties. But this likeness *(die ghelijcheit)* that God has given us all in common in nature makes us neither holy nor blessed, but grace and the gifts of God which come from above into us give us a virtuous life, and thereby God lives in us and we in him. And in this way we are like to God above our nature, and thus we remain eternally like unto God in grace and glory *(Ende alsoe ghelijcken wij gode boven onse natueren, ende aldus bliven wij gode ewelijc ghelijc in gracien ende in glorien)*.[39]

Likeness therefore has a natural dimension (our human nature resembles God in the Image of whom we have been made) and a graceful dimension (through grace we come to resemble God even more, but this growing resemblance also implies difference: we can never transcend our creaturely status, not even in glory). Insofar as we are merely created beings, we always remain "unlike" or dissimilar to God: "God's essence is uncreated, and our essence is created. And this is unlike without measure *(sonder mate onghelijc)*, God and creature. And therefore, even though it may unite *(vereeneghen)*, it cannot become one *(een werden)*."[40] Even in our union with God, the dissimilar character will not be abnegated, as Ruusbroec emphasizes time and time again: "Our createdness does not become God, nor does the Image of God become creature; for we are created to the Image, that is: to receive the Image of God. And that Image is uncreated, eternal: the Son of God."[41] The Image of God is the exemplary cause of our being without which we would immediately vanish into nothingness: it is, as Ruusbroec puts it in a Pseudo-Dionysian vein, "the supra-being of our being *(overwesen ons wesens)*."[42] Given our creaturely status, our relation with God is always only participatory,[43] and the likeness with God will never be transcended, not even in our utmost union with God:

> Likeness *(ghelijc)* sinks away from itself every moment and dies in God, and becomes one with God and remains one; for charity makes us become one with God, and remain and dwell in one-(ness). Nevertheless, we maintain likeness eternally in the light of grace or of glory, where we possess ourselves as active in charity and virtues. And we keep the oneness with God above our activity, in bareness of our spirit in divine light, where we possess God above all virtues in rest. For charity in the likeness must be eternally active, but oneness with God in enjoyable love will be forever at rest.[44]

As this quotation suggests, Ruusbroec distinguishes between resting in God's oneness in the bareness of our spirit and being active in likeness. As he puts it in the same context: "Every lover is one with God and at rest, and Godlike *(gode ghelijc)* in the activity of love." He then goes on to draw a comparison with the sublime nature of God that we resemble *(daer wij een ghelijc af draghen)*: God too dwells in enjoyable rest in the essential oneness and is active in the threeness of the Persons.[45] Therefore, the reason Ruusbroec expounds his trinitarian doctrine before outlining the contemplative life is because of the *analogous* nature of our created being, which will never be transcended, not even in the most supreme union with God. In short, Ruusbroec's objective descriptions of the life of the Trinity and our participation in it will fail to make sense unless we remember the analogous character of the latter.

Does this dialectic of absence and presence condemn us to perpetual solitude? It is no coincidence that Mommaers, a major advocate of a Jamesian reading of Ruusbroec's oeuvre, writes:

> As far as the crucial question about the ultimate destiny of man is concerned, it seems that the thinkers—and so many of the faithful instructed by them—run into a total impasse: either God is transcendent, and then man is doomed to remain alone; or else God is immanent, and then finally all that is human must merely disappear into the divine "Ground." According to Ruusbroec, there is only one way out of this aporia, . . . to take seriously the model experience which is the mystical union with God and not squeezing it immediately into a philosophical framework but *describing* it. He will complete the unsatisfactory reflection on the problem of God-and-man by a genuine *phenomenology* of the unitive experience.[46]

In later chapters I have more to say about this supposed phenomenology and the anti-intellectualism —also in the Jamesian tradition— that seeps through this quotation. There can be little doubt that Ruusbroec repeatedly emphasizes God's transcendence and that he equally stresses that we can never transcend our creaturely status or become God. In this sense we certainly remain "alone." However, insofar as we are transformed in response to God's grace and participate in God through love and knowledge (which is altogether different from "experiencing" God in the Jamesian sense), we definitely do not remain "alone." Thus, Ruusbroec's spirituality does not try to overcome the chasm that separates the created soul from God; it affirms it without meaning to imply that this allocates God to the realm of irrelevance. His spirituality too is based on a dialectic presence and absence, not unlike that of Gregory. As he puts it in *Vanden Blinkenden Steen:*

> We are poor in ourselves and rich in God, hungry and thirsty in ourselves, drunk and replete in God, working in ourselves and empty of all things in God. And so we shall remain through all eternity, for without practice of loving we can never possess God, and whoever feels or believes otherwise is deceived. And so we live completely in God, where we possess our bliss, and completely

in ourselves, where we practice our love towards God. And even if we live completely in God and completely in ourselves, yet it is only one life. But it is contrary and twofold according to experience *(van ghevoelne)*, for poor and rich, hungry and replete, working and at rest, those are contraries indeed. Yet in them resides our highest nobility, now and for ever. For we cannot become God at all and lose our createdness: that is impossible.[47]

Similarly in *Steen* 641ff. we read: "I just told that we are one with God, and Holy Scripture bears witness to this. But now I want to say that we must remain other than God for ever, and Holy Scripture bears witness to this as well. And we must understand and experience both points in ourselves, if we are to live right." In my view this is a healthy spirituality: it allows both God and creature to be what they are; it also implicitly questions the notion that God can be a source of spiritual consolations.

Although Ruusbroec does not offer a phenomenology of the experience of God, he describes in great detail the nature of the transformation of the human person in response to the stirrings of divine grace, and he thereby gives mystical theology an anthropological turn that seems quite new in the history of Western spirituality (a lead that was to be taken up almost two centuries later by John of the Cross). The effect of this "transformation" can best be described in terms of detachment (to borrow Eckhart's phrase, although Ruusbroec occasionally uses it too) and involvement or even "detached involvement"—another oxymoron—that indicates how the Christian relates to God and the world in a nonpossessive manner without, however, renouncing the world. Dying to the world and its idols (which is essentially a dying to self-centeredness and possessiveness) implies a new and more authentic engagement with the world. This theme, which has Augustinian roots, was developed, amongst others, by Eckhart, who argued that the human soul should become virgin and wife at the same time; that is, we should be detached from the world, yet engage with the world in works of charity. Turner has rightly emphasized that Eckhart's ideal of detachment does not refer to a specific emotion or experience beside other experiences but that detachment functions as a *category of experience;* that is, it shapes all our dealings with the world, all our emotions and experiences. Detachment does not mean that instead of loving creatures, we should now love God—for this too would reduce God to the status of an object of human-created desire. Nor does detachment for Eckhart refer to the fact that we should become desireless. The problem is not human desire but its possessiveness: "The strategy of detachment is the strategy of dispossessing desire of its desire to possess its objects, and so to destroy them."[48] As Turner puts it: "Detachment, for Eckhart, is not the severing of desire's relation with its object, but the restoration of desire to a proper relation of objectivity; as we might say, of reverence for its object."[49] Being aware that God should not be appropriated or instrumentalized to suit our own needs will change the way we relate to him and therefore to ourselves and the world. We should love God and his world the way God loves it—not out of a self-serving need but out of sheer gratuity (a theme central to the thought of Simone Weil in the twentieth century).

Interestingly, this traditional theme was developed more recently by Karl Rahner in incarnational terms. According to Rahner, the Christian reflects the divine goodness, which is both transcendent and allows the world to be and is yet radically involved with the world through the incarnation. Although Rahner's focus was more limited—the essay in which he developed this idea dealt with the nature of Ignatian mysticism in particular—its outline is fairly representative of the Christian attitude to the world in general.[50] Rahner wonders how we can make sense of the Ignatian *fuga saeculi,* on the one hand, and the joy in the world, on the other. How are we to understand that the joyous exuberance of baroque churches and the sacrifice of young Jesuit missionaries who died in agony in the bamboo cages of Tonkin both arise from the same spirituality? Rahner points towards divine transcendence and the incarnation to make this connection clear: "Ignatian piety is piety toward the God who is beyond the whole world and who freely reveals himself. In this . . . is to be found at once the reason for flight from the world and the possibility of an acceptance of the world."[51] This orientation of detachment and affirmation (or, in Ignatian terms, *indiferença*) allows the Christian to challenge the world without succumbing to escapism or denial of the world; similarly, the fact that God never coincides with any created thing or being keeps us from idolizing anything in the world. Throughout his writings Ruusbroec develops the same theme in trinitarian terms.

As these brief examples suggest, it is time to refocus the discussion of mysticism from "experience" to "transformation" for two reasons: first, because the notion of "transformation" (and the related notion of "deification") was traditionally more widely used than that of "experience"; and second, and perhaps more important, because it opens up the notion of mysticism to entail every aspect of life—unlike "experience" or "consciousness" its connotations are more universal and ethical than psychological. In the next section we will see how Ruusbroec too describes in some detail the process of the transformation of the self, using the metaphors of hired servants, friends, and sons to outline the relation of the Christian to God.

There are a number of conclusions to be drawn from the foregoing discussion. The Western tradition of mystical theology is probably too multifaceted and diverse to allow for a single framework or perspective of interpretation, in terms of "experience," "consciousness," or "hard" apophaticism (cf. Turner's understanding of apophaticism). However, if one wants to use the notions of experience or consciousness, one should be aware of their mediated character and be alert to one's own modern presuppositions (or even prejudices) that may be very different from the patristic or medieval perspective. This is why Turner's perspective is useful: he reminds us of the *difficulties* of reading mystical theological texts in terms of *immediate, unmediated* experience of God rather than in terms of experience full stop. He has also reminded us of Neoplatonic sources of mystical theology and the implications of the fusion of Neoplatonism with the Christian doctrine of *creatio ex nihilo* for our God-talk. Still, I feel the notion of "transformation" is a more promising central category to describe the nature of mystical theology than either (mediated) "experience" or "consciousness." It is now time to have a closer look at Ruusbroec's own writings in light of the issues discussed in this chapter.

Ruusbroec and Mystical Theology

In the remainder of this chapter I discuss whether Ruusbroec can justifiably be called "a phenomenologist of the mystical experience" or whether he should be situated in the medieval tradition of apophatic theology as elucidated by Denys Turner, albeit with the necessary qualifications. Ruusbroec offers a description of the transformation of the human person in response to God's grace, but he does not understand "union with God" in terms of immediate, passive experience of God. Similarly, a proper discussion of Ruusbroec's mysticism necessarily involves a wider engagement with his trinitarian theology and christology.

Ruusbroec's Trinitarian Theology

The intra-trinitarian life as expounded by Ruusbroec is extremely dynamic. In the following quotation he describes the processions of Son and Spirit and the return of the divine Persons in their shared unity: the Persons flow back into the divine essence or being *(wesen)* in a never-ending dynamic of ebbing and flowing.

> The noble nature of God which is the principal cause of all creatures, is fruitful; therefore it cannot remain in tranquillity in the unity of paternity because of the stirring *(gherinen)* of fruitfulness, but it has to give birth without cease to the eternal Wisdom, i.e., the Son of the Father. The Son is always being born, has been born, and remains unborn; yet it is one Son. Insofar as the Father contemplates the Son, the eternal Wisdom, and all things in the same Wisdom, he is born and is another Person than the Father. . . .
>
> Neither from the fruitful nature (this is paternity), nor from the fact that the Father gives birth to his Son, does Love — this is the Holy Spirit — flow; but because of the fact that the Son is born as another Person, distinct from the Father, in which the Father sees him as born and all creatures in him and with him, as the life of all things; and because of the fact that the Son beholds the Father as fruitful and giving birth, and himself [= the Son] and all things in the Father (this is a mutual beholding in the same fruitful nature): from this, Love, which is the Holy Spirit and a bond between the Father and the Son and between the Son and the Father, is brought about. With this Love the Persons are permeated and through it they embrace and flow back into the unity from which the Father is constantly giving birth. And when

they have flown back into the unity, there is nevertheless no rest because of the fruitfulness of the nature. This giving birth and flowing back into unity is the work of the Trinity; thus there is threeness of Persons and oneness of nature.[52]

Several observations can be made. First, the Father generates his Son out of his fruitful nature, whereas the Spirit flows from their mutual beholding as their Love. In chapter 3 I argue that Ruusbroec's language is reminiscent of that of St. Bonaventure who himself fused Pseudo-Dionysian elements (the divine nature as *bonum diffusivum*) and Augustinian elements (the Spirit proceeds from the mutual contemplation of Father and Son) as appropriated by Richard of St. Victor (Holy Spirit as the bond of Love of Father and Son).[53]

However, the most striking feature of the above quotation is that the Spirit permeates the divine Persons and is the principle of their return into the divine essence: this is known to theologians of the thirteenth century as *regiratio*, and Ruusbroec puts it at the heart of his theology of the Trinity.[54] Ruusbroec does not use the term *regiratio*—the return of the Persons into their shared unity—as he wrote in Middle Dutch. However, he translates it, quite accurately, as *wederboeghen*, usually used as a verb or occasionally as a noun, as in this passage:

> There, the Father with the Son and all beloved are enfolded and embraced in the bond of love, that is to say, in the unity of the Holy Spirit. It is this same unity which is fruitful according to the bursting-out of Persons and in the return, an eternal bond of love which can nevermore be untied.
>
> *(Daer es de vader, met den sone ende alle die gheminde, bevaen ende behelst in bande van minnen, dat es, in enecheit des heilechs geests. Ende dit es die selve enecheit die vrochtbaer es na den utebroeke der persone, ende in den wederboghene i ewech bant der minnen die nemmermeer onbonden en wert.)*[55]

A translation of this passage by Surius (1552), also found in the critical edition, is as follows: "Ibi Pater cum Filio, et cum eis electi omnes circumplectuntur vinculo charitatis, in divina unitate: quae quidem secundum personarum emanationem foecunda est, in earum autem reflexione sempiternus ac insolubilis est nexus amoris." Surius is sensitive to both the Neoplatonic *(emanatio, reflexio)* and the Richardian *(nexus amoris, vinculum charitatis)* vocabulary Ruusbroec uses. This vocabulary, especially when applied to describe the intra-trinitarian dynamics in its out-going and in-going aspects (described in terms of "flowing in" or "flowing out") reveals a distinct Pseudo-Dionysian influence in which Augustinian elements are then subsumed, similar to St. Bonaventure's approach. As I suggested earlier, Christian mystical theology draws on Neoplatonic sources to develop a discourse in which statements of indistinction do not necessarily refer to a "mystical experience" in which the human person loses himself in an immediate and passive experience of God. On the contrary, apophatic theology is based on the recognition that as God is radically distinct from his creation, statements of distinction and indistinction break down. Ruusbroec's claim that God and soul are one and indistinct is based on the recognition of God's utter transcendence.[56] This utter transcendence, of course, also implies that God cannot be "captured" in a mystical experience of whatever sort, or in any other way. This then raises the question whether being attentive to the Neoplatonic discourse Ruusbroec draws from helps us to interpret his descriptions of the union of God and soul.

Jamesian Experience or Apophaticism?

The dynamic of the trinitarian life shapes the spiritual goal Ruusbroec propounds, namely, "the common life" *(een ghemeyn leven)*. In the life of the "common" man activity and rest are perfectly integrated in an exact reflection of the intra-trinitarian dynamics in its out-going, in-going, and enjoyable or essential moments: "God's Spirit drives us [lit., "breathes us out"] towards loving and virtuous activity, and he draws us back in to rest and enjoy. . . . Therefore, to go in, in idle enjoyment, and to go out, in virtuous activity, and to remain constantly united with God's Spirit: this is what I mean."[57] In another passage, Ruusbroec describes the modelessness of the divine being and its relation to the human person:

> [T]here is no mode, no trail, no path, no abode, no measure, no end, no beginning, or anything one might be able to put into words or demonstrate. This is the simple blessedness of us all, the divine

being and our supra-being, above reason and without reason. If we are to feel this, our spirit must be transported into that same being, above our creatureliness, in the eternal point, wherein all our lines begin and end, the point wherein they lose their name and all differentiation, and are one with the point and the selfsame one that the point itself is. Nonetheless, in themselves, they always remain converging lines. So, you see, we shall always remain what we are in our created being; nonetheless, losing our own proper spirit, we shall always cross over into our supra-being.[58]

This passage has an unmistakable Neoplatonic ring to it. There is not only the terminology ("supra-being," "excessus"), but the very metaphor of a circle reminds us both of the famous proposition 2 from the *Liber XXIV Philosophorum (Deus est sphaera infinita cuius centrum est ubique, circumferentia nusquam)* and, even more, of a passage from *The Divine Names* 5.6, as I show below. Given this Neoplatonic background, are we entitled to understand this passage and similar ones as outlining an immediate, passive experience of God? This is the way Ruusbroec has been understood in recent decades. According to J. Alaerts, Ruusbroec's language is not Neoplatonic (or Pseudo-Dionysian): "What we are dealing with is a unitive-affective vocabulary, describing aspects of a union of loving experience. Moreover, our research seems to indicate that neither the conceptual framework of Scholasticism, nor the Dionysian framework (more philosophical than mystical) can yield an adequate interpretation of the mystical ascent of the soul, as Ruusbroec describes it."[59] The contrast Alaerts draws between "philosophy" and "mysticism" reveals a very specific, typically modern understanding of "mysticism" that differs significantly from the patristic and medieval understanding of "mystical theology." As we have seen, in this modern understanding, mystical texts are thought to present a description of a mystical experience that is characterized by immediacy, passivity, and a suspension of our ordinary cognitive faculties and awareness. It does not come as a surprise that Alaerts describes Ruusbroec's work as follows: "He presents us with a brilliant phenomenology of encounter and mystical union, which utterly surpasses the philosophical and theological framework that is, nevertheless, present. The true [*sic*] Ruusbroec focuses on life, and on the spiritually enlightened person who experiences in a direct and passive manner the presence of God."⁶⁰ As we have seen earlier, Mommaers also characterizes Ruusbroec as a "phenomenologist" who appeals to mystical experience to solve the "problem" of the ontological separation of God and creature, on the one hand, and the Gospel affirmation of their union, on the other (Jn 17:21; 1 Cor 6:17): "If the distinction between God and man is so strictly and irrevocably fixed as the current ontology holds, then can 'being one spirit with God' (1 Cor 6:17) ever be a reality?"⁶¹ Ruusbroec, "who does not present a philosophy but an experience,"⁶² "is more informed than those who rely only upon irreproachable and 'objective' thinking."⁶³ Mommaers claims that Ruusbroec completes the unsatisfactory reflection on the problem of God-and-man by "a genuine *phenomenology* of the unitive experience."⁶⁴

A similar approach was adopted by J. Feys to "resolve" apparent "contradictions" throughout Ruusbroec's writings, such as his emphasis on the unbridgeable chasm between God and creation (including the soul) and his equally emphatic assertion of the union between God and the human person—an assertion that was also made by the heretics of his time. In short, he argues that Ruusbroec describes a mystical *experience*, whereas the "heretics" he combats made *ontological* claims that were opposed to true faith. Commentators have correctly observed that Ruusbroec resorts to the same vocabulary as his opponents⁶⁵ but that he is not guilty of contradicting himself or of adhering to doctrines he himself rejects as "heretical," because, they allege, his vocabulary refers to a mystical experience: "The key to the problem of seeming contradictions in Ruusbroec's *Little Book (of Clarification)* then is the distinction to be made between doctrinal exposition and description of experience."⁶⁶ According to Feys and others, Ruusbroec speaks of "the experience of union, not of its metaphysical structure."⁶⁷ This interpretation needs to be questioned. To do this, it is important to see that Feys is really making two claims. He is arguing, with Mommaers, that Ruusbroec should be characterized as a phenomenologist of the mystical "experience"—understood along Jamesian lines in terms of passivity, immediacy, and so forth. He is also suggesting that the claims of Ruusbroec's opponents are more ontological than Ruusbroec's. I will first argue that Ruusbroec's expressions do not refer to an experience along the lines suggested [A]. After this, I will point out that Ruusbroec's ontology is more elaborate and sophisticated than that of his opponents [B].

[A] The argument that Ruusbroec talks of *experience* while his opponents make ontological claims is incorrect. Ruusbroec develops a fascinating theology of the image, which clearly has anthropological and ontological implications. Moroever, the apophatic nature of his descriptions of the union between God and soul compel us to question an interpretation of these descriptions in crude experiential terms. When Ruusbroec writes, "And all those who are elevated above their creaturehood into a contemplative life are one with this divine brightness, and they are the brightness itself," or "to comprehend and to understand God, above all similitudes, as he is in himself means to be God with God, without intermediary or any otherness which can create a hindrance or a mediation," he obviously does not mean to suggest that the soul literally becomes God.[68] Nor does he mean to suggest that the soul enjoys an immediate, unmediated experience of God. What he describes is how the soul becomes transformed or deified in an analogous fashion. Ruusbroec is careful to indicate that in the contemplative life we do not *feel* or *perceive* any distinction between ourselves and the Son—but that does not mean that there is not a distinction:

> In the abyss of this darkness in which the loving spirit has died to itself, there begin the revelation of God and eternal life. For in this darkness there shines and is born an incomprehensible light which is the Son of God, in whom one contemplates eternal life. . . . And without cease it becomes the very brightness which it receives. See, this hidden brightness in which one contemplates everything that one desires according to the mode of emptiness of spirit, is so great that the loving contemplative neither sees nor feels anything in his ground in which he rests except an incomprehensible light *(niet en siet noch en ghevoelt dan een ombegripelijc licht)*. And according to the simple bareness which encompasses all things, he finds and feels himself to be that very light by which he sees and nothing else. *(Ende nader eenvuldigher bloetheit die alle dinc beveet, soe vint hi hem ende ghevoelt dat selve licht daer hi met siet, ende niet anders).*[69]

Several observations, some of which will acquire their full significance in the following pages, need to be made. First, Ruusbroec obviously does not want to say that the spirit ontologically becomes the

Son of God. Deification is a transformation of the human person, not an identification with God.

Second, in self-transcendence the object-subject relation seems to disappear: there is no utterable or perceivable distinction between the soul and the Brightness that it sees and by which it sees.

Third, Ruusbroec clearly uses apophatic language, such as hidden brightness (*verborghene claerheit;* c 77) and an incomprehensible light (*een ombegripelijc licht;* c 80) to characterize the divine Light. It is therefore unjustifiable to interpret passages like this as somehow a departure from the apophatic tradition, as Dupré does: "Here Ruusbroec decisively takes his distance from any terminally negative theology. . . . For in himself God is not simply darkness or silence. His silence has brought forth the eternal Word; in his darkness shines the eternal Light."[70] The difficulty with Dupré's interpretation is that he seems to share the widespread notion that negative metaphors are an indication of negative theology whereas positive imagery would be an indication of a cataphatic theology. The fact that Ruusbroec continually contrasts the darkness of the divine ground with the brightness of the Son[71] should not be taken as an indication that Ruusbroec is not a negative theologian. Dupré's view entails that every theologian who puts the trinitarian dogma at the heart of his or her theology departs from the tradition of negative theology—which is clearly absurd. Ruusbroec characterizes the Son as an "incommensurable brightness" or an "incomprehensible light": clearly, the Son is as incomprehensible as the fatherly nature he reveals. Holding a different view would imply that the Son differs from the divine essence.[72] It is correct, as I show in chapter 3, that Ruusbroec contrasts the modelessness of the divine nature with the "modes" of the divine Persons, but that does not mean that we can meaningfully describe in positive language the divine nature as revealed by the Son: "The modeless being of God can be demonstrated neither by words nor by actions, by modes nor by signs nor by likenesses. It reveals itself, however, to the simple insight of the imageless mind."[73] The divine self-revelation in the Son is equally beyond words, above our understanding.[74] In short, even though we may not want to agree with the details of his analysis, Turner's claim that the use of negative or positive imagery in itself has nothing to do with negative theology in the full sense remains valid.

Fourth, when Ruusbroec uses metaphors that refer to the sense of taste this is not to describe an experience. Rather, he resorts to them because they clearly express the indistinguishable character of the unity between God and the soul (as opposed, for instance, to visual metaphors that imply a separation between subject and object, although he occasionally uses these too).

Fifth, considering the indeterminative and inexpressible nature of experience, interpreting Ruusbroec's texts as referring to an immediate experience of God will not allow one to distinguish heretical ontological claims from orthodox claims. On the contrary, interpreting Ruusbroec's texts as describing this sort of experience is grist to the mill of his opponents, because the supposed "experience" fuels the heretical claim that the soul has become God: "He finds and feels himself to be that very light by which he sees and nothing else." However, Ruusbroec tries to make clear that the soul that transcends itself perceives no difference between itself and God. Self-transcendence does not refer to a psychological experience but to a radical transformation of the human person whose self-centeredness has been "burnt away": "When the spirit *burns* in love it will find a distinction and an otherness between itself and God when it examines itself. But when it is *burnt* up it is onefold and there is no distinction left. And it will therefore experience nothing but unity for the unmeasured flame of God's love consumes and devours all it can capture inside its own self."[75] In the initial stages of our deification a distinction between God and soul is felt; but in the mature spiritual life (the contemplative life) this distinction has disappeared: the human person has become selfless, radically focused on God. Furthermore, this union is "habitual"—another indication of its nonexperiential nature: "For if we possess God in immersion of loving, that is: lost to ourselves, God is our own and we are his own and we sink away from ourselves for ever, without return, in our possession that is God. This sinking away is essential, with habitual love. And it happens whether we are asleep or awake, whether we know it or not. And so this immersion deserves no new degree of reward, but it keeps us in the possession of God and all the good we have acquired."[76] In short, although it is important to distinguish between the ontological level and expressions pertaining to the mystical union between soul and God, it is misleading to identify the latter with expressions concerning the *experience* of union. This is the very error Ruusbroec holds against his opponents: they focus on their "experiences" from which they draw ontological conclusions. This is what Turner has labeled "experiential positivism."[77]

[B] Throughout the following pages I question the contention that Ruusbroec is mainly talking about experience and not about *ontology*. It will become clear in the discussion of Ruusbroec's exemplarism that his ontology is actually more elaborate and sophisticated than that of his opponents. Whereas Ruusbroec's opponents refer to their experiences to back up the ontological claims they occasionally make, Ruusbroec does not refer to experience to refute them but to sound theology and the basic doctrines of Christian faith.[78] This point will become clearer in the discussion of Ruusbroec's criticism of the heresy of the Free Spirit.

In summary, this "phenomenological" approach and the Jamesian presuppositions on which it rests (namely, that there is something like an immediate religious "experience" that can be described in a meaningful way independent of a more comprehensive doctrinal and theological framework) are unconvincing. Mommaers's "phenomenological" reading of Ruusbroec does little justice to his developed ontological approach and is at odds with his emphasis on the role of Church and sacraments, with the role of Christ's redemptive work, and, finally, with his explicit denouncement of the Brethren of the Free Spirit one of whose main concerns was the pursuing of mystical experiences for their own sake separate from a wider theological and ecclesiological framework. Ruusbroec describes a transformation *(overforminghe)*, a conversion *(bekeringhe)*, a condition *(staet)*, not an experience. To underscore this position it is important to examine the ontological presuppositions of Ruusbroec's apophaticism in greater detail, occasionally indicating his use of Pseudo-Dionysian vocabulary.

Exemplarism and Transcendence

According to Ruusbroec, we have an eternal life in God's Wisdom or Image as divine idea, which is the formal, final, and efficient cause of our created being:

> In this Image God knew us in himself before we were created, and now that we have been created in time he knows us as destined for

himself. This Image is essentially and personally in all people and every person has it whole and entire, undivided; and all people have of it among them all no more than one person has. And thus are we all one, united in our eternal Image, that is the Image of God and the origin of us all: of all our life and our becoming; wherein our created being and our life are hung without intermediary as in its eternal cause. Yet our createdness does not become God, nor [does] the Image of God [become] a creature; for we are created unto the Image, that is: created so as to receive the Image of God, and that Image is uncreated and eternal: the Son of God.[79]

How can Ruusbroec affirm that God's Image exists "personally and essentially" in each person and assert in the same breath that our created being does not become God? Furthermore, how should we understand his claim that we already possess the Image within *and* that we are only created to the Image?

Ruusbroec's position within the apophatic tradition can best be clarified by examining his appropriation of the Augustinian teaching of exemplarism, which he fuses with a more Pseudo-Dionysian understanding of the indistinct (because radically transcendent) nature of God. Therefore, two elements in his appropriation of exemplarism will occupy our attention: on the one hand, there is the implication exemplarism has for our created being; on the other, there is the relation to the transcendent nature of God, which has important consequences for language about the union between God and the soul.

Ruusbroec emphasizes a strict unity between our life in God as idea and our created life: "For the being and the life which we are in God, in our eternal Image, and which we are in ourselves according to (our) essential being, are without intermediary and inseparate."[80] Two consequences follow from this strict unity between our uncreated life in God and our created being. The first is that our created being is naturally "attuned" to participating in the trinitarian life. We have a natural inclination towards self-transcendence as we are made to the Image, whereby "Image" always refers to the Second Person of the Trinity and not, or only in a secondary sense, to the soul.[81] This illustrates that for Ruusbroec too "grace perfects nature": our created being is already a trinitarian blueprint, which has to be perfected through hope, faith, and charity.[82] Because of this natural "attunement" to God the human person's created being shows a threefold inclination towards its own ground: "From this Image our life acquires three properties, through which we become like the Image of God that we have received. For our life is always being, seeing, and inclining towards the origin of our createdness *(wesende, siende ende neighende in den orsprong onser ghescapenheit)*."[83]

This "creaturely" inclination, which is the condition of possibility of natural mysticism, can finally result in a genuine self-transcendence in God: "And by means of the brightness of its eternal Image which shines in it essentially and personally, the spirit sinks away from itself, with respect to the highest part of its natural vigor, into the divine essence, and there abidingly possesses its eternal blessedness, and it flows out again, with all creatures, through the eternal birth of the Son, and is set in its created being by the free will of the Holy Trinity."[84]

To understand what this union with God's Image entails we need to discuss the second aspect of Ruusbroec's exemplarism, his understanding of the transcendent nature of God (an aspect that has important consequences for our language about the distinction between God and soul). In the passage from *Vanden Seven Sloten* quoted earlier in this chapter Ruusbroec describes the divine modelessness (and our relation to it) in language clearly reminiscent of that of Pseudo-Dionysius.

For instance, the metaphor of the eternal point from which and in which all lines emanate and converge is clearly Pseudo-Dionysian in inspiration, as the following passage from *The Divine Names*, 5.6 illustrates: "All the radii of a circle are brought together in the unity of the center which contains all the straight lines brought together within itself. These are linked one to another because of the single point of origin and they are completely unified at this center. As they move a little away from it they are differentiated a little, and as they fall farther they are farther differentiated. That is, the closer they are to the centerpoint, the more they are at one with it and at one with each other, and the more they travel away from it, the more they are separated from each other."[85] Dionysius uses this metaphor to explain that in the monad no differentiation or multiplicity exists: everything created participates in and preexists in a unified way in the first Cause in which there is utter simplicity. Ruusbroec concurs with this view and suggests that our created being is in its essence indistinguishable from the divine being that is nevertheless ontologically removed from everything created: it is our "supra-being." The quoted text does not outline a mystical experience but tries to indicate the implication of the non-distinguishability of God's essence/being in relation to the being of the soul. The Pseudo-Dionysian influence is quite discernible in *Vanden Seven Sloten*, 848–58 (quoted earlier), even in the terminology. Some of Ruusbroec's key notions (*overwesen*, or supra-being) appear to have been adopted from the author of *The Divine Names*, who writes that the "supra-essential being of God" is "at a total remove from every condition, movement, life, imagination, conjecture, name, discourse, thought, conception, being, rest, dwelling, unity, limit, infinity, the totality of existence."[86]

Ruusbroec states that created and uncreated being have nothing in common and are radically unlike each other *and* that God's ground and the soul's ground are one and indistinct. The first aspect—God's transcendence—is the very condition of the second. To understand more fully how God's transcendence can be the foundation of our union with him, Ruusbroec reminds the reader in his main work, *Die Geestelike Brulocht*, that it is not meaningful to distinguish between God and soul the way one can distinguish between two *loci* or two *res*, for that would be to misunderstand the relation between God'(s Image), who transcends our spatiotemporal categories, and the human soul:

> For wherever he comes, there he is; and wherever he is [there he comes; and where he never was], he never comes, for in him there are no chance nor changeability; and everything in which he is, is in him, for he does not go outside of himself. And therefore the spirit possesses God essentially in its bare nature, and God the spirit, for it lives in God and God in it. And with respect to its higher part, it is capable of receiving without intermediary, the brightness of God and all that God can give (it).[87]

This is a crucial quotation, for in it Ruusbroec quite explicitly indicates the implication of God's transcendent nature for the relation between God and soul and their union in particular: if God is truly transcendent, he is in the soul and the soul is in God.

Because God dwells in the soul and continually keeps it in existence and because God radically transcends his creation (to the extent that one can no longer distinguish between God and soul—for you can only distinguish between things that have something in common), Ruusbroec can establish an essential unity—the unity between our life as idea in God and the created soul. This unity always remains in God and is therefore beyond time and place and always acts after the mode of God. As such it "makes us neither holy nor blessed, for all persons, good and evil, have this within themselves, but this is certainly the first principle *(die ieerste sake)* of all holiness and of all blessedness."[88] Thus, there is a strict unity between our created life and our eternal life as idea in God's Image, because God radically transcends our spatiotemporal categories to such a degree that a distinction between God and soul becomes impossible. This essential unity, existing in both good and bad people but hidden from the latter, is both the origin and the fulfillment of our self-transcendence. This explains why Ruusbroec can assert that we both possess the Image and are made to it.[89]

In summary, exemplarism has two important implications: first, our existence as idea in God shapes our created being of which it is the cause; and second, our uncreated life in God's Image is one with and indistinct from our created being as God's nature radically transcends (and is therefore indistinct from) his creation. Therefore, our life as idea in God is both the condition of possibility *(die ieerste sake)* and the fulfillment of the contemplative life.[90] The contemplative life as a participation in the trinitarian dynamics via our uncreated life in the Image is the acme of a graceful transformation that perfects our natural disposition. To understand the nature of this transformation and to make clear why we should refrain from reading it in experiential terms we need to examine two crucial Ruusbroecian concepts, *meyninghe* (intention) and *ghebruken* (enjoyment).

A Single Intention and the Enjoyment of God

Ruusbroec deals in great detail with the graceful adornment of the soul throughout his works. As this is discussed at length in chapter 6, I will only give a brief outline at this stage. In his main work, *Die Geestelike Brulocht*, Ruusbroec distinguishes three lives: an *active* life, that is, a life of increasing virtue, modeled on the life and humanity of Christ; an *inner* or God-yearning life; and a *contemplative* life. The common life seems to be a crowning synthesis of the previous lives: it is a life in which activity and contemplation are harmoniously integrated. However we want to understand Ruusbroec's description of the contemplative life, it will have to accord with this wider ideal of perfect integration of "action" and "rest" or "contemplation."[91]

In the *inner* life two aspects are important: the transformation of the three faculties and the effects of divine grace on the essence of the soul (the divine touch). The memory is raised by grace above all multiplicity and busyness into a unified state of simplicity; the understanding is enlightened, resulting in the knowledge of many modes of virtues and the mystery of Scripture; and, finally, the will is enkindled in quiet love.[92] The effects of grace on the unity of the spirit (the divine touch) are described in colorful language by Ruusbroec—thereby inaugurating a new perspective later adopted by St. John of the Cross and others. The following passage from *Die Brulocht* illustrates this point.

> This is a divine stirring or touch in the unity of our spirit. And it is an irruption and ground of all grace and of all gifts and of all virtues. And this divine stirring is the innermost intermediary between God and ourselves, between rest and activity, between mode and modelessness, between time and eternity. And God produces this spiritual stirring in us first of all, before all gifts; nevertheless, it is the very last thing to be properly recognized and savored by us. For when we have sought God lovingly in all practices, into our innermost ground, then we feel the irruption of all grace and of all the gifts of God. And we feel this touch in the unification of our higher faculties, above reason, yet not without reason, for we perceive that we are touched.[93]

Nevertheless, Ruusbroec does not offer us a description of an experience of God: we feel the effect of this touch of divine grace, but he explicitly denies that we can grasp the source of it: "But if we wish to know what it is or whence it comes, then reason and all creaturely consideration fall short."[94] In chapter 6 I discuss the status of the "divine touch" in greater detail. The divine touch represents the last element in the inner life; that is, in the third or contemplative life, even the divine touch has been transcended.

This *contemplative* life is the topic of the third book of *Die Geestelike Brulocht*. That in the contemplative life there is no longer a discernible distinction between God and soul explains why Ruusbroec outlines this contemplative life in objective, theological language.[95] As a consequence, the third book of *Die Brulocht* is an excellent introduction to his trinitarian theology and its implications for our deification. If, as I argued, no distinction between God and soul is possible in the contemplative life, it comes as no surprise that Ruusbroec, in order to outline our participation in the trinitarian life, resorts to objective-theological language that sketches the intra-trinitarian dynamics. This illustrates that the contemplative life does not refer to an experience but describes how faith in the Trinity functions, to borrow a term from Turner, as "a category of experience."[96] As there is no discernible distinction between God and soul, the soul participates in the generation of the Son, the procession of the Spirit, and the return of the divine Persons in their "enjoyable" unity. In other words, in the contemplative life we know God (in the Son) and love him (in the Spirit) in the same way, albeit only in a necessarily finite, opaque, and analogous manner, as God knows and loves himself. Through faith and love we participate in our eternal life in the Trinity to which our created being is already attuned. Crucial in this participation is a selfless intention and focus on God solely. Therefore, when Ruusbroec describes the transformation of our faculties in the inner life, he does not aim at describing a particular experience in which the memory becomes empty, the understanding enlightened, and so forth, but he describes how grace effects a different intention or disposition towards God, world, and our fellow men. This is why he puts such an emphasis on *die eenvuldighe meyninghe (simplex intentio)*, or the single intention. The following quotation allows me to develop this in greater detail.

> Now understand how we should meet God in each work and increase in greater likeness (to him) and more nobly possess the enjoyable unity. Each good work, no matter how small it is, which is borne into God with love and with uplifted, single(-minded) intention, merits greater likeness and eternal life in God. The single intention draws the scattered faculties together in the unity of the spirit and places the spirit in God. The single intention is end and beginning and enrichment of all virtues. . . . That intention is

single that intends nothing but God and everything as ordered towards God. . . . It is the foundation of all spiritual life. It contains faith, hope and love within itself; for it trusts in God and is faithful to him.[97]

Ruusbroec clarifies how he understands the union between God and man: "Through the ground of a single intention, we go beyond ourselves and meet God without intermediary, and rest with him in the ground of simplicity; there we possess the inheritance which is prepared for us from eternity."[98] He always associates "rest in God" and "enjoyment of God's unity." Now we begin to see what he has in mind: we "rest" in God or "enjoy" him when we, whichever acts we perform (willing, knowing), intend God alone.[99] Resting in God means "offering God all our life and works in single intention." I will clarify the issue further by indicating, first, the connection with Ruusbroec's trinitarian theology and, second, the Augustinian roots of the main impetus of Ruusbroec's teaching on this issue.

The connection between the common life—in which activity and rest are perfectly integrated—and the life of the Trinity is explicitly made in numerous places. In the following passage from *Die Brulocht*, for instance, Ruusbroec explains how we are one with God in and beyond our activity: "We keep the oneness with God above our activity, in bareness of our spirit in divine light, where we possess God above all virtues in rest. For charity in the likeness must be eternally active, but oneness with God in enjoyable love will be forever at rest. And this is what it is to love. For in one now, in one instant, love acts and rests in its beloved. And the one is reinforced by the other. For the higher the love, the more the rest; and the more the rest, the more inner the love. For the one lives in the other."[100] Then Ruusbroec makes the explicit link with the Trinity: "Every lover is one with God and at rest, and Godlike in the activity of love; for God, in his sublime nature of which we bear a likeness, dwells with enjoyment in eternal rest, with respect to the essential oneness, and with working, in eternal activity, with respect to threeness; and each is the perfection of the other, for rest resides in oneness, and activity in threeness. And thus both remain in eternity."[101] The conclusion asserts the impossibility of "tasting" God if one is inordinately attached to creaturely things: "And therefore, if a person is to relish God, he must love; and if he is willing to love, then he can taste. But if he allows himself to be satisfied by other things, then he cannot taste what God is."[102] The link between "tasting" God and "resting with enjoyment" in God's unity can be clarified by referring to the famous Augustinian distinction between *frui* and *uti*. This will further explain what the single intention entails for our union with God.

Enjoyment, or *ghebruken*, is actually translated by Surius as "fruitio." In *On Christian Doctrine* Augustine had made a distinction between *frui* and *uti*, and in *De Trinitate* he refers to this same distinction but links it with the acts of willing and understanding. The text is of some interest because a clear association is made between willing, "resting," and fruition or "enjoyment" of God—exactly the sort of connections Ruusbroec makes throughout his writings: "Two of these, memory and understanding, contain the awareness and knowledge of many things; will is there for us to enjoy them or use them. We enjoy things we know when the will reposes in them because it is delighted by them for their own sakes; we use things when we refer them to something else we would like to enjoy. And what makes the life of men vicious and reprehensible is nothing but using things badly and enjoying them badly."[103]

Augustine thus links enjoyment and repose of the will with being focused on God alone.[104] This does not mean that we should not care for created things but rather that we should love them for God's sake only—not for themselves: *non propter se sed propter aliud*. God should be the sole "object" of our fruition or enjoyment, which implies a detached or selfless relation towards creatures.

In the closing pages of *Vanden Blinkenden Steen*, while criticizing those who engage in quietism, Ruusbroec reiterates his central message:

> All men are deceived who think they contemplate while they love, practice or possess a creature in a disorderly manner *(onordelijc minnen)*, or those who think they can enjoy before they have been cleared of images, or those who rest before they enjoy *(ghebruken)*: they are all deceived. For we must be turned towards God *(te gode ghevoecht zijn)* with open hearts, with a peaceful conscience, with a bare countenance and without deceit, in honest truth. And then we shall ascend from virtue to virtue and contemplate God and enjoy him *(ghebruken)* and become one in him as I told you.[105]

Another text illustrates the same point, namely, that we should enjoy *(ghebruken)* God solely and creatures in God. In a passage in which Ruusbroec emphasizes that we should love God for his own sake, he goes on to say: "Father and mother, wife and children, our own soul and body should not be enjoyed by us *(sele wi niet ghebruken)*; but we will love, be active and make ourselves useful in God's service.... Thus we will have things at our disposal, free from care and remain so [= free from cares] just as if they were not in our possession at all. This the world cannot attain for it has not made itself an offering to God."[106]

In summary, the transformation of the human person results in a different intention or focus in dealing with God and his world. This is what union with God means for Ruusbroec: to live a life of Christian faith and love, in which "rest" or "fruition" of God is perfectly integrated with our human activities (charitable works, prayer, etc.) in a perfect reflection of the trinitarian dynamics in their "active" and "enjoyable" dimensions. This explains a distinctive feature of Ruusbroec's description of the contemplative life: it is presented in objective language, outlining in an apophatic manner the intratrinitarian life with which the soul can become one beyond distinction.[107] This union beyond distinction is based on a specific understanding of the relation of the soul and God, who radically transcends created beings and who for that very reason is said to be indwelling in the soul. With this is connected another distinctive apophatic theme of the late-medieval period, that of annihilation of selfhood. A discussion of this theme will further enhance our understanding of being "intent" on God alone: truly "resting" in God (without turning him into another created "object" of worldly desire) entails a very specific relation to the self—one of selflessness. This will throw further light on the union beyond distinction and the objective language in which it is described. Indeed, participation in the trinitarian life refers to a selfless or detached way of acting in and towards the world: it means to love and to know God (and his creation in him) the way God knows and loves himself, with a common love, both "actively" and with "fruition."[108]

The terms "detached" and "selfless" are Ruusbroec's. Indeed, our transformation centers on "selflessness." Thus, the theme of self-transcendence is of crucial importance to understand Ruusbroec's apophatic theology.

Self-Transcendence in *Vanden Blinkenden Steen*

In his short work, *Vanden Blinkenden Steen,* Ruusbroec gives a concise, attractive, and eloquent exposition of the evolution from self-centeredness to annihilation of selfhood (*eyghen, hem selven, eyghenheit, eyghenscap,* etc.) using the metaphors of hired and faithful servants, secret friends, and hidden sons.[109] Hired servants love themselves so inordinately that they do not wish to serve God except for their own profit; they cut themselves off from God and keep themselves unfree and self-centered *(behouden hem-selven onvry ende in eyghenheiden),* because they seek themselves and are only intent on themselves in all their works *(want si soeken ende meinen hem selven in al hare werken).*[110] Their utilitarian approach is a sign of their lack of the authentic love "which would unite them with God and all his beloved."[111] Because they do not trust in God and because they are joined to themselves in a disorderly manner, they live a life of fear and toil and "always remain alone with themselves."[112] Although they appear to keep God's commandments, they do not keep the law of love: they act only to avoid damnation. Yet their very fear of hell arises from their self-love *(van eyghenre minnen die si tot hem selven hebben).*[113] When a person, with God's help, is able to overcome his selfishness or self-love *(sine eyghenheit)* he becomes a faithful servant who puts his trust in God.[114]

Faithful servants lead an active life *(een werkende leven),* in contrast to the secret friends who maintain a loving and fervent adherence to God for the sake of eternal glory, together with a voluntary renunciation of everything apart from God. God invites them to turn within, revealing to them the many hidden ways of leading a spiritual life.[115] The faithful servants lead an exterior, active life, but they remain interiorly unenlightened. Moreover, they are aware that they fulfill God's will and are therefore not free of self-satisfaction. Their exercises are more exterior than interior, more sensual than spiritual.[116] Predictably, Ruusbroec refers in this context to the Lucan story of Mary and Martha (Lk 10:38–42). Nevertheless, he stresses that the friends will always remain faithful servants in an explicit denouncement of quietism.[117]

However, the friends still possess their interiority with attachment *(die vriende besitten hare inwindicheit met eyghenscap).*[118] They cannot transcend themselves or their works to reach a state of imageless bareness, for their works and their very selves constitute an image and intermediary *(si sijn vermiddelt ende verbeelt met hem-selven ende met haren werken).*[119] They always keep their own self *(si behouden eyghenheit haers selfs),*[120] and they do not wish to die to the self-centeredness of their spirit *(eyghenheit van gheeste)*[121] in God or lead a life of complete conformity with God. They attach great importance to God's gifts and their own interior works—the consolations and sweetness they experience from within. Whereas the friends feel nothing inside but a loving, life-giving ascent that is marked by particular forms, the sons feel, beyond this, a simple deathlike passing over into a state devoid of form *(eenen eenvuldighen stervenden overganc in onwisen).*[122] Again, the interior life of the friends is an upward-tending exercise of love in which they wish to remain forever, together with something of themselves *(met eyghenscape),*[123] but they experience nothing of how a person possesses God through bare love in emptiness of self *(met bloter minnen in ledicheiden).*[124] In short, the sons have renounced themselves and their self-centeredness *(eyghenscap)* in their works, and with a bare imageless spirit they transcend all things and are led directly by the working of the Spirit.[125] When we transcend our self-centeredness we become God's property: "If we do possess God in the immersion of love—that is, if we become lost to ourselves *(dat es in verlorenheiden ons selfs)*—God is our own possession and we are his *(soe es god onse eyghen, ende wij sijn sijn eyghen),* eternally and irretrievably immersing ourselves in our own proper source which is God himself *(in ons eyghendom dat god es).*"[126]

Self-transcendence—"loss of self," as Ruusbroec calls it—does not mean that the soul loses its own activity, knowledge, and love.[127] Ruusbroec clearly rejects a spirituality in which a person focuses on the "consolations" themselves. Only when one is solely focused on God and is *not* attached to the *ways* that lead to God does one become "a hidden son" of God. A critique of people who focus on mystical "experiences" is implied. Loss of self, emptiness, and so forth, should not be construed as a psychological experience in which the intellect, will, and memory have become inactive. Rather, it is a state of the deified person whose focus *(meyninghe)* is radically theocentric or even christocentric in whatever he thinks, wants, or does. We have to purify our self-centeredness, conform to our human nature assumed by Christ so as to be clothed, in grace, with his personality, which will allow us to participate in the intra-trinitarian life: "We should also, through Christ's personality, with a onefold intention and with enjoyable love *(met eenvoldigher meyninghe ende met ghebrukelijcke minnen)*, transcend ourselves and the createdness of Christ, and rest in our inheritance, that is the divine essence, in eternity."[128]

Nevertheless, the fact that we should not focus on the "ways" that lead to the modeless divine being does not mean that we can dispense with them: we can only be united with the modelessness of God via intermediaries or modes—which allows us to question interpretations that stress the "special" character of the union between God and the human person as described by Ruusbroec. Indeed, what Ruusbroec appears to be saying is that we ought to transcend images and intermediaries through those very images and intermediaries: then our reason will succumb to *excessus* and admiration.[129] This interpretation is confirmed by a crucial passage from the *Spieghel* in which Ruusbroec describes "the common man" who beseeches God, "[T]ake me fully into yourself and consume me, so that I might become one life with you and in you and that I might be able to transcend myself in your life and above all modes and practices to a state devoid of modes *(boven alle wisen ende ufeninghe in onwisen)*—that is, to a state of modeless love where you are your own beatitude and that of all the saints. It is here that I will find the fruit of all the sacraments, of all particular forms, and of all holiness." But then he makes this significant addition: "However, we must seek this fruit in particular modes *(met wisen)*, in the sacraments, and in a holy life; only then will we find it modelessly and without measure *(wiselooes ende sonder mate)*, in eternal and fathomless love."[130] Thus, we can meet God in a modeless *(wiselooes)* knowledge and love that must always be mediated by different forms, modes, or intermediaries *(wisen)*. This raises serious doubts about interpretations that assume Ruusbroec offers a description of a mystical experience that supersedes the ordinary means of salvation or even offers "a phenomenology of the mystical experience" in which the soul knows God's essence with an "experiential knowledge."[131] The union with God is not an esoteric experience, but it takes place in faith: "God reveals himself to those he wishes, to those who transcend themselves *(die haers-selfs vertijen)*, who follow his grace in what they do and leave undone and in their practice of all the virtues, and who through faith, hope and love are elevated above all their works to their soul's bare act of seeing *(boven alle hare werke verhaven sijn in dat blooete ghesichte der zielen).*"[132] When Ruusbroec talks of union with God, what he has in mind is knowledge and love of God that we acquire through the ordinary means of Christian faith and worship. We find more evidence in support of this point in Ruusbroec's vehement criticism of the Brethren of the Free Spirit.

Ruusbroec and the Brethren of the Free Spirit

In almost all of his writings Ruusbroec criticized the Brethren of the Free Spirit and their practice of natural mysticism. According to Ruusbroec, the Brethren are guilty of "neglecting all the sacraments and all virtues and all practices of the Holy Church, for they think they have no need of them."[133] Furthermore, he repeatedly stresses that they turn mysticism into a technique: "But now consider the manner in which a person surrenders himself to this natural rest. It is a sitting still without (any) practice within or without, in emptiness, so that rest may be found and abide unhindered. . . . And this rest is nothing but an emptiness into which a person falls and forgets himself and God and everything with respect to any activity."[134]

If the natural mystic can empty himself of images and of all works, he can find rest in mere nature, without the grace of God.[135] But the loving spirit cannot rest in this, for charity and the inward stirring of the grace of God do not lie still.[136] Another problem he identifies is their alleged autotheism: they pretend to be one with God without grace. It has been argued that Ruusbroec criticized quietism in his early works and later also focused his attacks on autotheism.[137] More significant for my argument is the relation Ruusbroec observes between these errors: "For in the highest point in which they are turned, they feel nothing save the simplicity of their essence, hanging in the essence of God. This absolute simplicity which they possess they regard as being God because there they find a natural repose. This is why they consider themselves as being God in the ground of their simplicity, for they lack real faith, hope and love."[138]

The heretics thus draw ontological conclusions from their experience: quietism leads to autotheism. It is the "blind essential repose which they experience"[139] that leads them to believe, not only that they are God, but also that the Persons will disappear into the Divinity and "nothing else will remain in eternity but the essential substance of Divinity."[140] So they even draw conclusions about the nature of the Trinity from their experience.

It is now possible to clarify an issue raised previously, namely, that Ruusbroec often seems to reject statements of the heretics that he himself then seems to make regularly. If it is correct, as Turner claims, that there were spiritual movements in the fourteenth century and later that "cashed in" the apophatic language for religious experience, then it will be very hard to distinguish their approach from the more traditional apophatic writings. Undoubtedly, people like *The Cloud* author and Eckhart (occasionally) reacted against spiritual movements that they considered similar yet fundamentally different in nature from their own spiritual project. Whereas Ruusbroec and Eckhart offer a clear theological context, characterized by a specific theological discourse (apophatic language based on specific assumptions on the relation between God's transcendence and his creation), their opponents interpret their language in terms of an immediate mystical experience, severed from a theological framework. This explains why Ruusbroec condemns statements by the heretics that he himself seems to make.

For instance, we find that he rejects the claim of the "heretics" that they live without will and that they have died to their selves,[141] but this is exactly the sort of language he uses to describe the mature spiritual life. This bizarre feature is further evidence for the interpretation presented here: because Ruusbroec's opponents understand descriptions of the union of God and soul in experiential terms, his attack on them is clothed in terms identical to his own project. Yet their meaning differs considerably from his understanding of union. Some additional examples will clarify this point. When Ruusbroec writes that one ought to abandon one's own will his opponents interpret this literally, as an experiential datum ("to be in a state without will"), whereas he wants us to give up our *own* will/self-centeredness and lead a life that is radically theocentric.[142] The same applies to the transformation of memory (becoming imageless) and intellect (see chap. 6). Self-transcendence does not entail that a person has lost the use of his faculties. It is not an *experience* in which the faculties are being worked upon by God. It is essentially about *intention (meyninghe):* our faculties ought to be focused on God solely. This aspect is crucial for understanding his doctrine, and he leaves us in no doubt about its importance.[143] Insofar as a person is solely intent on God, he "rests" in God, but this rest is only possible in the midst of activity, whether this activity is a life of prayer or charitable works. The common man lives a life of actively loving and resting above activity.[144] God, writes Ruusbroec, "demands of us enjoyment and activity, and not that the one should be hindered by the other, but rather always fortified. Therefore, the inner person possesses his life in those two modes, that is, in resting and activity. And in each, he is whole and undivided, for he is wholly in God where he rests in enjoyment, and he is wholly in himself where he loves with works. And he is admonished and bidden by God at every moment to renew both rest and activity."[145] Ruusbroec's spiritual ideal is one in which activity and rest are perfectly integrated. Those who lose themselves exclusively in outward works or indulge without action in an inner emptiness cannot understand it.[146]

Ruusbroec rejects an experiential interpretation of his mystical theology. The hallmark of the experience described by the Free Spirit is that it is characterized by *passivity*. Of course, Ruusbroec acknowledges the role of grace in our deification,[147] but the heretics he combats interpret this as referring to mystical experiences in which the faculties become passive and empty. They separate spirituality from the broader theological, doctrinal, and ethical framework of the Church: "By means of the natural rest which they feel and possess in themselves, in emptiness, they maintain that they are free and united to God without intermediary, and that they are elevated above all practices of the Holy Church, and above the commandments of God, and above the law, and above all the virtuous activity that one can have in any way."[148] They consider the experience of emptiness nobler than all virtue and want to remain in it unhindered: "And therefore, they stand in a pure passivity without any activity upwards or downwards *(Ende hier omme staen si in eenen pueren lidene zonder eenich werc opwert och nederweert)*, just like a loom which itself is inactive and awaits its master, when he wishes to work. For if they did anything, God would be hindered in his activity, and this is why they are void of all virtue, and so empty that they wish neither to thank nor to praise God, and they have neither knowledge, nor love, nor will, nor prayer, nor desire."[149] They maintain that they are "empty of all works, and that they are nothing other than an instrument with which God works what he wills and how he wills. And therefore, they say that they are in a pure passivity without working."[150] Again, Ruusbroec himself had described the common man in *Vanden Blinkenden Steen* 943–44 as "a living and willing instrument of God with which God does what he wants, the way he wants." But whereas Ruusbroec has complete conformity to God in mind (the will ought to conform to God's will), his opponents take his words on their prima facie meaning (one ought to become willless).

Ruusbroec acknowledges that the creature undergoes the working of God's grace passively, but he rejects a passivity that accompanies a supposed immediate experience of God. Grace is a gift that one receives; the natural mystical experience is induced—it is a technique—aimed at resting passively in one's self. Ruusbroec explains that passivity should not be construed as if the creature lost its activity. The Brethren claim that God performs their works and they undergo God's working in emptiness.[151] Ruusbroec's answer is illuminating:

> This is altogether deceit and impossible, for God's working in himself is eternal and immutable, for (what) he works (is) himself, and nothing else. . . . But the creatures have their own activity, through the power of God, in nature and in grace and in glory. Now, were it possible—which it is not—for the creature to be annihilated with respect to its activity, and to be as empty as it was when it did not exist, namely that it would become one with God in every way as it then was, then it could not gain more merit than it did then; it would also be no holier nor more blessed than a stone or a stick—for without our own activity, love and knowledge of God, we cannot be blessed; but God would be (as) blessed as he was eternally, though it would be of no avail to us.[152]

Likewise, when Ruusbroec criticizes people who pay more attention to their external works than to God for whom they (should) perform them,[153] he does not want to suggest that therefore one should not strive for virtue or perform any works. Yet this is exactly how the heretics interpret Ruusbroec's message: "And therefore they say: as long as a person strives for virtue and yearns to do the dearest will of God, then he is still an imperfect person. For he is still gathering virtues, and he knows nothing of spiritual poverty, nor of this emptiness."[154] If one interprets Ruusbroec's discourse in psychological categories or as outlining a straightforward religious experience, false conclusions are easily drawn: "For they say that they live without will and that they have given their spirit to God in rest and emptiness and that they are one with God and are annihilated with respect to themselves *(ende datsi sijn een met gode, ende te niete worden ane hen selven)*."[155] This is indeed the sort of language Ruusbroec himself used to describe self-transcendence—but he does not aim at describing an experience but a state or condition that is characteristic of the deified person.[156]

According to Ruusbroec, heretics are guilty of "spiritual unchastity": "in their lust, they are entirely inclined towards inward savor and towards the spiritual ease of their nature."[157] The problem of the heretic is an unruly relation towards his *self*: he is "inclined towards himself with natural love, and he seeks and desires consolation and sweetness and whatever brings him pleasure. And this is like a merchant. For in all his work he is turned back upon himself, and he seeks and is intent upon his rest and his profit more than the honor of God. The person who lives this way in mere natural love always possesses his own proper self undetached from self-will."[158] He contrasts the heretic's attitude with Mary, whose life was one of perfect purity and who "never tasted consolation or any gifts with gluttony."[159]

Observations

I have argued that Jan van Ruusbroec ought to be seen as a representative of the medieval apophatic tradition that draws its inspiration from Pseudo-Dionysian and Augustinian elements. This tradition produced a specific discourse—embedded in the larger context of the faith and practices of the Church—on the union between God and soul in which we find the resources for a critique of the understanding of that union in terms of immediate, unmediated experience.

To buttress this claim, I have given a brief overview of essential features of Ruusbroec's theology, beginning with a brief analysis of his trinitarian doctrine with special attention to the notion of *regiratio*. Ruusbroec's understanding of the Trinity is highly dynamic: not only do Son and Spirit proceed, but they also flow back into the modeless divine being where they rest in enjoyment, in an eternal rhythm of ebbing and flowing: "God is a flowing, ebbing sea, which flows without cease into all his beloved, according to each one's needs and dignity. And he is ebbing back in again, drawing all those whom he has endowed on heaven and earth, together with all that they have and can do."[160] As this quotation suggests, we can participate in this trinitarian dynamics: this is Ruusbroec's spiritual ideal of the common life in which "activity" and "rest" are perfectly integrated. However, his description of this union between God and soul should not be construed as if it referred to a mystical "experience of God"—an interpretation inspired by William James and favored by most Ruusbroecian scholars in recent decades.

Ruusbroec also appropriates Augustinian exemplarism in an original manner by fusing it with elements that seem more Pseudo-Dionysian in inspiration. Thus, he uses exemplarism in a double manner: first, to explain how our created being is already naturally attuned to the life of the Trinity; and second, to show how our uncreated life as Idea in God accounts for the fact that God and soul cannot be distinguished. These two elements—which are closely interlinked—explain why our eternal life in God as Idea is both the origin (because it inchoately shapes our created nature according to the Image of the Trinity) and the fulfillment of our self-transcendence in God (where no distinction between soul and God is possible, as God's radical transcendence implies indistinguishability from created things).

Having clarified these ontological presuppositions of Ruusbroec's apophaticism, I have also examined his understanding of the union of God and soul. I have argued that Ruusbroec does not describe a psychological *experience* in which memory, intellect, and will have an immediate contact with God but a *state* of the deified person who relates in an entirely new manner to God and world. Crucial in this is the single intention or focus *(meyninghe):* "That intention is single that intends nothing but God and everything created as ordered towards God."[161] This interpretation is corroborated by understanding that "enjoyment" of God has to be seen in light of the Augustinian distinction between *usus* and *fruitio*. Augustine too associates "enjoying" God, "resting" in God, and taking God as the sole "object" of willing.

There is further support for my claim that the union between God and soul is above all a matter of theocentric intention in Ruusbroec's description of "loss of self" in his treatise *Vanden Blinkenden Steen*.

Taking God as the sole "object" of fruition implies annihilation of attachment to both self and "ways" to attain God. However, this detachment from "ways" does not mean that we are justified to dispense with them. Ruusbroec states that we can only attain God's modeless being via modes—and he shows little patience for people who claim to not need sacraments or who do not perform charitable works. This is the basis for Ruusbroec's criticism of the Brethren of the Free Spirit. Here it becomes abundantly clear that an experiential reading is at odds with his most central concerns. He explicitly denounces the Brethren, who engaged in natural mysticism outside the context of Christian faith, the Church, and its sacraments, thereby turning mystical theology into a technique aimed at undergoing mystical experiences.

In subsequent chapters I flesh out some of the issues that have not been dealt with in any detail in this introductory chapter. A more detailed exposition of Ruusbroec's trinitarian doctrine is essential for understanding the rest of his theology (chap. 3). We also need to examine in greater detail how the created soul can be called a trinitarian blueprint (chap. 4). In chapter 5, dealing with Ruusbroec's christology, I investigate the crucial role of Christ's redemptive work in enabling us to participate in the trinitarian life. In particular, I show how renouncement of self ties in with Christ's sacrificial work, which needs to be understood as a self-gift that generates (or better, restores) a loving relationship between humanity and God. In chapter 6, on deification, I attempt to bring some of those themes back together so as to shed further light on the topics discussed here.

CHAPTER 3

"A flowing, ebbing sea"
Trinitarian Doctrine and *Regiratio*

The notion of *regiratio*—the flowing back of the divine Persons into their shared unity—is central to Ruusbroec's trinitarian doctrine. Although it has been argued by J. B. Porion and others that Ruusbroec adopted the idea of *regiratio* from the beguine Hadewijch (ca. 1210–60) whose writings he almost certainly knew,[1] it seems to me that Ruusbroec's trinitarian doctrine is very much sui generis. To highlight the originality of Ruusbroec's use of this theme, I briefly indicate how some of his predecessors (St. Albert the Great and his followers, including Thomas Aquinas and, later, Meister Eckhart) developed this Neoplatonic notion and contrast some key issues from Ruusbroec's trinitarian theology (such as the role of the Spirit in the divine flowing-back) with the ideas of Richard of St. Victor and other major theologians. In unpacking Ruusbroec's theology, I pay specific attention to his characterization of the nature of the divine *being* or essence and examine the tension between the divine being and the Persons. The question of how the fruitful nature of the divinity relates to this modeless divine essence or being is also discussed in detail.

Regiratio

There are two reasons for putting the relatively unknown notion of *regiratio* in its proper theoretical context: because it is central to Ruusbroec's doctrine and because it will strengthen my argument that we have to be aware of the Neoplatonic themes present in the writings of most major mystical theologians, including Ruusbroec's. Therefore, below I briefly examine the notion of *regiratio* in the writings of Albert the Great, Aquinas, and Eckhart so as to make clear Ruusbroec's highly original perspective.[2]

Albert the Great

The notion of "return"—*reditus, reflexio, regiratio, regressus*—is of course a major theme in Neoplatonic thought, and it is therefore no surprise that this notion was adopted by the scholastics. However, less known is the way the notion of return affected, or did not affect, the trinitarian doctrine of major theologians at the end of the thirteenth and the beginning of the fourteenth century.

Although the notion of *regiratio* or *motus circularis* was well known to scholastics such as Albert the Great, Albert prefers not to apply it to the intra-trinitarian life. Instead, he applies the theme of *exitus-reditus* primarily to the created world—everything finds its origin in God and returns to him—but not to the divine processions. One of the main reasons that Albert refuses to apply the theme of *motus circularis* or *regiratio* to the intra-divine processions is that, in his view, it somehow suggests a deficiency in the *vis spiralis* of the Son. Why then does Albert in this context discuss the notion of *regiratio* in the first place? The link between the Neoplatonic notion of *regiratio* and intra-trinitarian doctrine was suggested by the traditional theme of the Spirit as the loving union between Father and Son. This idea of the Spirit as the bond of Love, or the mutual Love of Father and Son originates in the teaching of Augustine as developed throughout the Middle Ages, especially by Richard of St. Victor. Thus, the theme of the Spirit as the mutual Love between Father and Son was linked by Albert with the Neoplatonic notions of *egressus* and *regressus,* and this allows him to characterize the intra-trinitarian processions as a circular movement from the Father through the Son to the Spirit and back. It is only in this attenuated sense that Albert is willing to speak of *regiratio* or *regressus* within the Trinity, namely, insofar as the Father is the origin of Son and Spirit and insofar as the Spirit is their bond of Love, which represents a sort of union. It is in this context that he quotes proposition 1 from the *Book of the XXIV Philosophers* (*Deus est monas monadem gignens, in se unum reflectens ardorem*).[3] This link with the role of the Spirit provides a second reason why Albert does not attribute a genuine *regressus* or *regiratio* to the divine Persons: if the Spirit as mutual Love of Father and Son is the principle of the return of the divine Persons, then we are in danger of implying that the Father and the Son love one another through the Spirit; that is, the Spirit becomes the *principium diligendi* of Father and Son. However, it is inappropriate to state that the Father and the Son somehow "need" the Spirit to love one another, since the Father and the Son love another in the divine nature (and not in the Spirit who merely proceeds as their Love).[4] In short, Albert is willing to use the metaphor of return to describe the intra-trinitarian life insofar as the reciprocity of the love between Father and Son seems to suggest a sort of return of love to the Father, because of the union of the person loved with the person who loves. However, he does not want to entertain the idea that, properly speaking, the notion of *exitus-reditus* could be ascribed to the intra-trinitarian life itself, as if the Father was not just the origin but also the end of the divine processions—which is exactly how Ruusbroec sees it. Therefore, properly speaking, the idea of *reditus* should be applied only to creation: God is the goal of the return of *creatures* in God. Albert then develops these ideas in greater detail in his commentaries on Dionysius's works *The Celestial Hierarchy* and *The Divine Names*. In the first work, the concept of *circulatio completa* emerges as the basic structure of the angelic world, while the image of flux and reflux from the prologue to *The Celestial Hierarchy* allows Albert to present the Father as the origin and goal of all things. In his *Commentary on the Divine Names,* the theme of *exitus* and *reditus* also refers in the first place to the created perfections in the world, which illustrate the overflowing goodness of the divine nature.[5]

Aquinas

The views of the young Aquinas on *regiratio* do not differ substantially from those of Albert. According to the *index thomisticus* Aquinas uses the noun *regiratio* three times and the verb *regirare* only once. Only one passage, from his *Commentary on the Sentences,* is particularly relevant for our purposes. In this passage, Aquinas argues that we can speak of a circular movement or "return" *(circulatio vel regiratio)* insofar as *creatures* proceed from the first Principle, to which they also return. The out-going *(exitus)* of things from God and their return to God as to their end *(reditus in finem)* are both caused by the divine goodness.[6] The creation of things is described as an *exitus a principio* and creatures attain their perfection when they attain their goal, or *finis.* The *principium* corresponds to the *finis:* attaining your goal is returning to the *principium,* or beginning. Creatures attain their goal following an order that corresponds to and reflects the *processio* from their origin. Thus, the *exitus* and the *reditus in finem* take place *per eadem:* our return to God corresponds to the procession of divine goodness towards us.[7] Thus, Aquinas too prefers to apply the notion of *regiratio* to the effects of the divine processions in the *created* world, namely, the processions of wisdom and goodness in creatures, and our return through the gifts of wisdom and love. He makes a close connection between the intra-divine processions, on the one hand, and (re-)creation, on the other: "The procession of the Persons *(processio personarum)* is the cause of the production of creatures *(ratio productionis creaturarum)* ... and likewise, this same procession is the cause of the return towards the end *(ratio redeundi in finem),* namely, as we have been created through the Son and the Spirit *(per Filium et Spiritum sanctum),* similarly, we are being united to our ultimate goal through them *(ita etiam et fini ultimo conjungimur).*"[8]

Two things need to be pointed out in this context:

(1) Aquinas obviously draws a close parallel between the intra- and the extra-trinitarian operations, that is, between the processions, on the one hand, and creation and the mission of the divine Persons, on the other.
(2) Nevertheless, despite this close parallel, Aquinas is not willing to allow for an intra-trinitarian *regiratio: regiratio* only applies to

created things as they return to their origin—a position not unlike the one defended by Albert.

In short, *regiratio* does not refer to the intra-trinitarian processions but to the creaturely effects of these intra-trinitarian processions; or again: the structure *exitus-reditus* refers to the economic Trinity, not the immanent Trinity.[9]

Meister Eckhart

Meister Eckhart is the first major author who applies the structure of *exitus-reditus* to the immanent Trinity. Given the complexity of his thought, a short exposition of his main teaching is bound to be somewhat unsatisfactory. Nevertheless, I hope to make clear the contrast in relation to the theme of *regiratio* between Eckhart and the other figures discussed so far. Eckhart refers to proposition 15 of the *Liber de Causis* to explain how the Son flows back into the Father. Whereas Aquinas used proposition 15 ("Every knower knows its essence. Therefore it reverts to its essence with a complete reversion") to explain how God knows his essence (and all creaturely things) directly through himself—unlike the human soul which has to turn to phantasms in order to acquire knowledge[10]—Eckhart uses it in an altogether different, more trinitarian context, namely, to account for the "complete return" of the Son into the Father: "The first outburst and the first effusion God runs out into is his fusion into the Son, who flows back into the Father."[11] In many of his other works Eckhart refers to the *reditio completa*. What complicates the issue is that Eckhart, drawing on Aristotle's *De Anima*, affirms a connaturality between the human soul as intellect and God. According to Book III of *De Anima*, the intellect has to be universal, incorporeal, and separated from matter (*De Anima*, 429 a 24–25) in order for it to know things. As the intellect does not have a character of its own, it can take on the forms without distortion in the act of thinking. God too is intellect or spirit, according to Eckhart, and therefore the soul, insofar as it is intellect, is indistinguishable from God.[12] This indistinguishability of God and soul explains how the soul can participate in the "complete return" of the Word into the Father. Often Eckhart seems deliberately ambiguous, leaving it unclear whether he is talking of the procession and return of the Son or of the human soul.

A good example of this ambiguity is found in *Sermon XLIX*.[13] In this text Eckhart discusses the apex of the soul as God's image. He points out that an image cannot be separated from that of which it is the image: we cannot separate the image and its exemplar as if they were two substances, but the one is in the other. He goes on to say: "It is consequently necessary that the image be found only in intellectual nature where the same reality returns to itself in a perfect return *(reditio completa)* and where the one that gives birth is one and the same with the child or the off-spring, finding oneself in the other and the other in oneself." The context makes clear that Eckhart is not just talking about the Image of God—that is, the Second Person of the Trinity—but also about the soul (as intellectual or uncreated) insofar as it participates in the *generatio* and *reditio* of the Son, as God and soul are one and indistinct. This theme was developed in much greater detail in his German works: the spark of the soul refers to the intellectual, eternal, immaterial aspect of the soul that is indistinct and one with God and therefore shares in the birth or generation of the Word.

Clearly, while Albert refused to allow for a genuine intra-trinitarian *regressus*, Eckhart does not share Albert's reservations and is happy to state that the Son flows back into the divine unity. Also, whereas Albert associated *regiratio* with the Spirit as the mutual Love of Father and Son (cf. Ruusbroec), Eckhart, drawing on *Liber de Causis* and Aristotle's *De Anima*, focuses on the Word as the principle of the "complete return" into the divine unity.

Ruusbroec's Trinitarian Theology and *Regiratio*

Ruusbroec, like Eckhart, does not have any reservations about applying the Neoplatonic notion of *regressus* to the inner Trinity, but, unlike Eckhart, he associates the return of the Persons primarily with the Person of the Spirit rather than the Son. The best way to introduce key aspects of his teaching is by presenting a major section of his work.

> God is every being's super-essence *(overwesen)*. His Godhead is a fathomless whirlpool; whoever enters it loses himself in it. God is one in nature, threeness in Persons. Threeness is eternally remaining in oneness of nature, and oneness of nature in threeness of personhood. Thus nature is living and fruitful in eternity. The

being/essence of God is idle, eternal beginning and end, a living subsistence of everything created. And that same being is nature and fruitful and potentiality of the Persons. And that potentiality is personhood and personal in three properties, namely, paternity, filiation, and, entailed in them, the third property, namely, voluntary spiration.

The nature cannot exist without the Persons, nor the Persons without their substance, for it is a living support of the Persons. Therefore the nature is one in itself, fruitful in threeness, and threeness in oneness, and oneness lives in threeness, and threeness is fruitful in itself; and it is not distinguishable according to things, but according to reason. For threeness is oneness of nature. It generates the Persons, distinct according to reason and in reality, namely the Father, the Son and the Holy Spirit: they are three distinct Persons and one Godhead whom one should not divide or separate. Thus we confess one God in three Persons. . . .

The Father is an eternal beginning *(beghin)* of the Persons and that beginning is essential and personal. . . . He begets the eternal Wisdom, his Son who is equal and consubstantial with him. He knows his only begotten Son as eternally unborn in himself, as ceaselessly being born from him, and as having been born from him as another Person, always one God in nature with himself. The Son is the Wisdom of the Father. He beholds and contemplates his origin, namely, his Father. He sees himself as unborn within the nature, as out-flowing in personal distinction from the Father's substance, as a distinct Person from the Father and as always remaining with the Father within the nature. From this mutual contemplation of Father and Son flows an eternal pleasure, the Holy Spirit, the third Person, who flows forth from the other two. For he is one will and one love in both of them, eternally flowing out of them and flowing back in into the nature of the Godhead.[14]

As we have seen, the concept of *regiratio* is not unique to Ruusbroec, but the way he deploys it—by consistently applying it to the intra-trinitarian life and in particular to the Spirit as the active principle of the return of the divine Persons into their perichoretic unity—is; and it has bearings throughout his doctrine, on his understanding of the relation between God and humanity, the incarnation, passion, and eucharist, the gifts of the Spirit, and so forth, which have to be interpreted in light of the bestowal of gifts by God in order to establish a loving relationship with humanity in which we can reciprocate these gifts in a dynamic that finds its origin in the heart of the Trinity. In short, the Spirit is not just the "passive" Love, resulting from the mutual contemplation of Father and Son, but he is an active principle in their flowing back into the divine essence, so that the trinitarian life can be described using dynamic metaphors, such as a "flowing and ebbing sea," a circular movement, or even a "whirlpool," an image especially dear to Ruusbroec. Ruusbroec therefore distinguishes three moments in the intra-trinitarian life: (a) there is the activity of the divine *processions* of Son and of Spirit, from the fruitfulness of the fatherly nature; (b) there is the *return,* or *regiratio,* of the divine Persons into their shared unity or essence; and finally (c) there is the moment of "excessus," passing over or "yielding" of the divine Persons in their *enjoyable* or idle essence.

Another noteworthy aspect of this elaborate quotation is the distinction Ruusbroec draws between the divine nature as the fruitful source of the divinity and the divine essence or being *(wesen)*. "Nature" is associated with the "activity" within the Trinity, namely, the generation of the Son and the procession of the Spirit, while "Essence" or "Being" is associated with "idleness" and "rest." This distinction, which needs to be seen in light of his teaching on *regiratio,* is merely conceptual as in reality "nature" and "essence" are identical. A third interesting aspect is the emphasis on the primacy of the Father as the fruitful source of the divinity. This emphasis is by no means self-evident. It seems distinctly reminiscent of a major theme of Bonaventure's trinitarian theology, as I show below.[15] Simplifying matters, we can state that Bonaventure fused Augustinian elements, as developed by Richard of St. Victor in his work *De Trinitate,* with Pseudo-Dionysian elements, to develop a highly original trinitarian doctrine. The Pseudo-Dionysian element can be discerned in the role Bonaventure (and Ruusbroec after him) ascribes to the divine nature: this nature, always located in the Father, is the *fruitful* origin of the divinity. The Neoplatonic theme of *bonum sui diffusivum* is used to explain the first procession, the generation of the Son. There can be little doubt that Ruusbroec was familiar with this line of theological thinking, and

Ruusbroec's own ideas can be fully grasped only in relation to some of the main aspects of Bonaventure's doctrine. First, however, I want to examine how Ruusbroec characterizes the divine being or essence *(wesen)*, which is essential to understand the tension he sees between the enjoyable rest at the heart of the divinity, on the one hand, and the activity in the threeness of the Persons, on the other.

The Relation between the Divine Being, Nature, and Persons

The Modelessness of the Divine Being

Ruusbroec shares the conventional medieval thesis that the divine perfections (which are reflected in multiple ways in creation) are simple in God's essence. We can attribute the perfections we encounter in this created world to its Cause, but how they are actualized in God's modeless, undifferentiated essence is something we cannot know: we can only say that God is, not what he is.[16] Before exploring this notion, I need to clarify further the "modelessness" of the divine being or essence. Ruusbroec characterizes *wiseloos* as "without mode, neither this nor that, neither here nor there" *(zonder maniere, noch sus noch sooe, noch hier noch daer)*.[17] The concept is consistently used to denote the divine essence *and* our knowledge and love of it. Indeed, the vocabulary Ruusbroec uses to describe the "yielding" *(overliden)* of the divine Persons before their shared unity is much the same as he uses to describe the "yielding" of humans before God. Accordingly, Surius translates *overliden* as *excessus*, a Pseudo-Dionysian concept that expresses the acme of negative theology, in which human knowledge transcends itself:

> For the unfathomable modelessness *(afgrondighe onwise)* of God is so dark and so modeless that it encompasses within itself all divine modes *(wisen)* and activity and property of the Persons, in the rich embrace of the essential unity *(weselijcker eenicheit)*, and (that it) produces a divine enjoyment in this abyss of namelessness. And here is the enjoyable passing-over *(een ghebrukelijc overliden)*, an engulfment flowing away into essential bareness where all divine names and all modes and all life-giving ideas which are

depicted in the mirror of divine truth fall without exception into this simple namelessness, without modes and without reason.[18]

As I show in chapter 6, Ruusbroec draws a close parallel between the intra-trinitarian activity in both its moments (both in-going and out-going) and divine rest, on the one hand, and the human participation in it, on the other.[19] All discursive knowledge is transformed in the contemplative life in "a bottomless unknowing" *(in onwetene sonder gront)* if we, beyond all names which we can give to God or creatures, pass away into "the abyss of namelessness" in which we lose ourselves.[20] Again, the remote influence of the Pseudo-Dionysius, who wanted to investigate the divine names of "the unutterable and unnameable Deity," is discernible.[21]

The most fascinating aspect of Ruusbroec's trinitarian theology is his suggestion that even the divine Persons themselves have to "yield" before the modeless divine being. The "unfathomable modelessness of God" *(die afgrondighe onwise gods)* is so dark and modeless that it encompasses all divine modes and activity and property of the Persons. All divine names and all modes and all life-giving ideas that are depicted in the mirror of the divine truth (= Son) fall without exception "into this simple namelessness, without modes or reason." We are left in no doubt that the divine Persons themselves flow back into this dark stillness: "the Persons and everything that is in God must yield before this."[22] Below I discuss the role of the Spirit in this *regiratio* and the relation between the simple divine essence and the fecundity of the divine nature. For now it suffices to indicate that Ruusbroec shares a Neoplatonic understanding of the divine being or essence, which is the cause of all beings and yet transcends created being utterly.[23] He has radicalized the Neoplatonic emphasis on the undifferentiated (*wiseloos,* or modeless) divine essence/being to the extent that he even allows the Persons themselves to "yield" before their shared being. In short, Ruusbroec opposes the modelessness of the divine being in which all differentiation is transcended in rest and enjoyment to the divine modes (= Persons) and the intra-divine activity (= generation and spiration):

> Where the divine Persons de-spirate themselves in the unity of their Being, i.e., in the bottomless abyss of onefold bliss, there is no longer Father, Son, Holy Spirit, or creature. There is nothing

> but onefold Being, namely, the substance of the divine Persons. There we are all one and uncreated in our supra-being (...). There God is without activity in his simple being, eternal idleness, modeless darkness, unnamed isness, the supra-being of all creatures, and a onefold unfathomable bliss of God and all saints.[24]

Of course, Ruusbroec does not mean to convey that the Persons lose their ontological reality in this undifferentiated divine unity. He actually criticizes people who hold the view that "the Persons will disappear into the divinity and that, there, nothing else will remain in eternity but the essential substance of the divinity."[25] As explained in chapter 2, this line of reasoning has to be seen in light of his criticism of the Brethren of the Free Spirit and their pursuit (and justification) of quietist practices.

The divine being or essence thus represents the moment of rest and enjoyment while the Persons represent the intra-trinitarian activity: "The divine Persons are in the fruitfulness of their nature one God, eternally active; and in the simplicity of their divine being/essence *(wesen)* they are one Godhead, eternal idleness. And God is therefore in the Persons eternal activity and in the essence/being eternal idleness."[26] To understand this dichotomy we need to examine the concept of divine "nature," the fruitful ground of the Trinity, and its relation to *wesen* and the divine Persons.

Nature and Being

Ruusbroec opposes God to Godhead, Persons to being/essence, activity to rest.[27] This dichotomy between Persons and being is only conceptual, for it is the Persons who possess the divine being, who are the divine being. Likewise, the opposition of being/essence and nature is only conceptual: "The divine being is inactive, eternal beginning and end, and a living subsistence of everything created. And this same being is nature and fruitful and possession of the Persons."[28] Nature is always squarely situated in the Father. It is therefore wrong to surmise that Ruusbroec posits nature as an "intermediary" between the divine being and the Persons to resolve the tension between unity and multiplicity. This point needs to be discussed in some detail, because in his major study on Ruusbroec A. Ampe defends this particular thesis.

It is my contention that Ruusbroec's thought can only be properly understood in light of a continual tension in unity between the following polarities:

Essence/being	Persons
Godhead	God
Unity	Threeness
Modelessness *(onwisen)*	Modes *(wisen)*
Rest, enjoyment	Activity/work *(werc):*
	– Out-going
	– In-going
Father/Nature	Son, Holy Spirit

The position of the Father in the first column (while the divine Persons are in the second) indicates that for Ruusbroec there is no real opposition between the divine being/essence and the Persons. The divine nature, from which the Son is generated *per modum naturae,* is firmly located in the Father; this same nature is identical to the divine essence/being in which the divine Persons lose themselves in enjoyment. Every interpretation that argues that "because of his strong ontological stance, Ruusbroec has to put forward the fruitfulness of the divine ... nature as a link between the empty essence and the pure activity of the three distinct Persons"[29] misses the main point—that in Ruusbroec's view God is both activity and idle enjoyment in an unremitting tension. If Ampe's interpretation were correct it would also become hard to see how Ruusbroec's trinitarian thought could be free of "quaternity," a teaching that had been rejected by the Fourth Lateran Council. In short, the "mediating" role of "nature," which in Ampe's view is meant to bridge the gap between the unfathomable essence and the intra-trinitarian activity or Persons, is highly doubtful.[30] This interpretation, which understands the divine nature as an intermediary between the divine essence and the Persons, aims at resolving the tension between the unity of the One and multiplicity. However, such a Plotinian reading distorts Ruusbroec's teaching since it does away with the unremitting (dual) tension that forms the heart of his conception of God.

One of the arguments in favor of Ampe's understanding of the divine nature as an intermediary between the divine "essence" and the divine Persons is that it can supposedly be discerned in Ruusbroec's anthropology, which mirrors his trinitarian doctrine. I return to this parallelism in chapter 4, but because Ruusbroec's trinitarian thought and his anthropology are so closely intertwined, it is helpful to mention it here briefly. Thus, Ampe identified two "triads," one horizontal and one vertical, in both God and the human person:

In God	In the human person
Essence *(wesen)*	Essence *(wesen)*
Nature *(natuere)*	Ground *(gront)*
Persons:	Faculties *(vermoghens):*
– Father-Son-Holy Spirit	– Memory-Intellect-Will

The close connection between trinitarian theology and anthropology that this scheme presupposes is correct. Yet the parallelism is not as strict as Ampe assumes, for two important reasons. First, the relation between the divine Persons and their "essence" is very different from the relation between human faculties and their "essence." In the first case there is identity—the Persons do not differ from the divine essence—while in the second there is not. This is perhaps one of the reasons Ruusbroec does not want to call the soul the image of the Trinity—or only do so in a secondary sense. Also, and more important, when he does expound the image-character of the soul, Ruusbroec does *not* refer to the human person's three faculties, as I demonstrate in chapter 4. This telling observation raises serious doubts about the parallelism between the two "horizontal" triads Ampe puts forward.

Therefore, the divine "nature" does not represent a "link" between the divine essence and the activity of the Persons, because for Ruusbroec the nature of the divine is characterized by this constant dialectic between essence and activity, rest and Persons. His understanding of God lives on this tension, the source of divine dynamism. We must try to think both movements together and should not try to eliminate this tension. This is possible if we realize that God's *wesen* is not merely idle essence but being, both idle and fruitful—in which case it is called "fruitful nature," one and threefold. It is not surprising that Ruusbroec occasionally states that the divine being or essence and the fruitful nature are the same.[31] Thus, Ruusbroec views the divine nature,[32] shared by the three Persons, from two perspectives: on the one hand, the divine nature is essence; on the other, it is "fruitful" and the source of divine Persons. From the first perspective, nature is called onefold *(eenvuldigh)*;[33] from the second, it is always called "fruitful" *(vruchtbare)*. God is, according to the fruitfulness of his nature, pure activity *(een puere werken)*, while in the "essential" unity (perhaps better translated as "unity of being") he is eternal rest. Both elements are fundamental and should be thought together, "because God is always active *(werkende)* and constantly enjoying *(ghebrukende)*."[34]

In summary, Ruusbroec considers the divine unity from two angles: as the ground of the divine processions, that is, the fruiful nature situated in the Father; and as the end of the divine *regiratio* in which no distinction can be discerned. Nevertheless, the distinction between the Persons is never abolished: "And there you must accept that the Persons yield and lose themselves whirling in essential love, that is, in enjoyable unity; nevertheless, they always remain according to their personal properties in the working of the Trinity. And thus you may understand that the divine nature is eternally *active* according to the mode of the persons *(na wise der persone)*, and eternally *at rest* and without mode according to the simplicity of its essence/being *(na eenvuldicheit haers wesens)*."[35] The same tension in unity within the divine nature can be found in *Van Seven Trappen*, III, 270, where Ruusbroec writes that where the divine Persons die away in the unity of their being/essence, God is without work, eternal idleness, modeless darkness, unnamed *istegheit* (is-ness), and so forth, but in his fruitful nature the Father is a powerful God, Creator and Maker of heaven and earth.

The idea that we ought to think of God as both at rest and active seems to have Neoplatonic origins. In *The Divine Names* we find for instance that God "proceeds to everything while yet remaining within himself. He is at rest and astir, is neither resting nor stirring and has neither source, nor middle nor end."[36] Ruusbroec's originality lies in situating this tension within the Trinity itself, by associating "activity" with the (processions of the) divine Persons and "rest" or "enjoyment" with their shared being or essence.[37] The divine Persons express the modelessness of the divine being in modes *(wisen)*. They "grasp" as distinct Persons the undifferentiated divine unity in which they "rest" in enjoyment.

This tension at the heart of the Trinity has profound implications for Ruusbroec's understanding of our spiritual goal, which is to love actively and to rest enjoyably: "Every lover is one with God and at rest, and Godlike in the activity of love; for God, in his sublime nature of which we bear a likeness, dwells with enjoyment in eternal rest, with respect to the essential oneness, and with working, in eternal activity, with respect to threeness; and each is the perfection of the other, for rest resides in oneness, and activity in threeness. And thus, both remain for eternity."[38] The full implications of this and similar texts will become evident in the following chapters. Here I want to examine the rest of Ruusbroec's trinitarian doctrine in more detail, discussing the role of nature in relation to the First Person of the Trinity and the distinctive character of the two processions and the three Persons, with specific attention to the Spirit as principle of the divine *regressus*.

The Role of the Fatherly Nature in the Generation of the Son

It is evident that the intra-trinitarian life, as outlined in the works of Ruusbroec, can best be characterized as a circular movement, in which the Father, out of his fruitful nature, gives birth to his Son, and from their mutual contemplation the Spirit flows as their bond of love; and in which also the divine Persons flow back into their shared being/ essence through the Spirit.

How to distinguish between the generation of the Son and the procession of the Spirit—or how to distinguish between the Son and the Spirit themselves—was a problem that occupied theologians at least from the time of St. Augustine onwards. Thomas Aquinas, indebted in this respect to Augustine, clarifies the difference between the two processions by referring to the difference between the activities of will and intellect.[39] His approach differed considerably from that of Bonaventure, who explained the processions in a "naturalistic" way, in terms of self-diffusive goodness—an idea Ruusbroec would adopt, perhaps through Hughes Ripelin of Strasbourg.[40] Indeed, in Bonaventure's exposition the generation of the Son is ultimately conceived in terms of a necessary self-communication, which arises by reason of God's very nature as self-diffusive goodness *(bonum est diffusivum)*.[41] Thus, the primary principle of the Son's generation is the divine nature; the natural fecundity of the Neoplatonic tradition dominates his understanding. Similar to Bonaventure, Ruusbroec integrates the Augustinian tradition within this Pseudo-Dionysian framework, for example: "For as the almighty Father has perfectly comprehended himself in the ground of his fruitfulness, the Son, the eternal Word of the Father, has gone out, as another Person in the Godhead."[42] In summary, according to Bonaventure (and Ruusbroec after him), the fruitful nature is the primary principle in the generation of the Son. The divine nature is necessarily self-communicative (a Pseudo-Dionysian legacy), while the model offered by Richard of St. Victor allows Bonaventure (and Ruusbroec) to move beyond this natural emanation to explain the procession of the Spirit as an emanation from a fecund will. While the divine nature is the primary principle in the generation from the Son, the will is a real principle in the spiration of the third Person. Two emanations can be distinguished: one *per modum naturae* (the *fecunditas naturalis* of the Father is the "cause" of the communication of the divine nature through generation); and another *per modum amoris* (the *fecunditas voluntatis* in the Father and the Son "causes" the procession of the Spirit).

In the previous section I indicated that Ruusbroec always locates the fecundity of the divine nature in the Person of the Father. Indeed, in the major quotation above Ruusbroec actually identifies "paternity" with the fruitful nature. This may appear strange (one would have expected that he would have reserved this term for the relation of the Father to the Son). Ruusbroec's words here and elsewhere,[43] taken at their face value, are in opposition to the document of the Fourth Lateran Council that states that the divine essence is "neither generating nor generated, nor proceeding, but it is the Father who generates, the Son who is generated, and the Holy Spirit who proceeds, so that there are distinctions between the Persons but unity in nature."[44] However, in the same text Ruusbroec also states that the *Father* begets the Son—which seems to illustrate that he firmly locates the fruitful nature in the Father as origin of the Trinity without, however, wanting to imply a strict identity between paternity and fruitful nature.[45] Indeed, the Father is "the principle of the whole Godhead with respect to being and Persons,"[46] "the eternal beginning of the Holy Trinity."[47] Ruusbroec identifies the unity of the divine nature with the Father "because of the fruitfulness and the origin of its eternal works."[48] It also seems to indicate, although Ruusbroec does not deal with this problem in a systematic manner, that the Persons are primarily constituted *per originem* and not *per relationes:* the Father is unoriginated and fruitful source of the other Persons; the Son is from the Father, and from their *mutual* contemplation proceeds the Spirit. What Z. Hayes writes about the position of the Father in Bonaventure's thought also applies to Ruusbroec, who, as we have seen, squarely situates fruitful nature in the Father: "Logically prior to his full and actual paternity which is the active relation to the Son that constitutes him as Father in the full sense, he is Father already in an inchoative sense in as far as his personal property of being fecund source of all others has a logical priority to any actual emanations."[49]

From the lengthy quotation given at the beginning of this section (and innumerable other places in Ruusbroec's writings), we learn that Ruusbroec shares with Bonaventure this emphasis on the fecundity of the divine nature from which the Father generates his Word.

The Procession of the Spirit

Having dealt with the procession of the Son, it is now time to examine the procession of the Spirit. The verb Ruusbroec most frequently uses to describe the procession of the Spirit from the mutual contemplation of Father and Son is "to flow out" and, in the active sense, *gheesten*, "to spirate."[50] The procession of the Spirit occurs *per modum voluntatis*, unlike the generation of the Son, which is determined by the fruitfulness of the fatherly nature. The Spirit flows from their mutual contemplation; he does not flow out of the divine nature, or not of the begetting of the Son, but out of their mutual contemplation:[51] "The Father and the Son spirate one Spirit, which is the will, or love, of them both. And this Spirit neither gives birth nor is born, but, flowing out from both, he must be eternally spirated."[52] The Spirit in its out-flowing aspect is then shared with the whole of creation but resides above all in the Christian Church. Because of his very nature, the Spirit is very much involved with our world and its salvation. Therefore, a strict separation of the functions or operations *ad intra* and *ad extra* of the Holy Spirit is not possible: the Spirit is "a love outflowing *(ene uut vloyende minne)*, which has fulfilled heaven and earth with all that is good."[53]

As the preceding quotations suggest, Ruusbroec frequently refers to the Holy Spirit as the *Minne* of Father and Son: the Holy Spirit is not only the divinely personal love breathed forth by the Father and the Son but also a bond uniting them to one another and uniting all good persons with them, as we can read throughout Ruusbroec's works.[54] This language of the Spirit as a "bond of Love" recalls that of Richard of St. Victor who exerted considerable influence on Bonaventure.[55] A brief outline of their key positions will help to elucidate Ruusbroec's own view in which the most striking element seems to be the role he attributes to the Spirit as an active principle of *regiratio*.

Richard argued from an analysis of the divine essence as love to the existence of the Trinity. When two persons love each other mutually there is love on both sides *(dilectio)*, but there is no shared love *(condilectio)*. Shared love is properly said to exist when a third person is loved by two persons harmoniously and in community and the affection of the two persons is fused into one affection by the flame of love for the third.[56] This *condilectio* is defined as nothing other than "the mutual coming together of intimate benevolence and supreme harmony" *(nisi intimae benevolentiae et summae concordiae mutua concursio).*[57]

Richard discerns three modalities of love within the Trinity: *amor gratuitus*, found in the Father who gives without having received; *amor debitus*, found in the Spirit who receives all love without returning it; and *amor ex utroque permixtus*, found in the Son whose personal property it is to proceed from another and to have a Person that proceeds from him.[58] Of course, the Spirit can bestow *amor gratuitus* on a created person but not in its fullness, Richard argues, for it would not be appropriate to love in such a degree that which is not worthy of this full love. (One wonders whether this reservation is compatible with the divine love as made known in the God made man and with the nature of love in general.)[59] Because Richard identifies these modalities of love with the three Persons,[60] the Spirit from whom nobody proceeds cannot share his love actively with another Person. What, asks Richard, could the Spirit, to whom the fullness of divine love has been communicated, return of the love he received?[61]

It is here that Ruusbroec parts ways with Richard (and Bonaventure),[62] for according to him the Spirit is an active principle by which the divine Persons flow back into their shared unity or essence. For Ruusbroec, it belongs to the nature of love to return what it has received in order to enable the other to give once again, and so forth: *do ut des*. Thus, the Spirit is not just the "passive" Love, resulting from the mutual contemplation of Father and Son, but an active principle in their flowing back.[63] In Ruusbroec's view, the Spirit, who, to put it in Richardian language, receives the fullness of love from the other two Persons, returns what he has received to the other Persons of the Trinity. Likewise the Spirit will give himself to us (Ruusbroec deals at length with the gifts of the Spirit throughout his works) but will demand back from us whatever he has given us.

In short, with regard to the Spirit, Ruusbroec distinguishes two aspects or moments: first, the Spirit is called the Love of Father and Son as the result of their mutual contemplation; and second, the Spirit as principle of *regiratio* (the flowing back of the Persons in their shared, undifferentiated unity) then unites Father and Son in enjoyable or essential unity. Ruusbroec therefore affirms, in parallel to the two outgoing movements (generation and procession), two in-going movements, an active unity (the Spirit as a bond between Father and Son) and an essential unity.[64] This is why the Spirit pervades Father and Son both "actively and enjoyably."[65] Ruusbroec's terminology is consistent: "active" always refers to the level of the Persons, whereas "enjoyable" refers to the undifferentiated divine being or essence. The following quotation illustrates some of the main issues discussed.

> The lofty essence *(wesen)* of the threeness of God is eternally empty, without activity, and immoveable, according to essential being *(na weselijcken sine)*. But the nature of the Persons is fruitful, eternally active as to the mode of the Persons. For the Father gives birth to his Son as someone other (from him) by his nature; and the Son is born of the father as the eternal Wisdom of God, an other in Person and one in nature with the Father. And the Father with the Son pour forth from themselves the Holy Spirit, who is one nature with them both. And thus there is oneness in nature and otherness in Persons, for in the relations of the Persons there is mutual knowledge and love, flux and reflux between the Father and the Son by means of the Holy Spirit, who is the love of them both. But the oneness of the Holy Spirit, in whom the Persons live and reign, is active in the out-flowing and fruitfully operating all things according to free nobility, wisdom, and power of the Persons. But in the reflux of the Persons the oneness of the Holy Spirit is enjoyable drawing inwards and containing the Persons above distinction, in an enjoyment of fathomless love that God himself is in being and in nature. See, thus does God live in himself, with himself, in knowledge *(in kinnen)*, in love *(in minnen)*,

> in possession *(in besittene),* in enjoyment *(in ghebrukene)* of himself above all creatures. See, this is the highest mode of living that a person can express about God.⁶⁶

The full implications of this dynamic trinitarianism will be made clear throughout the rest of this study. I conclude this chapter with a brief discussion of the divine Persons.

The Persons

It is important to stress that the Persons never stand in opposition to the divine essence; they always and only stand facing each other. The divine essence is only in the other Person, and only *there* can Father, Son, and Spirit be one, as Mommaers correctly observed.⁶⁷ Father and Son take pleasure in each other and "embrace" each other, and this embrace reveals itself as bottomless abundance. This superabundance is the divine essence or being *(wesen).* According to Ruusbroec, then, the essence is nothing other than the inexhaustible transcendence of the other Person; beatitude is nothing other than a rest that reveals itself in activity.

The Father
We have seen that two elements are noteworthy in Ruusbroec's teaching on the Father. First there is the Father's primacy: he is "the principle of the whole Godhead with regard to being and Persons," "the eternal beginning of the Holy Trinity," "the first Person in the divine nature," "an eternal source of the Holy Trinity and all our faith," and so forth.⁶⁸ The second important element is that the fecundity of the divine nature is consistently associated with the Father.

Just as the fruitful nature is located in the Father as source of Son, and, with him, of the Spirit, so is the essence or divine unity in which the Persons flow back primarily associated with the first Person.⁶⁹ This illustrates that we have to think both movements in one moment (seeing that the Father is *both* the divine unity and the fruitful nature). From this it follows that when Ruusbroec is contrasting Godhead with God, he does not have in mind "a Godhead behind the Persons" but the divine essence/being that is shared by the three divine Persons and the principle of which is the Father. It is correct, however, that Ruusbroec describes the divine essence as a whirlpool in which the divine persons lose themselves. Again, this essence *is* the Father, from what we could call a nonpersonal or nonrelational perspective. Similarly, it is precisely because of this identity that Ruusbroec sometimes gives the impression that the divine nature generates the Persons. In this nonpersonal sense, God's essence/being remains incomprehensible and unfathomable, even for the divine Persons (who are *werc* in respect to the divine essence). God's essence can only be known in an essential, modeless fruition.[70]

The Son
Both Aquinas and Bonaventure consider "Son," "Word," and "Image" personal properties, and both seem to have a preference for the title "Word."[71] There are, of course, differences in their understanding of the two processions, especially with respect to the generation of the Son. We have seen that Bonaventure's and Ruusbroec's approach is more Pseudo-Dionysian, while the approach adopted by Aquinas in the *Summa* seems more Augustinian. When we turn to Ruusbroec, it is clear enough that he considers "Father," "Son," and "Holy Spirit" personal properties.[72] Can we say more? For instance, does Ruusbroec consider "Word" a personal property? He does not explicitly discuss this topic. What seems strange is that he appears to speak of the generation of Word and Wisdom indiscriminately.[73] However, there is at least one passage that clearly suggests Ruusbroec considered "Word" a personal property and "Wisdom" an appropriation. In *Brulocht* b 1045–65 he enumerates the appropriated attributes of the three Persons: the Father is called "almighty power and majesty," "creator," "sustainer," "mover," "beginning and end," and so forth. The Spirit is called "incomprehensible charity and generosity," "benevolence," "unfathomable goodness," and so on. With respect to the Second Person Ruusbroec writes: "The attributes of the Eternal Word: unfathomable wisdom and truth, exemplar of all creatures and (their) very life."[74] This passage seems to indicate that he considered "Word" a personal property whereas "Wisdom" is only appropriated to the Son. "Image" too is one of his preferred names for the Second Person. This central notion will be especially relevant for Ruusbroec's anthropology, as we are made to the Image of the God.

The Spirit
The Spirit proceeds from the mutual contemplation of Father and Son *per modum voluntatis*, as their mutual love.[75] We have seen that the

Spirit is both the Love of Father and Son and the principle of *regiratio*. This central notion of *regiratio* gives Ruusbroec's teaching its distinct character. This analysis of divine love as a mutual self-gift will have far-reaching implications for Ruusbroec's doctrine as a whole: the whole redemption has to be seen in light of the theme of *do ut des*.

Ruusbroec seems to consider *Minne,* or Love, a personal property of the Third Person (as do Aquinas and Bonaventure), although again he does not explicitly discuss the relation between Love as a personal property and as an essential attribute of the divinity. We can only observe that on the one hand he always identifies Love with the Third Person as he proceeds from the mutual contemplation of Father and Son and that on the other hand he clearly affirms that all dealings of God with his creation are an expression of divine love. Creation is an expression of divine goodness; the incarnation was the result of God's incomprehensible *Minne* and the neediness of all men, as was the passion, and so forth.[76]

The Spirit is also called the Will of the Father and Son. In the absence of an explicit discussion of the issue, we can only assume that Ruusbroec has only an appropriation in mind when he calls the Spirit the Will of the Father and Son.[77]

The role of the Spirit as principle of intra-divine *reditus* is mirrored in his graceful activity on earth. The seven gifts are a crucial instrument in our deification. Yet the most important gift is that of *Minne* itself: God has poured his grace and his *Minne* into our souls.[78] Ultimately *Minne* is God's gift of himself, although there are enough passages in the *Brulocht* where Ruusbroec makes an explicit distinction between our *minne* and God's *Minne* to prevent us from understanding it in a purely univocal sense.[79]

In short, the Spirit is both the fruit of the mutual contemplation of Father and Son and a bond of love that unites them and all the faithful with them in the unity of the Church.[80] Through the activity of the *Minne* the Persons are embraced and permeated and flow back into unity, from which the Father is ceaselessly giving birth.[81]

Observations

God is one in his nature, but this nature is fruitful in the threeness of the Persons: incessantly out-flowing, living, and working, with distinction of the Persons. At the same time they are incessantly flowing back into their essence/being, with eternal *Minne,* in the unity of the Spirit, where we, above ourselves, lovingly rejoice together with them.[82]

It cannot be denied that Ruusbroec's understanding of God has a certain grandeur. Most striking to modern readers are the ideas of the divine *regressio* or *regiratio* and the daring assertion that we can share in this intra-trinitarian dynamics.

The nature of Love is to give and take, writes Ruusbroec, and therefore we have to return to God in faith and works the love and grace we have received. Hereby a dynamic is generated of giving in order to enable the other to return the gift, and so forth, in a movement that is patterned according to the intra-trinitarian life in which the Spirit/Love is an active principle of love: the Spirit does not just "receive" the love of Father and Son but "returns" it and is thus the active principle of the divine *regiratio* whereby the divine Persons flow back into their shared unity, from which the Father out of his fruitful nature once more gives birth to his Son, and so on. This is Ruusbroec's central intuition, which he elaborates in almost each area of his theology. It is seen in his christology (the Son has been given to humanity to enable us to return this (self-)gift: in the incarnation and passion God bestows his Son, and man returns this gift (the two natures of Christ allow us to see the life and work of the Redeemer as a gift of God to humanity and, subsequently, as a gift of humanity to God). We also see it in his sacramental theology, for instance, in the eucharist where we are being eaten when we eat. It is evident in his spirituality in the strict sense. For instance, the life of the "common man," who is equally ready for contemplation or for action, displays the same tension in unity: "With God they will ebb and flow and (will) always be in repose, in possessing and enjoying. They will work and endure and rest in the supra-being *(overwesene).* They will go out, and in, and find nourishment both here and hereafter."[83] The full implications of this profound vision will become clear after we have examined Ruusbroec's anthropology and christology.

CHAPTER 4

"Made to the Image"
Ruusbroec's Anthropology

In chapter 2 I described some aspects of the Neoplatonic tradition of negative theology, and I argued that Ruusbroec's thought needs to be understood as part of that tradition. I suggested that Ruusbroec appropriates the traditional doctrine of exemplarism —we have an eternal life in God's Image or Word—and that this doctrine has important consequences for the way he characterizes our created being, which is already naturally "attuned" to participating in the trinitarian life. Ruusbroec teaches that the "essence" of our created being is not a substance but a relation to God. As God utterly transcends our spatiotemporal categories, it is not possible to distinguish God and soul from each other in the way we can distinguish between two created things. Ruusbroec adopts the Augustinian doctrine of exemplarism—we have an eternal life in God who is the (formal, efficient, final) cause of our created being—and transforms it in light of the Pseudo-Dionysian apophatic conviction which implies that a distinction between our life in God and the soul is inconceivable. In apophatic discourse (itself the result of the fusion of a Neoplatonic hierarchy of being with the Christian doctrine of the creation out of nothing) it is not contradictory to claim that our created being is essentially one with God and yet infinitely removed from him. Ruusbroec asserts both elements throughout his works.

In this chapter I want to develop these ideas in more detail. Ruusbroec does not have an interest in anthropological reflections for their own sake, yet a study of his anthropology is relevant for two closely related reasons: because it illustrates the centrality of his trinitarian doctrine and its implications for his understanding of the human person and because it allows us to explain the status of what scholars call "natural mysticism," or, in Ruusbroec's terms, "the natural way." First I expound Ruusbroec's teaching on the image-character of the soul and his discussion of the so-called three unities.[1] Then I examine Ruusbroec's evaluation of "the natural way." Finally, I briefly discuss the distinction between image and likeness, a distinction that will prove relevant to Ruusbroec's notion of deification.

In the Image of the Trinity

For Ruusbroec, created beings owe their existence to the knowledge and the will of God. Because God knew and willed us eternally in himself, he created us, not out of necessity, but out of the freedom of his will: "There is continuously new birth-giving *(ghebaren)* in new knowledge, new complacency *(behaeghen)* and new breathing forth *(gheesten:* spiration*)* of the Spirit in a new embrace with a new torrent of eternal love.... It is in this complacency that heaven and earth are suspended, being, life, activity and subsistence of all creatures, save only the aversion from God through sin, which comes from the creatures' own blind perversity."[2] As we have seen in chapter 3, Ruusbroec appropriates Wisdom to the Son and Will to the Spirit.[3] He can therefore describe the creative act as an extension of the processions of Son and Spirit: the Father knows his creation in his Son and wants this creation in his Spirit: "Just as the Father beholds all things anew, without cease, in the birth of his Son, thus all things are loved anew by the Father and by the Son in the outflowing of the Holy Spirit."[4] In short, by his free Will, through his eternal Wisdom, the Father has created all things out of nothing according to the divine Exemplar that he himself is.⁵ In the case of the human person the connection between createdness and the trinitarian life is even more evident as we are a trinitarian blueprint, created in God's image and likeness.

God the Father has known all creatures in the Son, their Exemplar, as life-giving ideas.⁶ In the divine Image all creatures have an eternal life outside themselves:

> This is the Father giving birth to his Son, the eternal Wisdom and the Image of the Father in which he knows himself and all things. This Image is the life and cause of all creatures because in this Image all things live according to a divine mode, and according to this Image all things are created perfectly; and through this exemplar all things are ordered wisely; and because of the ideas *(overmids redene)* of this Image all things are well tuned to their goal insofar as it depends on God.... But the rational creature, in its creaturely out-flowing, is not the image of the Father, for it flows out as creature and therefore it knows and loves with limitation *(met maten)* in the light of grace or glory.⁷

As this quotation suggests, and as I discuss in greater detail in chapter 5, it is Ruusbroec's view that the Word, not the human person (or only in a secondary sense), is the image of God. This position probably has to be seen in light of his denouncement of the heretical doctrines of the Brethren of the Free Spirit, who, according to Ruusbroec, were guilty of claiming to be Christ.⁸ Therefore, however much Ruusbroec emphasizes the unity of our eternal life and our created being, he will also equally emphasize the radical separation between created things and God—once again an indication that he has to be read in the tradition of negative theology in which such oxymorons abound: "And although you have an eternal life in God's Wisdom without yourself, you nonetheless do not become God's Wisdom. And although God lives in all creatures and all creatures in God, the creatures are nonetheless not God, nor does God become his creatures. For created and uncreated always remain separate, infinitely removed from each other *(Want ghescapen ende onghescapen die bliven altoes twee, ende sonder mate verre van een)*."⁹

Ruusbroec repeatedly states that only the Son and not the human person is the true image of God. His position differs therefore from that of St. Augustine who, appealing to 1 Cor 11:7, has no reservations, at least in some contexts, about calling the human person the image of God. Moreover, according to Augustine, we are made to the Trinity rather than to the Son.[10] Ruusbroec argues that we are made according to the Image, namely, the Second Person, and therefore to the image of the Trinity as a whole, since the Son (who is without cease being born from the Father) reveals the divine nature of the Father who is the principle of the entire Trinity; yet he has reservations about calling the human person "image" of God in an unqualified sense.

To understand the relation between our life in God as idea and our created being we now have to discuss two important passages from *Die Geestelike Brulocht*. The first, shorter passage is found in the first pages of Book II of *Die Geestelike Brulocht*. The second one, also from Book II, is more elaborate and will be discussed shortly.[11] It introduces the pages in which Ruusbroec describes how we can meet Christ. In the first passage Ruusbroec identifies a "triple unity" *(drierhande eenicheit)*, the "unity of the heart," the "active" or real unity of the spirit (the ground of the faculties), and the so-called essential unity. These three unities are naturally given, but the first and the second are capable of being supernaturally adorned. Book II of *Die Geestelike Brulocht* then describes in detail the transforming effects of grace on them. It is structured accordingly: first, it discusses the effects of grace on the lower unity (*Brulocht* b 212–971), then on the three faculties (*Brulocht* b 972–1405) and the (active) unity of the spirit (*Brulocht* b 1405–1817), and concludes with a recapitulation (*Brulocht* b 1818–2293) and a denouncement of a devious interpretation (*Brulocht* b 2294–584). Book III discusses the indistinct union with God, based on the essential unity between God and the soul.

The first "unity" refers to the life of creatures in God's Wisdom, on which depend their life and existence: if creatures should be cut off in this way from God, they would immediately fall into nothingness. This unity is in us essentially by nature, whether we are good or evil. We possess this unity both in ourselves and above ourselves, as a principle and support of our being and life.[12] Second, there is the unity of the higher faculties, where they take their natural origin as to their activity. In this unity we call the soul "spirit" *(gheest)*. From it, memory *(memorie)*, intellect *(verstannisse)*, and will *(wille)* originate.[13] The third natural unity is the soul in the strict sense *(ziele)* as the domain of the bodily faculties. From it originate all bodily activity and the five senses.[14]

Grace has to adorn the two last mentioned unities: the lowest by outward practice "in perfect conduct, after the manner of Christ and his saints, bearing the Cross with Christ, subordinating (human) nature to the commandments of the Holy Church and to the teaching of the saints, according to the strength of our nature, with discernment."[15] The second is enriched by the three theological virtues, following the example of Christ. Interestingly, Ruusbroec does not say that the third unity needs to be adorned. We need grace to possess our life in God—but this life itself is one of indistinct union with God: in receiving God's created gift of grace (which perfects our natural attunement to the trinitarian life) we receive God himself.[16]

In the second passage, which recapitulates some of the points in the earlier passage, Ruusbroec only deals with the active and essential unities as he treats of the grace-giving activity of God in the so-called unity of the spirit (as distinct from the lower, bodily unity). In this passage he outlines the relation between our uncreated life in God's Word as idea and our created life:

> The unity of our spirit exists in two ways, namely essentially and actively. You should know that the spirit, according to its essential being *(na weselijcken sine)*, receives the coming of Christ in its bare nature, without intermediary, and without cease. For the essence/being *(wesen)* and life which we are in God, in our eternal Image is immediately and indivisibly united with the being and life which we have and are in ourselves according to (our) essential being *(na weselijcken sine)*. For this reason the spirit, in the most intimate and highest part of its being, in its bare nature, ceaselessly receives the impress of its eternal Image and of the divine resplendence and becomes an eternal dwelling place of God.[17]

Ruusbroec then continues to explain that God radically transcends our spatiotemporal limits in a passage already quoted in chapter 2.[18] He then concludes: "And therefore the spirit possesses God essentially in its bare nature, and God the spirit, for it lives in God and God in it."[19] Again he distinguishes this essential unity from the active unity that is the ground of the faculties, the unity in which the spirit subsists in itself as in its created personal being, "the beginning and end of all creaturely activity," as he puts it.[20] As the ground of the faculties, this unity is not active, but the faculties derive their power and potency from their originating source, that is, from the unity of the spirit, where the spirit subsists in its personal mode of being.[21]

What is the relation between these two "unities," the essential and the active? To answer this question we have to examine the relation between our life in God as idea and the (active) unity of the spirit. The essential unity is not the same as our life in God, but it refers to the union between our life in God and our personal, created being or active unity. However, this union cannot be distinguished from our life in God's Wisdom as God transcends time and place:

> This essential unity of our spirit with God does not exist by itself, but it abides in God, and it flows forth from God, and it hangs in God, and it returns back into God as into its eternal cause, and in this mode, it is never parted from God nor will it ever do so. . . . And this unity is above time and place and always acts without cease after the mode of God, only it receives the impress of its eternal Image passively, insofar as it is God-like but creature in itself. This is the nobility which we have by nature in the essential unity of our spirit, where it is naturally united with God.[22]

Thus, the essential unity is not identical with our life as idea in God, but it is the unity between the ground of the faculties (the active or real unity) and our life in God's Image. Yet it cannot be distinguished or separated from this life in God's Image as this would imply a notion of God at odds with the transcendent nature of the divinity. This interpretation explains why Ruusbroec calls it a "unity" (*eenicheit ons gheests met gode,* in *Brulocht* b 1655)—something that implies the union of two poles, namely, our exemplary life in God and our created being, that is, the active unity as the ground (therefore "unity") of the faculties. This union also illustrates Ruusbroec's assertion that created and uncreated are radically unlike each other and yet that "our created being is suspended in the eternal being, and with respect to (its) essential being, it is one with it."[23] Ruusbroec is suggesting that the essence of our created being (the active unity) is not a substance but is essentially a relation to God, who is also not a substance (in our normal, creaturely understanding of the word, as characterized by spatiotemporal limits). This is why Ruusbroec asserts that we possess the essential unity both in ourselves and above ourselves—a statement that only makes sense if the essential unity is the unity of our created being ("in ourselves") and God's Image who radically transcends our creaturely confines ("above ourselves").[24] Again, it explains why Ruusbroec can equate the active unity (our personal, created being) and the essential unity and maintain the thesis that created and uncreated are totally unlike—an equation that is untenable if we understand the essential unity as referring to our life in God as idea.[25]

The interpretation put forward here—the essential unity refers to the union between our created being and our life in God, not just to the latter—is not controversial as such. Other Ruusbroec studies have agreed that the essence of the human person is a relatedness to God.[26] However, they have failed to see the important implication this position entails, namely, that it does not make sense to posit a human essence over against the divine essence. Even a perceptive scholar such as Ampe makes this mistake. He is aware that the essential unity is a relatedness to God, and yet he speaks of a human essence as if it is a self-contained substance, for instance when he explains how the soul mirrors the Trinity—a key idea in his major study on Ruusbroec. As I mentioned briefly in chapter 3, Ampe identifies two triads, one horizontal and one vertical:

God	Human person
Essence/being *(Wesen)*	Essence/being *(Wesen)*
Nature	Ground
Persons:	Faculties:
– Father-Son-Spirit	– Memory-Intellect-Will

I have already criticized Ampe's view on the intermediary role of "nature" in the Trinity. Now I want to point out that the human being does not possess its own "essence" separate from God's essence beyond his or her created ground. A better presentation would be

God's essence → ground of faculties: memory, intellect, and will
↓
Father-Son-Spirit

"Made to the Image"   107

In short, Ampe's presentation does not do justice to the human essence or being *(wesen)* as relatedness to God. I have argued that the union of our created being and our life in God is called the essential unity. The ground of the soul (= the active unity as source of the faculties) is one with and indistinguishable from this union or relatedness to God.

Similarly, in a study that has never been challenged, P. A. Van de Walle tries to exonerate Ruusbroec from accusations of pantheism, arguing that he does not allow for any ontological continuity between the essence *(wesen)* and life we have in God and the essence and life we have in ourselves. He speaks of a "double-life," a "merely psychological union" without any ontological significance: when Ruusbroec says these two lives are one and indivisibly united, he merely wants to point out a "psychological" union.[27]

Now it is entirely correct that Ruusbroec puts a particular emphasis on the chasm that separates God from his created world, including humans, but that does not necessarily mean that he had only a "psychological" union in mind. Van de Walle's argument fails to elucidate the ontological implications of our life in God for our created being. Thus, although this interpretation is correct in its identification of an ontological chasm between God and the human person, it is wrong in assuming that one can distinguish a human essence from the divine essence, not realizing that this distorts Ruusbroec's message. Ruusbroec argues that it is not meaningful to oppose a human essence to a divine essence, since the "essence" of a human person is a relatedness to God whose essence too cannot be opposed to the substances of this world as he radically transcends our spatiotemporal limitations.

This does not mean that God's essence becomes identified with the soul: creaturely being is not infinite, and it is related to God's being as to its supra-being, as Ruusbroec frequently states in language that has a distinct Pseudo-Dionysian ring: "God is his own Image and that of all creatures. He knows himself and all things with himself and in himself. He is the supra-being of all beings *(alre wesene overwesen)*.... The being of God is ... a living subsistence of everything created."[28] Indeed, Pseudo-Dionysius too had argued that God is "the substantive cause and maker of being, subsistence, of existence, of substance, and of nature."[29] Yet this Cause of all being precedes being and infinitely transcends creaturely beings.[30] In short, the divinity is "the Being pervading all beings and [it] remains unaffected thereby. It is the supra-being beyond every being."[31] Ruusbroec adopts Pseudo-Dionysian language and the idea that God's supra-being ceaselessly keeps created beings in existence and yet infinitely transcends them. If we understand Ruusbroec in the tradition in which he is writing, it becomes clear that he is not talking about a merely "intentional" or "psychological" order.

To understand more fully the relation between God and soul, we have to discuss Ruusbroec's usage of the traditional metaphor of the mirror of the soul reflecting the divine Image. It is useful to follow Ruusbroec's reasoning closely as he outlines it in the *Spieghel*.[32] After he has referred to Gn 1:26 ("the heavenly Father created all human beings to his image and likeness") he goes on to say:

> His Image is his Son, his own eternal wisdom. All things live in him, as St. John says: "All that was made was life in him" (Jn 1:3–4). That life is nothing other than God's Image, in which God has known everything from all eternity and which is also the cause of all creatures. This Image, which is the Son of God, is therefore eternal, prior to all creation. It is to this eternal Image that we have been made, for in the most noble part of our soul—namely in the ground of our higher powers—we have been created as a living and eternal mirror of God, on which God has impressed his eternal Image and on which no other Image can ever be impressed. This mirror remains constantly before the face of God and therefore participates in the eternity of the Image which it has received. In this Image God knew us before we were created, and now that we have been created in time he knows us in this Image as destined for himself. This Image exists essentially and personally in all persons. [33]

The metaphor of the mirror helps us to understand the relation between the human person's created being and his eternal life in God's Wisdom. In the ground of our higher powers, that is, in the active unity as unity, we have been created as a mirror that receives the impress of the divine Image (= the essential unity or the union between our created being and our life in God's Word). We find a clear indication that Ruusbroec has more in mind than a "psychological" union in his assertion that our created being (in particular, the ground

"Made to the Image" 109

of the faculties) participates in the eternity of the Image it receives. Also, the transcendent nature of God implies that God's Image exists both personally and essentially in all persons and yet transcends our created being: we are made *to* the Image. In a passage already quoted, Ruusbroec links the metaphor of the mirror to his exposition of the essential and active unity:

> And with respect to its created being, it [= the soul] constantly receives the impress of its eternal Image, just like a stainless mirror in which the Image remains constantly, and in which, without cease, in each new beholding, knowledge is renewed with new brightness. This essential unity of our spirit with God does not exist by itself, but it abides in God, and it flows forth from God, and it hangs in God, and it returns to God as into its eternal cause, and it never parts from God, nor can it do this in this mode, for this unity is in us according to (our) bare nature. If the creature were to part from God, it would fall into pure nothingness. This unity is beyond time and place and it works constantly according to the mode of God; only it receives the impress of its eternal Image passively, insofar as it is Godlike but creature in itself. This is the nobility which we have by nature in the essential unity of our spirit, where it is naturally united with God. This makes us neither holy nor blessed, for all people, good and bad, have this within them, but it is the first cause of all sanctity and blessedness.[34]

This quotation allows me to summarize some of the main points in this section: in our created being, that is, in the ground of our faculties (the active unity) we have been created as a mirror that receives the impress of God's Image. This impress—the union of Image and mirror—is the essential unity. It transcends time and place, since it is the relation between our created being and God's Image. It is the "place" where God's eternal creative activity and our temporal createdness meet. Therefore, Ruusbroec can state that this mirror of the soul becomes "eternalized" through the Image it has received.[35] Again, this does not mean that the creature becomes God: "Even though God's Image is in the mirror of our soul and is united with it without intermediary, still the Image is not the mirror, for God does not become a creature."³⁶ This union is entirely natural, but it is also the foundation of sanctity: grace still needs to perfect this natural givenness. It also explains the possibility of what Ruusbroec calls "the natural way" or what Ruusbroecian scholars call "natural mysticism."

"The Natural Way"

From the impress of the Image the soul acquires three dispositions or inclinations that mirror the Trinity and that are the foundation of "natural mysticism." In *Spieghel* Ruusbroec describes those inclinations. The first is an essential bareness devoid of images, which mirrors the Father. The second relates to the soul's higher reason, a mirror-like resplendence through which we resemble the Son and through receiving him we become one with him. The third attribute is the spark of the soul *(de vonke der zielen)*, the natural tendency of the soul towards its source: through this tendency we resemble the Spirit and in receiving him we become one spirit and one love with God.³⁷ Both the resemblance and the union are in us by nature, but in the case of sinners they are hidden in their proper ground because of the coarseness of sin, as we will see below.

It is in his first work, *Dat Rijcke der Ghelieven,* that Ruusbroec gave his most elaborate treatment of the natural way. It refers, on the one hand, to the adornment of the lower nature of the human person with the "natural virtues" of prudence *(vroetheyt)*, temperance *(ghematicheyt)*, justice *(gherechticheyt)*, and fortitude *(stercheyt)* and, on the other, to the threefold natural tendency of the soul's faculties towards their ground. The latter aspect illustrates how Ruusbroec's anthropology is shaped by his dynamic trinitarian doctrine—a trinitarian doctrine that has Augustinian roots but has become transformed in light of the central notion of *regiratio.*

Ruusbroec identifies an out-going and an in-going movement in the three faculties. Usually the memory is directed outwards, together with reason and will, and the three together govern the bodily powers. However, each of the three faculties can also turn within. The memory idly reposes in the soul's ground when it turns away from activity and multiplicity. When reason turns within, it becomes inactive and rests in nonactivity. The will permeates memory and reason, and they then incline towards their source. For when the faculties are unconcerned with temporal things and bodily pleasures and when they are lifted up in unity, from which a pleasurable rest originates that permeates body and soul, the faculties are being permeated and transformed into the unity of the mind, or memory *(dan werden de crachten doergaen ende overbeelt in die eenicheyt der ghedachten).*[38] The analogy with the life of the Trinity is obvious: in both cases there is an out-going, an in-going, and an enjoyable (or essential) dimension. Interesting too is the fact that the memory is both the ground of the faculties and the unity in which the faculties become onefold, thereby reflecting the role of the Father as origin and end of the intra-trinitarian dynamics. Another notable feature is that the will permeates memory and reason and thereby makes them incline towards their ground, just as the Spirit is a bond between Father and Son by which they are permeated and by which they flow back into their shared unity.[39]

We have seen that the soul is united with God by nature and has therefore a threefold inclination towards its ground in which God resides. Although this "natural way" is not bad in itself [40]—Ruusbroec holds the traditional view that everything created is good—it can lead to aberrations when people become fixated with this natural rest that they can experience in the ground of their being.[41] When "mysticism" is turned into a psychological "experience" of stillness it is no longer recognizably Christian but degenerates into a self-seeking technique:

> These are the people who do not practice virtue and whose understanding is exempt from images. They find their essential being in themselves and possess it in the naked idleness of their spirit and nature. For they lapse into an idle blind emptiness of their essential being and they no longer pay attention to any good works, outer or inner. For they spurn all inner works, such as wanting, knowing, loving, desiring and all the works that join them with God. But if they had loved God for one hour in all their life and if they had tasted true virtue, they would not have been able to come to this unbelief. For the angels and the saints and Christ himself will work, love and desire, give thanks and praise, want and know for all eternity. And without these works they would not be able to be blessed. And God himself would not be able to be either God or blessed if he did not work. And this is why these wretched

> people are sorely deceived. For they pass away and sink away from themselves in essential natural rest. . . . These people's way is a quiet sitting down of the body without work, with idle, unimaged sensuality turned inward into themselves.[42]

Throughout his career Ruusbroec increasingly criticized those people who "have strayed into the empty and blind simplicity of their own essence and wish to become blessed within the limits of their own nature. For they are so simple and so inactively united to the naked essence of their soul and to the indwelling of God in themselves, that they have neither ardor nor devotion towards God, neither without nor within. For in the highest point in which they are turned, they feel nothing save the simplicity of their essence/being hanging in the essence of God."[43]

We have learned already that the fact that God resides in the soul's being is both a natural datum and the first cause of all sanctity. What then is Ruusbroec's problem with those people who "rest" in the emptiness of their own being in which God resides? On the one hand, he reproaches them that "they have united themselves to the blind, dark emptiness of their own being; and there they believe themselves to be one with God."[44] On the other hand, Ruusbroec himself affirms in numerous places that the being of the soul is one and inseparable from God's being. He even states as much in the passage just quoted: "They are so simple and so inactively united to the naked essence of their soul *and to the indwelling of God in themselves,* that they have neither ardor nor devotion towards God, neither without nor within."[45]

Ruusbroec acknowledges that the soul has been created as a trinitarian blueprint (which explains the natural tendency of the faculties towards their ground), but this natural datum has to be perfected by grace. Without grace the human person is inclined to rest in her own "being" without being drawn by God, who indwells this being, into a true Christian life of charitable works and true devotion: "Above the essential repose which they possess they feel neither God nor otherness. For the divine light has not shown itself in their darkness and that is because they have not sought it with active love and supernatural freedom."[46] In short, they are not open to the full nature of God who resides in the soul and yet transcends it but prefer to engage in a self-seeking technique of quietism. Although human nature is already predisposed to participate in the Trinity, an exclusively "natural" mysticism that focuses on a natural repose of the faculties, although not sinful in itself, often leads to spiritual vanity, self-complacency, and lack of Christian commitment.[47] Indeed, this is perhaps the only doctrinal area in which we can discern a shift in Ruusbroec's thought.

In his first work Ruusbroec had argued that the natural way is not bad in itself but that it is very hard to reach perfection without the grace of God: "This is the way of the natural light, which one can attain with natural virtues and with emptiness of spirit; and it is called natural because one can follow this way without the stirring of the Spirit and without supernatural divine gifts; yet only seldom is it being attained in the way I described to you, without the aid of God's grace."[48] In later works Ruusbroec's appreciation of this natural way became more explicitly negative: "And therefore, as I have told you before, watch out for the conceited men, who, through their vacant imagelessness, with their bare simple vision, have found within themselves in a natural manner the indwelling of God and pretend to be one with God without the grace of God and without the practice of virtues and in disobedience to God and to the Holy Church. And with all this perverted life, . . . they wish to be a son of God by nature."[49]

I indicated in chapter 2 that Ruusbroec's spiritual goal is a condition of the deified person who is active and involved in this world and yet "rests" in God, a person who perfectly integrates contemplation and action, who exercises his faculties and yet is always radically centered on God in whatever he does. I develop this idea in greater detail in chapter 6, dealing with deification. Here it suffices to indicate that Ruusbroec refers to his trinitarian doctrine to refute the assertions of heretics and their quietism. Although it is correct that the being of God is not active, nevertheless, Ruusbroec argues, the Holy Spirit is active. The heretics therefore sin against the Spirit when they pursue idle rest without charitable works and when they claim that all will become God's undifferentiated being at the end of time. Thus, they justify their erroneous beliefs and practices on the view that God is nothing but a simple, blessed being without activity. They even claim, according to Ruusbroec, "that all people, whether good or bad, and God himself will become God's being at the end of time, empty and inactive in eternity. And therefore they do not want to know or understand, nor they do want to will or love, thank or praise, desire or possess. . . . But those who are born from the Spirit and live the Spirit, they practice all virtues. They know and love, they seek, they find; they taste and possess glory and grace, eternal rejoicing without measure, which is God himself."[50] Although we are a natural blueprint of the Trinity, we need grace to perfect this natural datum, so as to know and love God and his creatures in him.

Sin, Image, and Likeness

Because we have been made in the image of God, we have a natural inclination that resembles the trinitarian movements in their in-going, out-going, and enjoyable aspects. These natural inclinations are the basis of what Ruusbroec calls the natural way. However, the natural way, although not bad in itself, can degenerate into a self-seeking technique of passivity and quietism. To grasp the relation between nature and grace in Ruusbroec's thought, we must consider the distinction he draws between image and likeness and the obstructive role of sin.

We are not only made to the Image, but also to the likeness. Likeness refers to God's grace-giving activity that deifies the human person.[51] Whereas Ruusbroec establishes a close link between the human being *(wesen)* and the Image of God, the likeness refers to God's grace-giving activity to which we should respond in an active manner through works of charity. As he puts it in *Vanden XII Beghinen:* "But you are to mark that we are made not only unto the image of God and to be one with God, but we are also made unto the likeness of God, that is, to be ordered in affection, in love, in charity and in all virtues."[52] In the same work he links the oneness of the image and the active, gracing aspect of likeness as follows: "You have created us unto your image, that is, to be one with you in love. And you have created us unto your likeness, that we, by your grace, might be like you in all ways of virtue."[53] As noted in chapter 1, the theme of likeness implies both similitude and difference. Through grace we can grow in likeness:

> God has made us to his image and likeness *(te sinen beelde ende te sinen ghelijcke)*. And when we die to sin and deny ourselves and our self-will in the will of God, then we are like God *(gode ghelijc)*

and capable of growing and increasing always in greater likeness. Between ourselves and God there is no intermediary but his gifts and our good works.... With him we work all our virtues and good works; without him we can do nothing good. And against our will and without our contribution, we cannot resemble God, nor can he make us either holy or blessed. This is why we must gladly resemble God in virtues and in unfeigned charity: thus God lives in us and we in him. And our rational soul with all its faculties is filled with grace and spiritual gifts; thus we always remain rich in virtues and like unto God *(gode ghelijc)*, in his eternal complacency; and above likeness *(boven ghelijc)*, united to him in love without delay.⁵⁴

As the above quotation suggests, "likeness" refers to our growing deification in response to God's grace. We become more Godlike, but this "likeness" will never become dissolved in identity. "Image" relates to the union between the soul and the Son with whom the soul is united without distinction through the creative act of God, as explained earlier. If the concept of "likeness" is intrinsically linked with grace, sin makes us dissimilar to or "unlike" God. In the language of *Die Brulocht,* Ruusbroec explains how sin puts a screen between the faculties and the essential unity, which can only be overcome by grace:

> Now all holiness and all blessedness reside in the fact that the spirit, through likeness and mediation of grace or of glory, is introduced into rest in the essential unity. For the grace of God is the path we should always travel if we are to enter into the simple being in which God gives himself with all his richness, without intermediary. And therefore the sinners and the damned spirits are in the darkness, because they lack the grace of God which would enlighten and lead and instruct them to that enjoyable unity. Yet the essential being of the spirit is so noble that the damned cannot choose to be annihilated; but sin constitutes such a great obstruction and unlikeness between faculties and being—in which God lives—that the spirit cannot achieve union with its own being, which would be its own (domain) and its eternal resting place, were it not for sin. For whoever lives without sin lives in likeness and in grace, and God is his own (domain).⁵⁵

This quotation illustrates the point made above that the essential unity does not refer to our life in God as such (as divine idea) but to the union of our created life and our uncreated life in God, given the fact that Ruusbroec states that the being of the soul is "our own" and yet the place where God dwells. This is another indication that God's being and the soul's being are one and indistinct. This quotation also illustrates the fact that, according to Ruusbroec, sin constitutes an obstruction between the faculties and the being or essence of the soul in which God lives. It is clear that God "resides" in the soul by nature but that sin obstructs the soul's access to the being which is the dwelling of both God and soul.[56] A discussion of Ruusbroec's anthropology therefore points to our need for grace in Christ. This is the topic of chapter 5.

The Originality of Ruusbroec's Teaching on the Soul as Image

Ruusbroec's anthropology has its own distinctive character. The originality of his contribution can be seen from a brief contrast of his teaching on *ad Imaginem* with the doctrine of Aquinas and Bonaventure.[57]

Ruusbroec's doctrine shares with St. Bonaventure's the distinction between the (natural) image and the likeness. This distinction does not have the same importance in Aquinas's doctrine, although he is of course familiar with the notion of likeness as a perfection of the image.[58] A Bonaventurian influence on Ruusbroec is not improbable: in his first work, Ruusbroec compares the created world to God's vestige *(een voetspore Gods)* before dealing with image and likeness—a typical Bonaventurean setting.[59]

Also, both Bonaventure and Ruusbroec consider memory, intellect, and will three distinct faculties. The memory then has a special status as the ground of the soul. Aquinas explicitly rejects this interpretation.[60] The soul is image, Thomas argues, not because it reflects the three Persons but because it mirrors the divine processions of understanding and will. More particularly, when the human person knows and loves God the image is truly actualized. For Bonaventure the three faculties mirror the three Persons, especially when they take God as the object of their operation.[61]

Ruusbroec considers the Second Person the Image of God. The soul is not the image but only to the Image. Only in a secondary sense (and only very occasionally) the soul is called image.⁶² This position differs from that of Aquinas and of Bonaventure who do not have any reservations about calling the soul image of God. (As suggested earlier, this reticence on Ruusbroec's part may have something to do with his attack on the heretics of his time, who supposedly claimed to have become the Second Person.) Also, Aquinas would argue that we are in the image of the Trinity, whereas Ruusbroec argues that we are in the image of the Son and *therefore* in the image of the Trinity: the soul reflects the Second Person who reveals the nature of the Trinity as a whole.

Unlike Bonaventure or Aquinas, Ruusbroec prefers to speak of the soul as *to* the Image and usually restricts the use of the term "image" to the Second Person. Nevertheless, when discussing the soul as made to the Image or the soul as image in a secondary, derived sense, he does not draw a parallel between the three Persons and the three faculties but refers to a threefold inclination of the faculties towards their ground—an indication that his dynamic trinitarian doctrine shapes his anthropological thought: as the Persons flow back into their shared unity, so too the soul displays a threefold inclination towards its ground. Yet those same faculties also engage in outward activities. Again the message seems to be that we ought to engage our faculties in their external operations while "resting" in their ground at the same time.

This dynamic presentation differs from the more static one of Bonaventure, who finds the image character of the soul mainly in the three faculties, and from that of Aquinas, who focuses on the processions of intellect and love but does not develop the notion of *regiratio*. As we have seen, Ruusbroec draws a parallel between the will that permeates memory and intellect *(de wille die hevet omvaen die ghedachte ende dat verstennesse)* and functions as a principle of their inclination towards their source, on the one hand, and the Spirit who is a bond between Father and Son and the principle of *regiratio* of the Persons into their shared being, on the other.⁶³ It seems that Ruusbroec has appropriated traditional Augustinian teaching on the Trinity, more specifically, on the Spirit as bond of love between the Father and the Word, and has incorporated it into his own doctrine, thereby transforming it in light of his central notion of *regiratio*. This natural inclination, which needs to be perfected by grace, is the foundation of deification. Through grace we will become more *like* God and participate in the Trinity, that is, know and love God as he knows and loves himself and all things in him, both actively and with fruition. This is developed further in chapter 6.

Observations

The most remarkable element in Ruusbroec's anthropology is his teaching that the essence of our created being is not a substance but a relation to God. Ruusbroec clearly states that the essential unity—the unity between our created being and our eternal life in God's Image—is the same as the active unity (the ground of the faculties). Our eternal life in God is one with and indistinguishable from our created being as it transcends all spatiotemporal categories. It is therefore wrong to claim that Ruusbroec has only a "psychological" or "experiential" union in mind, because this claim presupposes that Ruusbroec posits a human essence over against a divine essence. This presupposition is wrong on two accounts: first, because one cannot posit God's essence as a distinct substance over against the created substances as God utterly transcends all creaturely categories; and second, because the human essence itself is not a substance but a relatedness to God. Nevertheless, as explained in chapter 2, this does not mean that Ruusbroec somehow conflates God and the created order; on the contrary, his whole thought hinges on the idea that since God radically transcends our spatiotemporal categories, he therefore cannot be distinguished from created things and the human soul in which he resides. Therefore, Ruusbroec adopts the traditional doctrine of exemplarism—we have an eternal life in God and this is the (formal, final, efficient) cause of our created being—but transforms it in light of an idea that seems more Pseudo-Dionysian in inspiration, namely, that a distinction between God and the soul is impossible. Because God radically transcends our spatiotemporal categories he resides in the soul, or rather, the soul dwells in God. In Ruusbroec's language: the active unity (i.e., the ground of the soul as the source of the faculties) is the same as the essential unity (i.e., the unity of our created being and our eternal life in God as idea) or, to put it differently, the human person is essentially a relatedness to God.

Because we are naturally created "to the Image" our faculties display a triple inclination towards their ground—a reflection of the trinitarian life in which the Persons proceed and yet flow back into their shared nature. This natural datum needs to be perfected by grace. However, this grace has only become available in Christ. By sharing in Christ's life and works we are enabled to share in the "common" life of the Trinity, a life characterized by movement and stillness, rest and activity. It is now time to examine Christ's mediating role in greater detail.

CHAPTER 5

"He, remaining God, became man for man to become God"
Ruusbroec's Christology

Ruusbroec's christology has not received the attention it deserves as commentators, if they treat of Ruusbroec's theology at all, prefer to focus on his trinitarian thought, which is supposedly far more original. Undoubtedly, Ruusbroec's christology contains many aspects that can be situated squarely in mainstream Catholic theology of the Middle Ages, for instance, those issues relating to the ontology of the hypostatic union and enhypostasization. Even so, a relatively elaborate treatment of Ruusbroec's christology is desirable for three reasons. First, it further legitimizes reading Ruusbroec's works in theological terms. Second, in Ruusbroec we encounter, perhaps for one of the last times in the medieval period, an author who combines a more popular, pietist approach, with a distinct emphasis on the humanity, life, and Passion of Christ (an emphasis that would be adopted by the *Devotio Moderna*), with a more speculative approach.

Third, as Ruusbroec's christology is closely linked to his trinitarian doctrine, it is to be expected that in this area too he will have an original contribution to make. Indeed, I argue that according to Ruusbroec the whole of Christ's redemptive work needs to be understood in light of the trinitarian love as mutual self-gift *(do ut des)*.[1]

This chapter consists of four parts. Before examining our redemption in Christ, we need to discuss Ruusbroec's description of our fallen, sinful condition. This first part is therefore somewhat prolegomenary. The second part treats of christology in the strict sense, focusing on the nature of the hypostatic union and on the function of Christ's humanity as an instrument of our salvation. The third part investigates the implications of the nature of the trinitarian love for Ruusbroec's understanding of Christ's redemptive work in the passion and eucharist. Finally, in part four, I examine Ruusbroec's views on how we can become incorporated in Christ's redemptive work by examining his understanding of "sacrifice." As this chapter reveals, Ruusbroec does make an original contribution to christology.

Nothingness and the Nature of Evil

In *Vanden XII Beghinen* Ruusbroec links the nothingness out of which creatures were made with the notion of evil as *privatio boni* in an acrimonious passage directed towards the Brethren of the Free Spirit. The Brethren supposedly claimed to rest in a nothingness that mirrored the divine nothingness.

> Everything that is, is either God or creature. Now some mad people claim that they are nothing and that God is nothing, but that is impossible. For being and non-being are mutually exclusive. . . . For God made all things out of nothing and the nothingness they are was left over to God, and that he could not make. For that is sin, false emptiness and disobedience: that nothingness was made by them. Everything God made is something. But the nothingness of sin is made without God, as St. John says. The first nothingness of sin was made in heaven, when God made the choirs and hierarchies of angels, commanded that they ought to work and be active and obey, love, thank and praise him. Those who did

this, remained steady in their works and are eternally blessed in God's glory. Those who in their pride were disobedient and despised God's command and his works fell out of heaven in the dark nothingness of sin and in false emptiness, so that they can never know, love, thank or praise God, nor can they work any virtues: the nothingness of sin and false emptiness induces separation between them and God, so that they cannot be united.[2]

Before I comment on this passage I would like to point out that my (literal) translation differs from most other readings. Van Mierlo, in the edition of 1933, understands "Ende dat niet dat si sijn, *dat bleef hem over; dat en conste hij niet ghemaken*" to mean "the nothingness that they are, was *too much for him.*" This interpretation is adopted in the English translation in the recent critical edition, where we find "and that nothing that they are was too much for him, so that he could not make it."[3] Even more implausible is the suggestion by Ampe who argues that *hem* is a dative plural and refers to the heretics: the nothingness they are is left to them; that is, God left it to them.[4] There is, however, no need to read this text differently from its prima facie meaning: Ruusbroec wants to link the nothingness of creation with the nothingness of sin. God created out of nothing; whatever he did not create was "left over" or uncreated, including sin. Surius translates accordingly: *Id autem nihilum, quod ipsi sunt. Deo mansit reliquum, nec illud facere potuit.* Another problem is the last sentence. I follow manuscript D, which reads "the nothingness of sin induces separation" *(niet der sonde . . . middelt tusschen hem ende gode).* Manuscript F, favored in this instance by the editors of the critical edition, has "nothing but sin induces separation" *(niet dan sonde . . .).* In this context where Ruusbroec has linked creation out of nothing and sin, manuscript D seems more accurate. Surius reads *peccati nihilum.* It is beyond doubt that Ruusbroec associates the nothingness of creation with the nothingness of sin, which is closely related to pride and the inclination of the will toward things other than God: a self-centered will is the root of evil, "it creates hell, a life in self-centeredness, and separates us from God."[5] Ruusbroec portrays the sinner as somebody who is separated and caught up in the multiplicity of evil.[6] The sinner is unable to renounce his self-will and to rule his own life according to the divine will.[7] A crucial aspect of Christ's redeeming work will consist of renouncing his own will in the will of the Father. By being intent on God solely and by renouncing our own will, we will share in Christ's redeeming work.

Sin is nothingness, but the converse does not hold: as Ruusbroec explicitly states, nothingness in itself is neither good nor bad, neither God nor creature.[8] This observation is important if we want to avoid the conclusion that since we are made out of nothing there is therefore a natural tendency towards evil in our metaphysical makeup. In fact, the opposite holds true: our will is actually drawn towards God *(synderis)*.[9] This is entirely consistent: we can only meaningfully speak of a deficient will when this will is, in principle, inclined towards something good: a "deficient bad will" is a meaningless notion.

This association of the nothingness of creation and the nothingness of evil is not original to Ruusbroec, although the way he develops it in this context certainly is, namely, by making the connection with the quietism of the Brethren of the Free Spirit who rest in "nothingness," that is, in their own idle sinfulness. Indeed, we find a similar analysis of evil in the works of Bonaventure, an analysis that differs considerably from that of Aquinas.[10]

Because self-will is the root of sin, the obedience of the God-man was crucial in our salvation. To understand Christ's redeeming activity we first have to examine the nature of the hypostatic union. One of the main questions that will occupy us with regard to this issue is whether the incarnation effected an ontological change in human nature (the "theory of physical redemption").

The Person of Christ

A Theory of Physical Redemption?

Ruusbroec balances redemption as an ongoing process and as a historical event; he puts equal emphasis on objective and subjective redemption, and discussing one separate from the other therefore partly distorts his doctrine. Similarly, it is impossible to discuss his views on redemption in Christ without at the same time dealing with the eucharist and the life of the Church in general.

In *Spieghel* 881 ff. Ruusbroec enumerates four signs of God's love: the fact that we have been created in God's image and likeness; the fact that the Son of God assumed human nature in the incarnation; the passion; and the presence of God in the sacraments, especially the eucharist. Ruusbroec does not explicitly deal with whether the Word would have become incarnate even if man had not sinned, but there can be little doubt that he sees the incarnation primarily as an expression of God's love.[11] Similarly, from the introduction to *Die Geestelike Brulocht* we learn that God sent his Son to wed human nature, his bride, who had been corrupted by sin. Here it is being suggested that the goal of the incarnation is union between God and humanity and not, or not in the first place, a reparation of the divine justice in this world. Apart from the issue of the cause of the incarnation—was it primarily an expression of divine love or rather a restoration of justice?— there is the issue of its redeeming value. Some scholars have claimed that Ruusbroec holds the view that the incarnation itself effected our salvation: as the Word assumed a universal human nature, we have already been objectively redeemed in the incarnation itself. I take issue with this view, as it seems at odds with Ruusbroec's emphasis on the redeeming activity of Christ as a whole and because it is, in my view, based on a misunderstanding of his notion of *ghemeyne natuere*. It is also in opposition to some of the main representatives of the Catholic tradition of the thirteenth century. It is hard to see how this interpretation can avoid the conclusion that we are de facto redeemed in the incarnation, a conclusion that is at odds with Ruusbroec's emphasis on the role of grace and sacraments.

In his study on Ruusbroec, Ampe has argued that the incarnation itself deifies human nature in general, although this objective redemption still needs to be appropriated by the individual person. He was followed in this view by Fraling.[12] These views have never been challenged. What appears to have generated this opinion is that Ruusbroec regularly speaks of "our common humanity" *(onse ghemeyne menscheit)* that Christ shares with us,[13] or that we have "to follow our nature deified in Christ." In this view, Ruusbroec supposedly argues that the incarnation effects an ontological change in human nature: "We are one life in God, in our eternal Image beyond our createdness. We are also one humanity, created by God, and one human nature in which God has impressed his Image in Threeness and which he assumed out of love so as to be God and man with us."[14] The following text, in which Christ addresses the soul, seems even more persuasive: "I have created you according to my Image and likeness. I have assumed your nature and have impressed my Image in it, for you to be one with me without intermediary in the glory of my Father."[15] In this passage the act of the incarnation appears to be presented as an imprint of the divine Image. These are the most persuasive passages in support of Ampe's interpretation. Of course, forced by clear textual evidence,[16] Ampe acknowledged that the incarnation did not deify each human being. Yet he adds: "Nevertheless, we are entitled to call this new structure of the human nature 'a christianized humanity' as this nature-contact with Christ is the essential connection by which Christ can bring about in us his 'causalitas instrumentalis.' . . . This deification is initially only ontological, physical, in as far as it affects only (human) nature as nature."[17]

However, if Christ assumed a universal humanity with which individual human beings are one in the same way as the Persons are one with their divinity, as Ampe claims,[18] then it becomes unclear why there could be any need for a subjective redemption. In other words, if one favors a collective or universal interpretation of "humanity" *(menscheit)*, then human beings are de facto redeemed by the incarnation—a position Ruusbroec does not teach. Thus, if one interprets *ghemeyne menscheit* as a collective humanity that, when assumed by the Word, is ontologically or physically affected, we are left wondering which role we could possibly attribute to the cross, the sacraments, faith, and charitable works. Therefore, Ruusbroec's emphasis on "our common humanity" should not be understood in universal terms but in solidaric terms. Our common nature does not refer to a collective humanity but to a particular human nature, which shares all its characteristics with the nature of other human beings, apart from the proneness to sin. Thus, the Word assumed our common or shared humanity: Christ's passions were those of a truly human being but were not mankind's.[19]

Our common nature has been exalted in Christ, not in the sense of a universal or collective human nature, but in the sense of a complete human nature, with all its properties, and in everything similar to ours, apart from sin. Thus, when Ruusbroec says that we should "always, with God's grace, transcend ourselves and our own personality and conform to our nature deified in Christ" *(soe sele wi ons-selfs ende onser eigenre persoenlecheit altoes vertien end volgen eenvuldechleke na, onser gegoodder naturen in Christo)*,[20] he wants us to imitate the man

Christ whose particular human nature was deified by its assumption by the Word. He does not mean to suggest that human nature, collectively understood, has become deified: "Although the Son of God has assumed our nature and has made himself human, he has not made us God."[21]

Moreover, even Christ's humanity is not "ontologically" or "physically" divinized. To hold the opposite view would be in conflict with the Chalcedonian Creed, which teaches that the two natures exist "without confusion or change." Therefore, Ruusbroec will teach that although in Christ the divine nature is "naturally" united to a human nature, even in him the union amounts merely to deification by grace and not by nature. A fortiori, our common human nature has not been deified (ontologically or otherwise) by the incarnation.

That Christ shared a "common" human nature with us is the absolute prerequisite of our salvation, in line with the traditional dictum that only that which has been assumed by God in Christ can be redeemed. Therefore, when Ruusbroec writes that we are "one humanity, created by God, and one human nature in which God has impressed his Image in Threeness and which he assumed," I do not take this to mean that human nature underwent a divine impress in the incarnation: it is only in creation that the human nature received the divine impress. The Word subsequently assumed this nature which is already a trinitarian blueprint. Similarly, when Christ addresses the soul with "I have assumed your nature and have impressed my Image in it, for you to be one with me without intermediary in the glory of my Father,"[22] Ruusbroec only affirms the possibility of the re-creation of humanity through the Word's assumption of *a* human nature. Therefore, although Christ, our Image, is one with humanity through the incarnation, this does not deify us, but we need to imitate his life and works, through grace, so as to be incorporated in Christ: "Although we are one in our image, through God's assumption of our nature, we have to resemble him in grace and virtues, if we want to be one with God in our eternal Image that God himself is. And therefore the humanity of our Lord Jesus Christ was and is raised and is one with God's Wisdom, and his soul and faculties were and are filled with the fullness of gifts: he is to us a living fountain from which we receive everything we need."[23] Having clarified that the incarnation did not effect an ontological change or a "physical" redemption, we must now investigate the nature of the hypostatic union (enhypostasization) and the role of the humanity of Christ as an instrumental cause of our salvation.

Enhypostasization

After creation, the second sign of God's love, necessitated by the Fall, was the sending of the Son to share our nature. Christ thus became a fellow human being and brother to all of us. To introduce some of the main elements of Ruusbroec's view I first give this relatively elaborate quotation:

> Christ humbled himself but exalted us, made himself poor but us rich, and brought disgrace upon himself but honor to us. But even though he humbled himself, he did not thereby lose his nobility, for he remained all that he had been when he took upon himself what he had not been: he remained God in becoming a human being, so that human beings might become God. He clothed himself with the humanity of us all, just as a king might clothe himself with the garments of his household and of his servants, in order that all of us might wear the one garment of human nature together with him. But in a special way he clothed in a royal garment, namely, in his divine personhood, the soul and body which he received from the immaculate Virgin Mary. This garment belongs by nature to no one but him alone, for he is both divine and human in one Person. If we are to be clothed with him, this can come about only through his grace. If we love him so much that we are able to deny ourselves and transcend our created personality, we will be united with his Person, which is eternal Truth.[24]

The full significance of this quotation will be brought to light in the following pages. Now I merely want to draw attention to several important elements that are being hinted at in this text: (a) the incarnation is an act of humility (a favorite topic with Ruusbroec); (b) the Word assumes a human nature that is like ours in all respects, apart from sin; (c) we can only attain the same relation to the divinity as Christ has "by nature" through grace; and (d) to be united with his divine Personality *(godleke persoonlecheit)*, our love of Christ and abnegation of our "created personality" *(ghescapene persoonlecheit)* are essential.

In another passage we find the same idea that we have to conform to the human nature as it was united to the Word. This implies abnegation of self. After he has indicated that Christ's humanity had no subsistence on its own but conformed to its divine Personality, Ruusbroec writes: "And therefore we will always, with God's grace, transcend ourselves and our own personality and conform to our nature deified in Christ."[25] "Our nature deified in Christ" refers to Christ's particular human nature that was shaped by its union with the divinity and which we can attain only through graceful incorporation in Christ. We have to purify our self-centeredness, conform to our human nature assumed by Christ so as to be clothed, in grace, with his Personality, which will draw us into the divine essence or being beyond the Persons. To understand Christ's role in this transformation, I must discuss what Ruusbroec has to say on the nature of the Person of Christ.

Ruusbroec's views on the Person of Christ are firmly in line with the doctrine of the incarnation stated at Chalcedon. In some passages we discern a clear echo of the declarations of the council of A.D. 451, for instance in *Spieghel,* 1936 ff., which says that in Christ there are two natures, remaining distinct, united in one divine Person *(die .ij. natueren onvermingt sijn vereeneght in eenen godleken persooen).* This aspect of his christology does not differ demonstrably from that of Aquinas or Bonaventure when they argue that the union occurred through oneness, not of nature, but of person.[26] A thorough comparison would therefore be superfluous: the three authors share the belief that the hypostatic union is an act of grace and can only in a special sense be called "natural" to Christ. They also agree that Christ's humanity is the instrumental cause of our salvation, that Christ confers his grace as Head upon all his members, and so forth. In what follows the reader should not expect to find any strikingly original contributions by Ruusbroec; it is not without importance, however, to show that his writings contain these traditional theological elements. Nevertheless, Ruusbroec develops this traditional teaching with a particular emphasis, for he wants to stress both the solidaric and the unique character of the Redeemer in opposition to the heretics of his day. As he puts it: "The humanity of Christ does not subsist in itself, for it is not its own person—as is the case among all other human beings—but instead the Son of God is its hypostasis *(onderstant)* and form *(forme)*. It is therefore of one form *(eenformegh)* with God. . . . The humanity of our Lord is thus taken up into God."[27]

Whereas other human beings are constituted in their personhood by their humanity, Christ's humanity is not the basis of his Personhood; on the contrary, his humanity is shaped by his divine Personhood. Ruusbroec's vocabulary—Christ's humanity is "one form with God"—is not as striking in the original as it is in a literal translation. As I indicated, "one form" renders the Middle Dutch *eenformegh*, which is used as an adjective and which Ampe proposes to translate as *unipersonalis* or *conpersonalis* (in analogy with *consubstantialis*).[28] Surius's translation, *conformis*, is the least technical and the most elegant: Christ's humanity conforms to his divine nature. Wiseman's translation of *onderstant* as "hypostasis" offers an important clue: Ruusbroec has enhypostasization in mind. He fully acknowledges that Christ has two natures (one human and one divine) in one Person, and he means to convey that the divine hypostasis of the Word is constitutive of the union in the God-man, taking up into that union a perfect human nature, which was not a hypostasis on its own but achieved hypostatic and personal reality in the union.[29] In other words, Christ's human nature is one with the eternal Word, for the Word is its *suppositum* and its personality *(persoenlecheit)*.[30] While in "ordinary" human beings human nature finds its connatural "personality" in the individual human person that subsists on its own, Christ's human nature is taken up in a higher, preexistent personality, whereby it receives a union with God that surpasses all human merit and dignity. Nevertheless, this does not mean that Christ's humanity was not "real"; the possibility of union necessarily entails that both natures retain their own character:

> The humanity of our Lord had no suppositum *(onthout)* of its own, but it conformed to its [divine] personality. For Christ possessed his personal being in two natures: he had an eternal birth from the Father and therefore he is Son of God and true God; and he had a birth in time from his mother Mary, and therefore he is son of man and true man. Nevertheless, each nature remained in itself everything it was: for the divinity did not become humanity, nor did humanity become divinity, but they were united

in the divine Person of the Son, and each of these natures belonged to him, for he was truly God and man. Therefore, with God's grace, we have to renounce ourselves and our own personality and conform to our nature deified in Christ. Thus we are transformed by the eternal truth, which is Christ himself.[31]

The last two sentences anticipate a theme that will be developed later. Here Ruusbroec describes the necessary ontological preconditions for our rebirth in Christ: two natures united in his personality in such a way that the human nature conforms to (lit., "goes after, follows") the divine nature, which exists from all eternity in the Second Person. Christ's humanity does not subsist on its own but is "shaped" by the preexistent "personality" of the Word. The image of the garment that Ruusbroec used in *Spieghel*, 980 ff. is apt, for a garment is shaped according to the figure of him who puts it on, and yet the one who puts it on is not changed from his form on account of the garment. So likewise the human nature assumed by the Word of God is ennobled, but the Word of God is not changed.[32] This is not to deny the humanity of Christ; on the contrary, through this enhypostasization human nature finds its true fulfillment. Other people do not have a personal union with the Word because they exist as individual human persons; they cannot "naturally" share Christ's riches but only through graceful participation in Christ.[33]

The "Personality" of the Word belongs intrinsically to Christ's being because he received it in the incarnation. Yet this union was brought about through sheer grace. According to his divinity, Christ is consubstantial with the Father; according to his humanity, however, Christ is one with the Father in essential love,[34] and his humanity can never become God. Even Christ's humanity is not naturally one with God but only through grace, for created being never becomes identical with God's supra-being. In short, enhypostasization does not mean that Christ's humanity itself is "ontologically" divinized; it only means that his humanity is "transformed" according to his divinity in love and grace. This transformation was only "natural" to him in the sense that it intrinsically belonged to him as the one who united both the divine and the human nature, while we can only attain it through a graceful participation in the Person of Christ. Through the Sonship of the Word Christ receives in his nature his inheritance, namely, the divine being that he passes on to humanity.[35] Thus, we become sons of grace and coheirs with Christ. Ruusbroec compares the incarnation to a window that looks out to the divine realm, which was opened for us at the appropriate time (Gal 4:4). In this union the Father has out of love given his Son, and out of love the Son has given himself and ourselves to his Father in his death. Out of love the Father and the Son have bestowed their mutual love, the Holy Spirit.[36] This mutual gift and exchange is a key idea in Ruusbroec's writings, and the whole redemptive work of Christ can be interpreted from this perspective, as I show below. Having clarified the status of the Person of Christ and the meaning of enhypostasization in Ruusbroec's christology, let me conclude by showing how Christ's humanity can function as an instrumental cause of our salvation.

Christ, Source of Grace

Christ fills our faculties with his grace, which he receives in abundance because his humanity is deified through the union with the Word: "Thus the humanity of Our Lord Jesus Christ was and is exalted and is one with the divine Wisdom, and his soul and all his faculties were and still are filled with the fullness of his gifts; he is the living fountain from which we receive everything we need."[37] (Later I will have something to say about the present tense Ruusbroec uses here.) From the fullness of grace in his soul Christ distributes his grace to our faculties:

> I have seen you eternally before all createdness in myself, one with me and as myself; there I have known, loved, called and chosen you. I have created you according to my Image and likeness. I have assumed your nature and have impressed my Image in it in order for you to become one with me without intermediary in the glory of my Father. I have created my soul with its faculties and filled them with every gift so that I could serve and obey my and your Father, your God and my God in our shared humanity, with all my might, unto death. From my fullness of grace and mercy I have filled your soul and your faculties, so that you are like me and are able, with my power and gifts, to serve, pay thanks and praise our God, in all eternity without end.[38]

This is a quotation rich in meaning: Christ points out that we were "chosen" before all creation; after having obscured the Image in which we were created in the Fall, Christ has restored us to our previous state and has bestowed the means to never again fall away from God. However, we have to play an active role in our redemption, that is, in our becoming one with God, by leading a life of virtue. Of course, our charitable works themselves are dependent on Christ's grace, which is available to the individual believer in Christ's Body, the Church, and in the sacraments in particular:

> Now observe, my dear, what else I have done for you. I have left you my Flesh and my living Blood, as food and drink, filled with a heavenly pervading taste, according to each single one's desire, taste and disposition. I have nourished [a] your desire and your sensual life and filled it with my martyred, glorious body. I have nourished and filled [b] your love and your rational life with my spirit, and with all my gifts and merits whereby I have pleased my Father. I have nourished [c] your contemplation and the topmost of your spirit and filled it with my personality, so that you live in me and I live in you, God and man, in likeness of virtues and union of enjoyment. My Father and I have filled the world with our Spirit, our gifts and our sacraments according to each one's desire and needs.[39]

Christ fills our sensual life with his humanity (the active life), our faculties with his habitual grace as Head of the Church, and the topmost of our spirit with his Personality[40] (inner life), whereby our personality is transformed so that we can live the trinitarian life with the Son (contemplative life). This occurs especially in the eucharist. At communion Christ gives himself in a threefold way: "He gives his flesh and his *bodily life*, glorified, full of joy and sweetness. And he gives us his *spirit* with its higher faculties, full of glory and gifts, truth and justice. And he gives us his *personality*, with (its) divine clarity which raises his spirit and all enlightened spirits into the sublime enjoyable unity."[41]

The first aspect transforms our *sensual* life. The believer has to be "enriched and fed in the lower part of his humanity with Christ's glorious humanity." He should behold how Christ inclines towards him with loving affection and great desire and consider his precious body, tortured, pierced, and wounded through and through for our sake. Faith has a transformative power. If we identify ourselves with Christ's life and works, we are changed accordingly: "When, in this receiving, a person recalls the martyrdom and the suffering of the precious body of Christ which he receives, at times he comes to such loving devotedness and felt compassion that he desires to be nailed with Christ on the cross, and that he desires to pour out his heart's blood in honor of Christ. . . . And this is how we satisfy Christ with respect to the lower part of his humanity."[42] I will come back to this demand of reciprocity, but here I want to observe that the life of faith is an ever-deepening penetration into the mystery of the God-man, which molds the believer accordingly.

In the sacrament, he also bestows his spirit, full of glory, rich gifts, virtues, and charity. Herewith we are enriched in the unity of our spirit and in the higher *faculties,* through the indwelling of Christ and his riches. In response to this we should dwell in the unity of our spirit and flow with expansive charity in heaven and earth, whereby we bear a likeness to Christ with respect to the spirit and give him satisfaction.[43]

Finally, in the sacrament of the altar, he gives us his exalted *personality* in incomprehensible brightness. This transports us to the Father who receives his chosen sons along with his natural Son. Thus we come into our inheritance of the Godhead in eternal blessedness. As Ruusbroec says, referring to the single intention and fruitive love (the relevance of which is discussed further in chapter 6): "We should also through Christ's Personality with single intention and fruitive love transcend ourselves and the createdness of Christ, and rest in our inheritance, that is, the divine essence, in eternity."[44]

A schematic presentation might help to clarify how Ruusbroec combines aspects drawn from different doctrinal areas, such as anthropology, christology, and his views on deification.

Anthropology	Christ's Redemptive Work	Aspects of Spiritual Life
unity of heart	life and humanity of Christ	active life
active unity		
a) faculties	grace of Christ	inner life
b) ground	Personality of Christ	
(unity of spirit)		
essential unity	one with the Son in Trinity	contemplative life

Through Christ's humanity (which has the fullness of grace in its active unity) we are enabled to come to his Personality and thus be united with the Son and live the trinitarian life. This corresponds to the three dimensions of the spiritual life (active, inner, contemplative). Because the God-man's humanity is "naturally" united with his divinity, it is permeated with the fullness of divine grace and can therefore be a source of grace for all people. In good Augustinian fashion Ruusbroec notes that God's grace operates from within outwards, while its effects are felt by us from without inwards:[45] first, our sensual life and our faculties are transformed before we encounter in the center of our being the source of all grace, the Person of Christ, which allows us to enter the trinitarian life.

Let me recapitulate. In the incarnation the Word has assumed a particular human nature that shares all features with ours apart from proneness to sin. Christ's human nature did not exist independently but was shaped by his divine Personhood. Christ offers the individual believer the possibility to share in his Personality in which there is no "screen" (sin) between his divinity and humanity. Christ affects human nature through his humanity (which is the instrument of his redemptive work and the channel of divine grace), without however "physically" or "ontologically" deifying it. In *Van Seven Trappen* Ruusbroec makes clear how Christ, filled with habitual grace, shares this grace with humanity: "God has honored, blessed and raised his [= Christ's] humanity, which is one with ours, and united it with himself above everything created. Because of this high union with God his soul and body is filled with all gifts and graces, which he possesses in their fullness. And from his fullness we, who are his disciples and his followers, receive grace upon grace and everything we need for a holy life."[46] God's grace is mediated through the assumed humanity. In short, our redemption in Christ as Head of the Church has an objective and subjective foundation: objectively, we are redeemed in Christ as he is the perfect offering made to the Father (see next section), but through faith and sacraments we have to identify with the Person of Christ who, as Head of the Church, gives life to all his members.[47]

Trinitarian Love and Christ's Redemptive Work

In chapter 3 I tried to make clear how Ruusbroec understands trinitarian love as a mutual self-gift. I also suggested that the work of Christ in the passion and eucharist has to be seen in light of the reciprocal nature of love. I would now like to flesh out this fascinating aspect of Ruusbroec's theology, first by discussing the nature of love and the ways it affects us and then by showing how the eucharist, both as nourishment and as sacrifice, has to be understood in light of the intra-trinitarian love whose essence is to give and take and yet remain in "emptiness" *(Minnen natuere es altoes gheven ende nemen; maer si es selve een ledich wesen).*[48] In discussing Ruusbroec's views on the eucharist as a reenactment of the sacrifice of the passion I also explain how Ruusbroec adopts and transforms St. Anselm's theory of satisfaction.

Love as *do ut des*

Love as "giving" and "taking" is described in terms of generosity and greed: as God bestows his grace, he also demands back what he has bestowed: "God's grace is not being purposelessly or idly given. If we observe it, it will flow and give us all we need, but it demands in return everything we can achieve. . . . We are united with him through his grace and our good works. He lives in us, and we in him, through mutual love, namely his grace and our works. . . . His spirit and his grace perform our good works more than we do ourselves. His grace in us and our love for him is a practice *(werc)* which we perform together."[49]

This exchange of gifts is an idea particularly dear to Ruusbroec: God bestows his grace and we return our works; thus grace and good works continually grow and are being renewed:[50] "God speaks to the interior man: 'I give you my grace; give me your works.' And he speaks further . . . : 'Give yourself to me, I give myself to you; if you want to be mine, I want to be yours.'"[51] This bestowing and demanding is a reflection of the trinitarian life itself: God *is* both "generosity" and "greed," which has to be understood as an illustration of the in-going ("greed") and out-going ("generosity") movement of the divine life. Our heavenly Father is both avid (Jordaens: *cupidus;* Surius: *avarus*) and generous: he bestows his grace, but he demands good works and gratitude in return, for "God's grace is not being idly given." If it belongs to the nature of love "to give and take," God's essence must be likewise: "But beyond all works and practices of virtue our heavenly Father shows his beloved that he is not only generous and avid in giving and demanding, but that he himself is avidity and generosity, for he wants to give himself and everything that he is to us, and he wants us to return to him everything we are. And thus he wants to be ours and he wants us to be his. Yet each remains what he is, for we cannot become God, but we can be united with God, with intermediary and without intermediary."[52]

This reciprocal nature of the operation of divine love therefore finds its origin in the trinitarian dynamic itself, in particular, in the movement of divine love, which flows out towards creation and draws creatures in at the same time. In *Dat Rijcke der Ghelieven* Ruusbroec describes how the person who has spiritual strength (one of the seven gifts of the Holy Spirit) ought to observe how good people and saints in the eternal realm are permeated with divine gifts of grace and glory and how God like the wide sea pours out and flows out with incomprehensible abundance in all those who are receptive to it and is drawing and ebbing back into the wild sea of his unity. They cannot dally in themselves when contemplating this unity, for it makes them flow out and flow back in appropriate love. And this results in an even greater desire to meet (fulfill) justice.[53] In short, our love mirrors the trinitarian life. The same theme is developed in a famous passage from *Die Geestelike Brulocht*:

> This flowing of God always demands a flowing-back for God is a flowing, ebbing sea, which flows without cease into all his beloved, according to each one's needs and dignity. And he is ebbing back in again, drawing all those whom he has endowed on heaven and earth, together with all they have and can do. And of some he demands more than they can do. For he shows himself as so rich and generous, and so fathomlessly good, and in this manifestation he demands love and honor in proportion to his dignity.[54]

In chapter 6 I return to this "failing" of the spirits to love God according to his nobility (which results in a modeless love),[55] but here I want to observe that the theme of generosity and greed is clearly linked to the dynamics of the trinitarian life, as this quotation illustrates. In short, God gives his grace to enable us to return this love (externalized in good works) to him, which results in him bestowing even more *Minne*, and so forth.

It goes without saying that Ruusbroec does not mean to suggest God is stained with an egoistic mentality ("You scratch my back..."), but he tries to clarify the relation between God and his people: a *do ut des* in the sense of "I give for the purpose of enabling you to give back to me." The reciprocal nature of love is not to be misunderstood: Love is its own reward and life.[56]

The Eucharist as Spiritual Nourishment

The passion and the eucharist abundantly illustrate this reciprocal nature of love. In the eucharist, two ways in which Christ has given himself are distinguished: as nourishment and as sacrificial offering.[57] The first aspect, the Body of Christ as our spiritual nourishment, is introduced with an explicit reference to the nature of love as *do ut des:* "Now it is the nature of love always to give and to take, to love and to be loved; these two aspects are found in everyone who loves. Christ's love is both avid and generous. Although he gives us all that he has and all that he is, he also takes from us all that we have and all that we are and demands of us more than we accomplish: he consumes us right to the depth of our being for he is a voracious glutton."[58]

In a passage very similar to the one referred to earlier from *Die Geestelike Brulocht,* Ruusbroec continues to describe how Christ first purifies us (he prepares his food by burning our sins and transgressions) and how he nourishes us in return: at the very moment he consumes us, he also nourishes us. He gives us his Body (which transforms our lower nature) and his soul (transformation of our faculties), and he reveals to us his divinity.[59] Thus, we are drawn into God's unity where we enjoy blissful rest. In short, sharing in the Body of Christ is entering into the dynamic of "giving and taking." Christ has given us his Flesh and Blood to eat and drink him, but he permeates and flows through our soul and body to such an extent that he eats us, that he draws us into himself, so that he possesses us. In eating Christ we are being eaten by him.[60] After he has related the out-going and the in-going movement of the divinity to spiritual hunger and satiation in the human person,[61] Ruusbroec immediately links this idea with the eucharist and the humanity of Christ, who was raised to the Father with great desire (inward movement) and turned down towards his fellow men and sinners (outward movement): "And he was and is so lovingly turned toward all good people that he wanted to buy us and pay for us with himself. And he has given his flesh for food and his blood for drinking, so as to permeate us in body and soul and all our faculties, yes, to eat us, this means that he wants to draw us in himself and possess him with desirous love; and he can then again possess us in turn with an all-permeating flavor. This is eating and being eaten."[62] Thus, the trinitarian love in its dual aspect is exemplified in Christ and in the eucharist as spiritual nourishment.

Sacrificial Offering and the Theory of Satisfaction

The second aspect of the eucharist refers to Christ as our consecrated sacrificial offering. This aspect is closely linked with the third sign of God's love, the passion. In the prologue to *Spieghel der Eeuwigher Salicheit*, a treatise that is explicitly eucharistic in inspiration, Ruusbroec anticipates some of the main issues he discusses in greater detail throughout the work:

> He will there reveal you how his humanity is a worthy offering to his Father. He has given you this humanity together with everything he suffered, so that with it you might boldly appear at the court of his heavenly Father, for he has brought about peace and set us free. You should therefore present and offer Christ, your sacrifice with a humble and generous heart as the treasure through which you have been delivered and redeemed. He in turn will offer you, with himself, to his heavenly Father as the beloved fruit for whose sake he underwent death, and the Father will receive you, with the Son, in a loving embrace. . . . But if the Son has offered you to the Father together with himself and his death, then you are embraced in love. This love has been given you as a pledge with which you have been purchased for the service of God and as a security with which you have been made an heir in God's kingdom. . . . Take great care, then, to hold fast to your pledge and your dowry in a unity of love with Jesus, your beloved Bridegroom.[63]

A dynamic of reciprocity can be discerned in Christ's redemptive work: the Son assumes a human nature, which is then being returned to the Father. Also, we offer Christ and Christ offers us, with himself, to the Father. In the following pages we will see how we are redeemed in Christ's sacrifice and how the cross (and the eucharist) need to be understood in light of the trinitarian love as *do ut des*. By examining Ruusbroec's understanding of "sacrifice" as essentially a renouncement of self-will, we will also see how we can be incorporated in Christ's redeeming work.

The following quotation, which deals with the sacrifice of Mass, although it is almost identical to texts in which Ruusbroec describes the passion as a sign of love, illustrates that our author regarded the sacrifice on the cross and during the eucharist essentially as the same event: "Greater love was never seen than when God's Son handed over his life to death and through that death bought us from the Father's justice so that we might live with him for all eternity. In his lowly death he offered himself and us to his Father's mercy, while the Father received us together with him into his Son's eternal inheritance."[64] As this passage suggests (especially the reference to the divine justice), Ruusbroec seems to propound a *theory of satisfaction*, although this too needs to be understood in light of the reciprocity of divine love in relation to humanity. Ruusbroec puts it as follows: "The Son's coming was not enough for the forgiveness of sins, for the Father wanted to requite sin in accordance with justice *(die sonde wreken na gherechtegheit)*. He therefore delivered his Son to death because of sin, and the Son was obedient to him even unto death, while the Holy Spirit brought this work to completion through love."[65]

Ruusbroec's language is clearly reminiscent of that of St. Anselm, the first to emphasize the theme of satisfaction to account for Christ's redemptive work. St. Anselm's theory is open to criticism but not the sort that is usually raised against it. Indeed, it is often alleged that Anselm introduced the notion of a vindictive God who exacted the sacrifice of his Son in order to meet the demands of his justice—a view E. Schillebeeckx calls "a blood-myth." I will briefly deal with some of the main issues and point out both the similarities and the differences between Anselm's seminal work, *Cur Deus homo*, and Ruusbroec's own appropriation of the theory of satisfaction.

The popular misrepresentation that in St. Anselm's view God requires Christ's sacrifice on the cross to appease his paternal wrath need not detain us, as the notion of a mutable God is an absurdity in medieval theology.⁶⁶ However, one could argue, in a somewhat more sophisticated manner, that God foresaw from all eternity the redemptive work of Christ and took it into account (which safeguards his immutability), so as to make the point that Anselm's view is not incompatible with that of a wrathful God. Nevertheless, this interpretation remains wrong on a subtler level, for it presupposes that Christ's sacrifice effects something in God. Yet Anselm emphasizes that redemption is *pro nobis* in the strongest possible sense (and not *pro Deo*). The cross affects the relation between humanity and God, but it does not affect God as such: God's honor is, in itself, "incorruptible and altogether immutable."⁶⁷ Those critics who assume that, in Anselm's view, redemption effects something in God actually reverse the cause-and-effect order. Redemption is the result of God's immutable goodness, but it does not effect anything in God's nature.⁶⁸ Thus, the cross affects the relation between humanity and God but does not affect God.⁶⁹

Closely linked to the foregoing is the observation that Anselm's central notion, "satisfaction," is not a feudal category, as is often alleged. It has patristic roots (e.g., Tertullian, *De Poenitentia*, chap. 5) and is, of course, a crucial aspect of the penitential system of the Church that was developing at that time.⁷⁰ Moreover, Anselm's and even more so Ruusbroec's understanding of sacrifice or satisfaction is influenced by the Augustinian notion of sacrifice. In *De Civitate Dei* X, 5, St. Augustine had argued that God does not need any sacrifices for his own gratification ("It is man, not God who is benefited by all the worship which is rightly offered to God"), but he only desires what sacrifices signify: "a heart that is broken and humbled" (Ps 51:18).⁷¹ "Thus," writes Augustine, "the true sacrifice is offered in every act which is designed to unite us to God in a holy fellowship, every act, that is, which is directed to that final Good which makes possible our true felicity." True sacrifices are "acts of compassion, whether towards ourselves or towards our neighbors, when they are directed towards God."⁷² In offering our sacrifices "we shall be aware that visible sacrifice must be offered only to him, to whom we ourselves ought to be an invisible sacrifice in our hearts."⁷³ And the Church, being the body of Christ, learns to offer itself through him.⁷⁴ Thus, for Augustine sacrifice has to be seen as a form of (self-)gift that mirrors the sacrifice of Christ. Understood against this larger context it becomes clear how

Anselm's (and Ruusbroec's) terminology can vary from "paying our debts," "making satisfaction," and "offering" to the language of "(self)-giving" without any noticeable differences. Examples of the latter can be found throughout Anselm's text.[75] For Anselm, following Augustine, Christ's sacrifice is both a divine self-gift and a gift of humanity to God: "Since he himself is God—viz., the Son of God—he offered himself to himself (just as to the Father and the Holy Spirit) for his own honor. That is, (he offered) his humanity to his divinity." [76]

In short, we need to understand "satisfaction" not as something directed towards God, but towards the relationship between God and humanity: satisfaction is a cleansing of the sinner in his relation to God.[77] Therefore, even if God were to forgive sins without further ado, the relationship between God and humanity would not really be restored. It comes as no surprise then that Anselm states that even if God were to forgive sins without asking for penance, we would not arrive at happiness.[78] In Christ God allows *humanity* to restore the relationship with its Creator.[79] As we could not achieve the restoration of humanity and were nevertheless obliged to do it, a God-man was necessary. The criticism that Anselm subjects God's mercy to his justice is therefore entirely unjustified: he quite explicitly states that one of the main concerns of his work is to resolve this tension between the divine justice and mercy, or rather, to show how it has been resolved by the God-man.[80]

Ruusbroec's version of the theory of satisfaction will bring out more clearly this harmony of justice and love. It only acquires its full meaning in the context of the theme of exchange between God and man (the Word assumed a human nature that we share with him) and their mutual self-giving. Christ's sacrifice has to be seen from the perspective of reciprocity: the sacrifice on the cross is the most radical illustration of the theme of *do ut des*. God gives his Son who does penance for the whole of humanity, which in itself constitutes a self-gift of humanity to God. More particularly, the cross allows for the reciprocity: we are not capable of restoring the relation with God, for we are imprisoned in our fallen nature, but the God-man accomplishes this *pro nobis*, and in return God makes himself present to humanity in faith and the sacraments. It is therefore not a question of appeasing the Father but of restoring a true relation in reciprocity between God and humanity through the self-gift of the Son who "breaks open the bars" of our imprisonment in sin. For a truly mutual relationship, both divine justice (which allows *us* to put it right) and divine mercy are necessary. In Ruusbroec's terminology, only the dialectic of "generosity" and "avidity" allows for a truly mutual relationship. The divine justice is not oriented towards an internal, divine scheme of things—this would indeed entail that God subjects himself to his own law—but it is directed towards us, to allow us to give God his due so that a relationship in mutuality is generated in which gifts succeed gifts. If one wants to smooth out the divine justice in a well-intentioned attempt to safeguard God's love from "despotic" traits, one does away with human autonomy in its relation to God and finally, perhaps, with love itself—for love "demands" reciprocity as its very foundation. Without reciprocity the dynamic of giving and returning cannot come into being. God graciously takes the initiative (prevenient grace), but if we do not respond, God cannot enforce his will. Thus, Ruusbroec too seems to be saying that divine love (mercy) requires that divine justice is not being done away with. Our salvation required more than a paternal fiat, if only for the fact that we have to cooperate for our salvation.[81] However, since humanity itself was not able to abolish sin, the cause of its alienation from God, the Trinity itself initiated our salvation in Christ, the God-man, without abolishing divine justice. The Father gives his Son to humanity, and Christ, the second Adam, offers us and himself to the Father: "Through my death I have sacrificed you to my Father," says Christ.[82] In his lowly death Christ offered himself and us to his Father's mercy, while the Father received us together with him into his Son's eternal inheritance.[83]

The foregoing explains why Ruusbroec calls the fact that "the Son saved us by his death, purchasing and redeeming us before the countenance of his Father with his precious blood so that we might have life through his death," a sign of love.[84] In this context it is relevant to note that the reason the Son became incarnate is "because God pitied the sufferings of his beloved." Christ has broken down the prison of sin and put to death our death by his death.[85] In the same book, *Die Geestelike Brulocht*—and this title in itself is revealing—we read:

> The reason why God became man was his incomprehensible love and the neediness of all men; for they were corrupted by the fall of original sin, and they could not repair it. But the reason why

Christ wrought all his works on earth, according to his divinity and also according to his humanity, is fourfold: that is, his divine love which is incommensurable; and the created love which is called charity, which he had in his soul through union with the eternal Word and the perfect gifts of the Father; and the great neediness of human nature; and the honor of his Father.[86]

We need to observe two things here. First, *ere* (honor) can also be translated as "glory,"[87] in which case the whole life of Christ (including his passion) has to be seen as his meritorious self-gift to God and a revelation of his love. Honoring God means loving God: "If one honors God, one is being honored by him. To honor God and to be honored is the practice of love. Not that God needs our honoring him for he is his own honor and glory and his own immeasurable bliss. But he wants us to honor and love him, so that we might be united with him and be blessed."[88] This quotation also illustrates the reciprocal nature of love, the gratuitous character of God's love, which does not need us, and the reason why he shares his love with us.

Second, Ruusbroec does not mention satisfying the demands of God's justice (the Anselmian *rectitudo*) when he considers the causes of the incarnation; in his life and death Christ "honors" the Father, but this was not the cause of his incarnation. Ruusbroec places love first and sees "satisfaction" in the perspective of this divine love (and our alienation). All this indicates, as suggested earlier, that according to Ruusbroec, God did not aim at appeasing his wrath through the sacrifice of the God-man. On the contrary, like Anselm, Ruusbroec suggests that in Christ's redemptive work the tension between divine mercy and justice is entirely resolved. However, there are differences in emphasis between the two theologians.

Anselm argues that expiation for sin was necessary, not only because a mere fiat would dispense with human autonomy (we would not have been happy if *we* had not been allowed to "repay our debt"), but also because this would upset the order in the universe that God had to uphold to be consistent with himself and with his justice.[89] Ruusbroec acknowledges that sin causes disorder in the world, especially in the relation between humanity and its Creator: it is *avekeer*, a turning away from God. He is also fully aware that we ourselves could not reestablish this loving relationship with God, but he does not express a view on the (im)possibility of other ways of redemption. More fundamentally, whereas Anselm argues that only Christ's death represents a work of supererogation, Ruusbroec suggests that both Christ's life and his death have redeeming value because they are a gift (sacrifice) to the Father whereby a loving relationship is being reestablished. The reason Anselm argues that only Christ's death represents a work of supererogation is that only the offering of the most perfect created being, namely, Christ, outweighs all sins.[90] This seems problematic, especially in light of the Augustinian understanding of sacrifice as self-gift that Anselm adopts. After all, Anselm himself had argued earlier that making satisfaction is above all the subordinating of the will to the will of God—something Christ had obviously done throughout his life.[91] He would argue, however, that every created being owes total obedience to God anyway, and therefore obedience does not have any supererogatory value as such. In my view this is the main weakness of Anselm's theory.

From it follows another problematic consequence: the fact that, in Anselm's view, Christ's obedience as such had no supererogatory value explains why he fails to make clear the organic link between Christ and other human beings. In Ruusbroec's works this link is clear since he holds the view that both Christ's life and his death have supererogatory value. We can share in Christ's sacrifice by renouncing ourselves in the will of the Father the way Christ did. Ruusbroec indicates on innumerable occasions the role of Christ as our Brother, as the Head in whose Body we share, and so forth. He is able to make this connection because the sacrifice on the cross and the eucharist (both as a reenacting of this sacrifice and as a source of grace by which we become one with Christ) are closely intertwined and call for a similar renouncement and obedience in response to it. If the cross is the place where God's gift to humanity (his only Son) and man's gift to God (Christ offers up himself and in him, our humanity) meet and whereby a union is reestablished between God and man, the two dimensions of the eucharist fit harmoniously with the event of Good Friday.

Ruusbroec's originality in christology lies mainly in the linking of Christ's life and death to the trinitarian love that reestablishes this union between God and ourselves. *The trinitarian love requires reciprocity and it is in the cross (and the eucharist) that we are given the possibility of reciprocating God's love.* The cross is the most sublime sign and cause of the restoration of the reciprocal love between God and humanity, a love that has to be mutual or reciprocal because it mirrors the trinitarian life in its dual aspect of movement and stillness, threeness and oneness, flowing forth and drawing in, "generosity" and "avidity." The Spirit flows out towards creation but also draws creatures in God's unity: all our works, prayers, gifts are a "returning" of God's love. God's love demands reciprocity (in the sense that it can only flourish in continual and mutual giving-and-returning-of-gifts), but only the God-man, the second Adam, as the sinless representative of humanity, could return this love and thus reestablish this reciprocity. It is in this sense that the Father is "satisfied" with Christ's and our work. "Ours" indeed, for Christ shares our humanity and he sacrifices his and our humanity to God who had given his Son to the world in the first place. In a passage from *Van den Geestelijken Tabernakel*, a highly allegorical work, this link between the mutual self-gift and the passion is explicitly made:

> The fourth property we find in God is called window. We understand this to mean the union between the eternal Word and our nature. This window of union keeps God's realm open to us. The window to this union had been open to God from all eternity and it was opened for us at the appropriate time. In this union the Father has given his Son to us out of love and the Son has returned himself and ourselves to his Father through his precious death and out of love. And out of love the Father and the Son have bestowed on us their mutual love, which is the Holy Spirit.[92]

This reciprocal character of love mirrors the trinitarian love that is born from the mutual contemplation and pleasure of Father and Son. Elsewhere Christ's passion is again described as a gift: "When he had given everything he was or could give he called out with a loud voice: 'It is fulfilled,' and bowing his head, he gave up his Spirit. And we should do likewise" (namely, deny ourselves and totally surrender to the will of God).[93] In short, human nature, perfected in Christ, is returned to God on the cross after having "received" the divinity when the Word assumed human nature. The cross is obviously not an event whereby a wrathful God demanding justice would be transposed into a merciful God, but it is a gift of obedience of humanity to God through Christ, as a response to the gift of his Son to humanity.

Participation in Christ's Redeeming Activity

The issue of how we can participate in Christ's sacrifice is particularly significant as it allows us to see how Ruusbroec's christology impinges on his views on our deification, for it is through our participation in Christ that we become transformed. Of paramount importance is the role Ruusbroec attributes to Christ's redemptive work as a *revealer and example* of divine love, humility, and self-effacement. The incarnation, life, and death of Christ reveal the nature of the Christian God himself. If we enter in faith into this revelation and live accordingly, we will be transformed and saved. This is a perspective that will later be taken up by the *Devotio Moderna*. Geert Grote was particularly fascinated by this aspect of Ruusbroec's teaching, despite his reservations regarding the more speculative aspects of Ruusbroec's mystical theology. According to Ruusbroec, the Father sent his Son to teach us love for God and our fellow men (love as its own reward), humility (especially important to Ruusbroec: the whole life of Christ teaches us and exemplifies this humility),[94] self-effacement, and renunciation of self-will.[95]

According to his divine nature the Son's humility is illustrated by the very fact of the incarnation—that is, he assumed human nature that was banished to "the depths of hell"—and by the fact that he chose "a poor maiden" (not a king's daughter) as mother. Also, one may say that the humble works Christ performed were actually performed by God through him. According to his humanity (by reason of grace), Christ's humility is exemplified in many ways: in his worship of the majesty of the Father, for whose honor he wrought all his works; in his submission to the Old Law; in his choosing poor people for his company; and so forth.[96] Charity kept him ceaselessly uplifted to his Father, with reverence, praise and worship, and inner prayer for the needs of all mankind. Yet it also made Christ flow down with loving fidelity and benevolence to the bodily and spiritual needs of all.[97] Ruusbroec also pays great attention to Christ's suffering in patience, especially during the passion.[98]

The imitation of Christ's life and works is more than the external following of a moral example set by a virtuous person. Through it and through the renunciation of our created humanity, we are, with divine aid, transformed in Christ, so that we live in him and he in us.[99]

Ruusbroec uses the metaphor of being clothed in Christ (Rom 13:14) to describe how we become incorporated in Christ: "If we want to be received and chosen in the eternal bliss of God, then we have to be clothed with the life of our Lord Jesus Christ and be united with him through grace and our good deeds."[100] In his last work, *Vanden XII Beghinen*, Ruusbroec mentions several garments or habits of Christ with which we need to be clothed.

The first is an *external* habit, which refers to Christ's virtuous life and activity. It signifies his humble life, his self-abnegation, his charity and obedience, and his service for all people.[101] In short, Christ exemplified the perfect "active" life of virtue and charitable works, and we have to imitate it and live accordingly.

The second is an *inner* habit *(inwindich abijt)*, which Christ's humanity had received from his Father and which he conferred on his disciples, namely, the power and authority to baptize, teach, convert, forgive sins in his Name, and so forth, on the one hand, and the communication of his spirit in the counsels of poverty of spirit, purity, and obedience, on the other. Both aspects seem to suggest that in this passage Ruusbroec was addressing clerics only. However, the apostolic counsels are usually interpreted in such a general vein that they can be considered applicable to all those who want to live the Christian life in its fullness. Although there are some passages in his writings that suggest he shared the view that the religious state, if authentically lived, is the best expression of Christian discipleship,[102] it cannot be doubted that Ruusbroec wrote for both religious and laypeople. For instance, the second, fourth, and fifth *Letters* were written for laywomen. The first of these deals in some depth with the contemplative life, which suggests that Ruusbroec did not hold the view that laypeople were excluded from a mature spiritual life. This point is further corroborated if we remember he often associates the commandments with the active life and the counsels with the inner life,[103] but he definitely does not suggest anywhere that laypeople cannot attain the inner and contemplative lives. More fundamental than the distinction between commandments and counsels is the imitation and following of Christ's rule that comprises them. This rule is Christ's life, and it entails the commandments and counsels, understood in a more general sense as renouncement of the world (poverty), self-abnegation (purity), and abnegation of our self-will in the freedom of God (obedience).[104] This illustrates that Ruusbroec did not consider the religious state separate from the wider Christian life aimed at following Christ and his *regule*.

In the passage we are presently considering, Ruusbroec once more gives a broad interpretation of the counsels. Christ bestowed his spirit and his inner life, namely, a *poverty* of spirit by which his disciples with joyful heart could scorn riches, worldly glory, and whatever profits the world might yield. Thus they acquired perfect equanimity, ready to endure whatever God would make them undergo. Poverty of spirit makes us detached from the world and its vain pursuits *(de werelt versmaden)*.[105] To imitate Christ we also need to abnegate our sensual nature through *purity* of body, soul, and spirit. This implies that we do not develop any feelings of inordinate attachment to creatures *(ongheordender liefden)*, indulge in worldly or bodily pleasures, or become encumbered by worldly images *(verbeelden)* or preoccupations.[106] In this context Ruusbroec reiterates his message (examined in greater detail in chapter 6) that, in order not to become engrossed in worldly distractions *(verbeelden)*, we need to focus on Christ's life and redemptive work: "If we bear the image of Christ, as God and Man in our heart *(ghebeelt in onse herte)*, crucified, martyred, living and dying out of love for our sake, then he lives in us and we in him."[107] Yet through and beyond these sense images of Christ we need to attain "an imageless, nude contemplation *(onghebeelde, bloet ghesichte)*, in divine light, of the eternal Truth which is Christ: there purity of heart and spirit is achieved."[108] In short, we attain to Christ's divinity through the medium of his humanity. Similarly, we become imageless *(onghebeelde)* when we "bear Christ's image"—the Dutch is stronger and implies that we ourselves become shaped according to a Christlike pattern *(ghebeelt)*— or mirror Christ, the Image of the Trinity. The third aspect of the inner habit is *obedience* and willing detachment *(ghehoorsamheit ende willighe ghelatenheit)*, which the Son brought from heaven as he descended to fulfill the Father's will unto death and with which he ascended into heaven after having endowed his disciples with it.[109] Again, this obedience does not refer exclusively to the apostolic counsel in the strict sense to be followed exclusively by people living in religious orders: it refers to all those who die in God to their self-will.[110] It reflects Christ's obedience to his Father's will and the renouncement of his own will on the cross.

The bloody habit of our Lord's *passion* is dealt with in the context of a vehement denouncement of the contemporary abuses of the Church,[111] in particular, the sloth, greed, and unchastity in monasteries and among the priesthood. Ruusbroec concludes this tirade in a characteristic fashion:

> The rich of the world are faithful and merciful to the sick and the poor. But the rich in cloisters, who by rights have no goods proper to them, let their sisters and their brothers lie near them, sick, hungry and thirsty, and perishing from poverty. Pride, infidelity, avarice, indignation, greed, aversion, hatred and envy: of these the orders and cloisters are full; not only those who live from the common goods, but also the praying orders, who live from daily alms. Now Christ is unrecognized. His life, his teaching and his works are unloved by all those who serve sin and indulge their own will *(die den sunden dienen ende eyghens willen pleghen).*[112]

L. Moereels rightly observes that "to sin" and "to indulge one's own will" are almost treated as synonymous.[113] By contrast, Christ's life and death reveal how one should submit one's own will to God's will. The habit of Christ's passion was purple and red, symbolizing the union of his soul with the divine will and love, which found expression in his sacrifice. All the disciples who are one will and love with Christ will be clothed with the same habit:

> Christ has humbled himself in our humanity below every creature and has made himself a worm (Ps 21:7). . . . He has renounced himself according to his humanity, and put to death his own will in the will of the Father. And thus he is one will with God. He put to death, annihilated *(vernieut)* and burnt in love *(verbernet in minne)* his created spirit *(gheest)* and thus he is one spirit with God's Spirit. . . . He has put to death and annihilated in love his created will: thus he has found freedom in God. He is one with the will and love of God. This is his garment, which is doubly flaming red, with which he and all those who are united with him in love are dressed.[114]

Crucial in this union of will and love is "a nude, imageless eternal love; not to possess anything, including ourselves, with inordinate love either within or without. We have to be empty of ourselves *(ons selfs ledich syn)* and all things, conformed to God *(eenformich met gode)* and transformed in essential love."[115] To be clothed in Christ's habit means to have died to self-will and self-love. This explains how we can share in Christ's sacrifice: by dying to our selves in God and by renouncing all self-attachment, we share in Christ's life and work and become Christlike *(in Cristo ghetransformeert)*.[116] It also corroborates the point made in chapter 2 that self-transcendence and being intent on God are crucial aspects of the mature spiritual life. Christ exemplified this perfect selflessness and theocentric focus. Through grace we can attain the same selflessness that mirrors in turn the self-giving nature of the Trinity.

This union between Christ and all those who are united with him in faith and charity explains why Ruusbroec understands the seamless garment of Christ (Jn 19:23) as a symbol of the unity of the Church. He says: "This garment belongs to him by nature, from his Father and Mother: if we are his disciples and remain united with him in Christian faith and charity, until our moment of death, we will be clothed with him. For one cannot tear or divide the noble garment: for we are his living members and he is our Head."[117] In his earlier commentary on the creed, *Vanden Kerstenen Ghelove,* Ruusbroec had already elaborated on this idea of the Church as the Body of Christ and the communion of saints.[118] All believers together are the Holy Church, "for through the Holy Spirit, who is a bond of love, they are all gathered in one faith, one baptism and one law of commandments and sacraments."[119] If the Spirit, the bond of love of Father and Son, effects the continuing unity of the Church, this unity is itself founded on Christ's redemptive work: "The united community of all believers is holy, for they have all been washed with the blood of our Lord Jesus Christ, and anointed with the grace of the Holy Spirit and sanctified because the Holy Trinity dwells in them."[120] As all the faithful are one body of which Christ is the Head, Christ nourishes every limb of the Church "and so do all good people with their works."[121] For this reason, "the good works of all saints and all good people penetrate all members of the holy Church, even though their good works remain their own in honor and praise. For all saints and all believers are one in our Lord Jesus Christ. And they are all each other's limbs."[122] When Ruusbroec writes that our works remain our own he does not want to suggest that they have any redeeming value independent of Christ's redemptive work.[123] On the contrary, as we are one body in Christ our works derive their value from Christ only. It is only through Christ that we can share in the divine reward: "For every good work that is carried out in God, he gives to the good an incommensurable reward, namely, himself, whom no creature can merit. But because he collaborates in the work of the creature, the creature then, in virtue of his power, merits (God) himself as reward; and that with fitting justice."[124] God cooperates with us—the Spirit works through us—and therefore we deserve eternal life *de condigno*. The value of a meritorious work, inasmuch as it proceeds from the grace of the Spirit, is meritorious of life everlasting condignly: the worth of the work depends on the dignity of grace. In *Spieghel*, 399–404, we find the same idea expressed as follows: "We cannot redeem ourselves, but when we follow Christ to the best of our ability in the way I have shown, then our works are joined with his and are ennobled through his grace. He therefore redeemed us not through our works but through his, and through his own merits he saved us and set us free."[125]

I have explained how we become clothed in Christ by renouncing ourselves and submitting our will to the Father in Christ. I will now analyze more specifically how we share in Christ's sacrifice, both as an offering and in a priestly role. The first aspect, how we share in Christ's *sacrifice* as an offering, has already been alluded to. If we renounce our own will in Christ we become one will with Christ.[126] Christ's sacrifice refers in the first place to the utter renunciation of his own will: "The highest offertory which we can offer to God and which Christ performs before his heavenly Father, is the dying to our own will in the will of God."[127] Ruusbroec explains that Christ's inner work (his obedience) had more redeeming value than his external sufferings since the former was the cause of the latter.[128] Christ's human will, with which the will of every good person is one, is the true altar—more so than the cross itself. Commenting on Ex 30:4–5, he explains in an allegorical fashion: "The two shafts of acacia wood represent the eternal knowing and loving of God, which held and holds our altar, the free will of our Lord's humanity. It was held through four gold rings that symbolize his and our works of love. For his free will has lovingly surrendered him to do and to suffer everything which God had known and wanted from him from all eternity. And we too should be similarly disposed."[129] If we imitate Christ in love and knowledge, we make the two other gold rings, which then "surround" Christ's knowledge and love.[130] Thus, Christ's human will is our common altar on which Christ and his followers "sacrifice precious herbs and burn incense," symbolizing Christ's and our virtuous deeds: "Those will be offered to the Father by Christ and by ourselves with him."[131]

The last quotation implies that Ruusbroec allows for a *priestly role* for every believer. This idea is developed especially in *Van den Geestelijken Tabernakel*. After he has explained that we have to be perfect in Christian faith, free of deadly sin, fruitful in "outflowing charity" (note the trinitarian language), and obedient to God's Spirit and that we need to renounce ourselves and love God for God's sake, without other reason *(God minnen ommen Gode, sonder waeromme)*, he goes on to state: "And thus we shed our own blood on God's altar and die in the hands of the priests who make us, dead and united with our Lord's death, an offering to the heavenly Father."[132] Whereas under the Old Law only the priests were allowed to enter the Tabernacle and eat the offertory bread (Ex 25:30), under the New Law "all those who are clothed in the garment of his grace" have access to the Tabernacle. In short, "all those who are priests in spirit, namely all those who have been anointed and sanctified with God's grace, enter the Tabernacle and present and sacrifice to God Christ's suffering and holy death, and Christ himself is their food and drink, the sanctity of all saints."[133] Every Christian whose obedience and virtuous works are integrated with those of Christ assumes a priestly role: we all offer Christ and our works with him, to the Father. In that sense all the believers are *priestere in den gheeste*. Nevertheless, as some of these quotations suggest, Ruusbroec does not play down the unique role of priests in the strict sense as mediators between God and his people, in imitation of the Son, the perfect Mediator both in the Trinity and in the world. The priest on whom Christ has bestowed his power has to bear the sins of the world with Christ and beseech forgiveness on behalf of his people. The priest does not belong to himself but has become "an eternal offering to God."[134] Ruusbroec draws a parallel between the investiture of Aaron and his sons by Moses and the investiture of priests. Moses accepted the sacrifice of Aaron and his sons and then put it back into their hands. They then returned it to Moses who burned it in God's honor (Lv 8:27–28; Ex 29:22–25). Similarly, Christ takes the sacrifice of his priests on behalf of his people and burns it with himself in the fire of divine love.[135] Likewise, the priests receive the sacrifices of the people, unite them with the sacrificial Lamb of God during the eucharist (they "return" them to Christ, the eternal Priest), and sacrifice them through him to God. Christ is thus both Priest and sacrificial Lamb.[136] Just as the Jews daily burned a lamb for the forgiveness of sins, Christ, the Priest, sacrificed the Lamb of his human nature for the forgiveness of our sins and as our nourishment.[137]

Under the Old Law, which prefigured the truth of the New Law, the faithful brought their gifts, which were offered by priests, apart from the meat that was kept for their nourishment. Similarly, in the New Law,

> the good priests are nourished spiritually by the internal sacrificial gifts of the holy Church. The synagogue made offerings of cattle, goats, sheep and pigeons; the priests took those gifts and offered them to God. The holy Church offers to God penitence, inner devotion, innocence, abstinence, renunciation of the world, love and justice. These are the gifts the priests receive because they are, by appointment of Christ, mediators between God and his people. Thereby they are spiritually nourished. Although it is true that all good people serve in the holy Church and in the heavenly dwelling before God's countenance, and that they bring their offerings, it is the prerogative of the priest to present these sacrificial gifts to the heavenly king.[138]

The sacrifice of Mass incorporates the individual life of virtue into the life of the Christian community. The sacrifice of the Church entails also an offering of all members of Christ's Body.[139] All our sacrifices—above all a renouncement of our own will—acquire redeeming value only through the connection with Christ's perfect sacrifice. This is the reason Christ can offer our works, together with his own, to his Father. Thus, we offer Christ and his works, and Christ offers himself and us "as his own fruit for which he died."[140]

In short, we participate in the sacrifice Christ performed at Calvary, both as priests and as offertory.[141] However, if the sacrifice of the Church during the eucharist is a true reenactment of Christ's sacrifice, then it follows that the Church assumed a priestly role, not just during Mass, but also at Calvary. Does that not diminish the unique character of Christ's sacrifice on the cross? And how can the Church be said to participate in Christ's Passion? In an absorbing article, H.U. Von Balthasar meditates on the relationship between the absolute uniqueness of the offering made by Jesus Christ on the cross and the acts of representation by the sacrificing Church at Mass: "If an essential aspect of the sacrifice of the Cross is that it is offered by Christ alone, then it seems that at any rate *this* sacrifice is not made present when another offers it now." Von Balthasar argues that the tension can be resolved by pointing out the contribution of the earliest Church in its assenting or saying "Yes" to the sacrifice of Christ on the cross.[142]

Ruusbroec would fully concur with this view. This should not surprise us, given his adoption of the Augustinian view of sacrifice as gift and renouncement of self, as well as his views on the reciprocal nature of love and the close link in his thought between the passion and the sacrifice at Mass. In the passion the early Church identified its will with Christ's will, and that is how it performed the sacrifice with Christ. Christ's human will renounced itself in the sacrifice—and we have to do the same. Mary, symbol of the Church, exemplified this behavior at the cross of her Son. Ruusbroec describes how she was pierced by grief and sadness "unto death." When Jesus noticed this, he sent his Spirit and made her remember the words of the angel Gabriel, namely, that her Son would be the Son of the almighty God. After Ruusbroec explained how Mary recalled his miracles, his words, and the words of the prophets, and the Scriptures that her Son had to suffer and die for the sins and the bliss of all humans, we find the following remarkable statement: "And God's Spirit gave her such charity that she herself was willing to die this bitter death for all people's bliss and neediness, if it had been possible; if the nails had bounced out of his hands and feet, she would have hammered them in again for the remission of our sins."[143] Standing in the shadow of the cross, Mary at first was overwhelmed by sadness, but then she renounced her own perspective and identified her will with Christ's. In this renunciation she finds "happiness and peace for all eternity."[144] Christ as Head allows the members of his Body to participate in his sacrifice. His sacrifice on the cross was unique, but he allows us to participate in the reenactment of this salvific event at Mass:

"He, remaining God, became man for man to become God"

We will always see before us our Lord's humanity raised above everything and united with the eternal Word of his Father in divine clarity. And yet, according to this same humanity, Christ offers himself up with all his works and all those who will belong to him, from the first man to the last, to the pleasure of the Father. And he wants us to experience this in ourselves and bring this sacrifice together with him. Therefore we have to sacrifice him, who is humble, obedient, filled with all virtues, for our sake living and dying in the honor of his Father. We have to sacrifice him as a precious vessel filled with noble balsam of his worthy merits and as our own treasure with which we are purchased and redeemed. And he again sacrifices us to our heavenly Father as his own fruit for which he has died: and in this mutual offering the Father finds eternal enjoyment.[145]

Because God identified himself with humanity to the extent of assuming our nature, we can offer this perfected humanity up as a worthy offering made on behalf of humanity "as our own vessel with our balsam."

Observations

It is necessary to have a closer look at the development of our spiritual life in response to the saving work of Christ. Examining this subject completes the treatment of Ruusbroec's thought that began by looking at the nature of union with God. In chapter 2 I have argued that this union should not be understood in terms of "mystical experience" but rather in terms of transformation. We cannot properly comprehend Ruusbroec's description of this union without reference to his wider theological doctrine, especially his trinitarian doctrine and his anthropology. In this chapter I have focused on the redeeming work of Christ, which allows us to actualize our natural predisposition towards participation in the life of the Trinity. This participation, Ruusbroec's ideal of the common life, is the subject of chapter 6.

CHAPTER 6

The Common Life
Deification according to Ruusbroec

This chapter on Ruusbroec's view of the "transformation" or deification of the human person in response to God's grace brings together several themes of previous chapters. For example, in the last chapter we saw how the essence of Christ's redemptive work was a renouncement of his own will in total obedience to the Father. We can participate in this redeeming work by sacrificing ourselves (especially our own will) in Christ. This ties in with the suggestion, made in chapter 2 and examined in greater detail below, that for Ruusbroec we should strive to be intent on God in whatever activities we engage in. In doing so we will participate in the "activity" and "rest" of the Trinity in the Image of which we have been made. Created as a trinitarian blueprint, we need to be perfected by grace in order to know, love, and rest with the Trinity through Christ.

The previous chapter commenced with a discussion of the nature of evil. Similarly, in the first part of this chapter I deal with the justification of the sinner, as a sort of preamble to the actual subject. In the second part I examine Ruusbroec's description of the goal of deification, the common life, that is, a life of harmonious integration of charitable activity and "enjoyment" of God. To understand this ideal of the common life I discuss the contemplative life in which we are one beyond distinction with God's knowing and loving and explain how Ruusbroec appropriates the traditional theme of *epektasis* in an anthropological way. I return to the crucial notion of the single intention or theocentric focus to make clear how we can simultaneously rest in God and engage in outward activity. Finally, in the third part I give an example of how Ruusbroec describes the earlier stages of the process of deification, namely, the active and inner lives.

As this chapter takes up many issues that have been dealt with before, some repetition is inevitable. However, it is relatively complicated to consider the various strands of Ruusbroec's theology in their totality, and some aspects acquire their full meaning only in light of his synthesis as a whole.

The Justification of the Sinner

Ruusbroec gives a relatively detailed account of the justification of the sinner in *Brulocht* a 56–178. He argues that three points are required for somebody who is to see supernaturally: the light of God's grace, a will freely turned to God, and a conscience untainted by mortal sin. Because God is a "common" good and because his fathomless love is "common," God freely bestows his grace in two ways, as prevenient grace and as meritorious grace. "Common" translates as *ghemeyne*, the same concept Ruusbroec uses to characterize his ideal of the common life. Ruusbroec is convinced that God bestows his prevenient grace universally upon all people, "pagans and Jews, good and evil." By means of his universal love *(ghemeyne minne)*, which God has towards all, he has caused his name and redemption to be preached and revealed to all the ends of the earth. Whoever wishes to turn can convert, Ruusbroec writes. All of the sacraments are at the disposal of all those who wish to receive them, each according to his needs: "For God wishes to save all, and to lose none."[1]

Prevenient grace moves all, but not all respond to it with free conversion and purification of conscience, and for that reason they lack the grace of God by which they would merit eternal life. Ruusbroec has a fairly broad understanding of prevenient grace. It affects us from without "by sickness or by loss of eternal goods, of family or of friends; or by public disgrace; or he is stirred by sermons or by good examples of the saints or of good people, by their words or by their deeds, so that a person might come to know himself."[2] From within we can be stirred by observing the marvel of God's creation, by fear of death and fear of hell, by considering our sins, the brevity of life, by recalling the sufferings of our Lord and the good that God has done for us. We are positively disposed towards these stirrings of grace as we have a natural fundamental inclination towards God (because of the spark of the soul in the will and because our higher reason always desires the good and hates evil). All this results in a self-confrontation whereby we become disposed to receive meritorious grace: "By these points, God moves all according to their needs and each one individually as he requires, so that at times a person is thereby stricken, reproved, alarmed in dread, while he remains standing within himself, observing himself."[3] In short, prevenient grace results in compunction for sin and a good will.

If the sinner does what he can and if he can do no more on account of his own weakness, God "whom no creature can merit before possessing him,"[4] bestows his sanctifying grace, which results in a free conversion of the will, "in the wink of an eye." For Ruusbroec, conversion is a harmonious process in which we cannot separate God's gift of grace from the conversion of the will: "These two are so interdependent that one cannot be completed without the other."[5] From the grace of God and from free conversion of the will enlightened by grace there arises charity, and out of this divine love there arises the third point, purification of conscience.[6]

The main points are summarized as follows:

1) God bestows prevenient grace upon everybody. Ruusbroec is very clear on God's universal salvific will, with no reservations.
2) Prevenient grace, in its diverse forms, may result in compunction and a good will but not necessarily. If we want to persevere in unbelief or cling to a perverse disobedient will in relation to the commandments of God, we will not receive meritorious grace.
3) If we do not persevere in selfishness, God bestows his meritorious grace, not because we have any claims toward God—we can only

begin to merit eternal life after we have received this grace—but because God, "out of free goodness and generosity," shares himself with those who are worthy of his gifts.[7]

4) Although it has been argued that Ruusbroec's view has semipelagian traits[8] and seems distinctly reminiscent of John Cassian's views (especially *Conference* XIII), it ought to be observed that God's grace is essential and primordial in our conversion. Therefore, with regard to the justification of the sinner it is important to remember that Ruusbroec emphasizes the universality of God's salvific will and the harmony of God's graceful activity and the conversion of the human will in response to it.

On this basis we can now turn to Ruusbroec's description of our deification, with special attention to the nature of the common life as the harmonious integration of virtuous activity and contemplation.

The Goal of Deification: The Common Life

To focus the discussion, let me begin from a brief outline of deification according to Ruusbroec's exposition in his Apology, or *Boecsken der Verclaringhe*, before examining in more detail the nature of the contemplative and common lives, as well as Ruusbroec's appropriation of the theme of *epektasis*.

A Brief Overview

Union with God is multifaceted, consisting of several dimensions that should not be taken in isolation, so as to avoid a misinterpretation that singles out one particular element, for instance, the dimension of "resting" in God. Ruusbroec gave a concise characterization of union with God in *Boecsken der Verclaringhe*, a short treatise written at the request of Carthusian monks who had sought clarifications on some of Ruusbroec's teaching in his first book, *Dat Rijcke der Ghelieven*. In the former, which offers an excellent introduction to his thought, Ruusbroec describes a threefold union with God: all contemplatives are united with God (a) through an intermediary *(overmidst middel)*, (b) without an intermediary *(sonder middel)*, and (c) without distinction or difference *(sonder differentie ochte onderscheet)*.[9] This mirrors the divine love as it flows out with all that is good, as it draws into unity, and as being supra-essential and without mode in eternal rest.[10]

[a] In the inward vision *(insiene)* of the contemplative, God's love is seen as a common good that flows out in heaven and earth. God bestows the *intermediary* of his grace on us, a gift we need to reciprocate by virtuous activity: "Thus they are united with God by means of the intermediary of divine grace and of their holy life."[11] This mediated union will never be abolished: "This union, with fullness of grace and glory in body and soul, begins here and lasts eternally."[12] This last observation qualifies our understanding of the unmediated union and the union without distinction: clearly, they do not refer to a union in which we directly and immediately experience God. Or rather, we can only be one with God without an intermediary and beyond distinction through that very intermediary. This view is corroborated by the fact that throughout his career Ruusbroec criticized those who claimed they could dispense with the normal intermediaries of the Church.[13]

[b] The union *without an intermediary* is even more explicitly linked to the intra-trinitarian dynamics. As the Father and the Son embrace themselves through the Holy Spirit, the elect are drawn into this divine unity. Accordingly, their three faculties become interiorly transformed: as God bestows his grace in the unity of the spirit or the ground of the soul's powers, the understanding is pervaded with eternal resplendence just as the air is penetrated by the light of the sun; the will is transformed and pervaded with fathomless love, as a piece of iron is penetrated by fire, while the memory finds itself set firm in a fathomless state devoid of images. This union too occurs "by means of grace and love returned to God" *(overmids gratie ende wederboechde minne in god)*. *Wederboechde* is of course a trinitarian concept, referring to the *regiratio* of the Persons through the Spirit.[14] As I explain below, Ruusbroec here describes a transformation of the faculties effected by grace, which allows us to share inchoately in the Trinity and which results in a radically different intention or focus. The higher faculties are drawn into their unity and become "simplified" *(gheeenvoldecht)*, but they are nevertheless "overflowing." Instead of leading a merely active, virtuous life, we become "interior, enlightened persons" *(inneghe, verclaerde menschen)*. Again, that does not mean that we now enjoy esoteric religious "experiences": it means that grace has made us more theocentric in all our activities and dealings with the world.

[c] Finally, as God's love is not only flowing forth with all that is good and drawing back into unity but is also above and *beyond all distinction* in a state of essential enjoyment *(weselec ghebruken)* in accordance with the bare essential being of the Godhead, enlightened persons find within themselves "an essential inward gazing *(een weselec instaren)* above reason and without reason, and an enjoyable inclination *(.i. ghebrukelec neighen)* surpassing all modes and all essence, sinking away from themselves into a modeless abyss of fathomless beatitude, where the divine Persons possess their nature in essential unity."[15] Ruusbroec continues:

> All spirits thus raised up melt away and are annihilated by reason of enjoyment in God's being *(wesen)* which is the supra-being of all beings. There they fall away from themselves and are lost in a bottomless unknowing. There all light is turned into darkness, there where the three Persons give way to the essential unity and without distinction enjoy essential beatitude. This beatitude is essential to God alone and to all spirits it is superessential.[16]

In the following pages I will try to clarify the nature of this union without distinction on the basis of Ruusbroec's more elaborate treatment of it in *Die Geestelike Brulocht*. There Ruusbroec describes how the soul (whose ground is one with and indistinct from God's Image who reflects the fatherly nature of the divinity) shares in the intradivine processions of knowledge and love in an analogous manner.

The Contemplative Life and the Union with God beyond Distinction

In the contemplative life, the subject of Book III of *Die Geestelike Brulocht*, the soul is one with God beyond distinction. This union is based on the fact that God's ground is one with and indistinct from the ground of the soul. We have an eternal life in the Image of God who is the cause of our created being and the foundation of our re-creation and our participation in the trinitarian life:

> For we find indeed that the bosom of the Father is our own ground and our origin, in which we begin our life and being. And out of

our proper ground,—that is, out of the Father and out of all that is living in him—there shines an eternal brightness, which is the birth of the Son. . . . And all those who are elevated above their creaturehood into a contemplative life are one with this divine brightness, and they are the brightness itself. . . . And thus the contemplative persons are attaining their eternal Image to which they were made, and they contemplate God and all things without distinction in a one-fold seeing, in divine brightness. And this is the noblest and most profitable contemplation to which we can come in this life.[17]

As the ground of the soul is one with and indistinct from the divine ground, we participate in the generation of the Son, or even more boldly: we are the Brightness that we see and by which we see.[18] As explained in chapter 2, Ruusbroec does not mean to suggest that we ontologically become the Word of God. In an apophatic discourse assertions of indistinct union go hand in hand with the assertion that God and creature are "infinitely removed" from each other. I argued in chapter 4 that the human soul is created as a mirror, which receives the impress of the Second Person of the Trinity. It is not meaningful to speak of a human essence over against a divine essence: God's ground and the soul's ground are one and indistinct. God transcends the soul to the extent that he cannot be distinguished from it: therefore the soul lives in God and God in the soul.[19]

Moreover, when reading Ruusbroec's descriptions of the contemplative life, we have to keep in mind their analogous character. To describe the contemplative life, Ruusbroec either resorts first to objective-theological language; that is, he sets out the main aspects of his trinitarian doctrine in an almost scholastic manner. This objective-theological language points to the analogical nature of our union with God: the intra-trinitarian life functions in a paradigmatic manner in the contemplative life. Or else he uses metaphorical language (which we obviously should not take literally). As he puts it in *Vanden Seven Sloten*, speaking of the contemplative person: "Beyond all the divine modes, with the same beholding *(insiene)* without modes, he shall understand the modeless essence of God, which is a modelessness, for it can be demonstrated neither by words nor by actions, by modes nor by signs nor by likenesses. It reveals itself, however, to the simple beholding of the imageless mind. We may also set out signs and likenesses *(geliken)* along the way, to prepare man to see the kingdom of God."[20] This proviso—we can only speak of union with God by using similitudes and metaphors—should be kept in mind when reading Ruusbroec's texts. One of his favorite metaphors to describe the divine touch is that of a storm, but we should refrain from understanding this metaphorical language as an immediate description of union with God. Similarly, when Ruusbroec describes the contemplative life in terms of fire, this should not be interpreted in physical or sensual terms as outlining a mystical experience:

> Imagine *(ymagineert)* it this way: as if you saw a glow of fire, immensely great, wherein all things were burnt away in a becalmed, glowing, motionless fire. This is how it is to view becalmed, essential love, which is an enjoyment of God and all the saints, above all modes and above all activities and practice of virtue. It is a becalmed, bottomless flood of richness and joy, into which all the saints together with God are swept in a modeless enjoyment. And this enjoyment is wild and waste as wandering, for there is no mode, no trail, no path, no abode, no measure, no end, no beginning, or anything one might be able to put into words or demonstrate.[21]

All of this is metaphorical language, drawing on similitudes and analogies, trying to express the inexpressible. Ruusbroec appeals to the imagination and uses metaphors to outline a contemplative life, which is beyond similitudes. It is crucial to keep the metaphorical and analogous nature *(ghelijc)* of these descriptions in mind and refrain from interpreting them as immediate, first-order descriptions of mystical union. But what does he aim to express, if it is not an experience? I have suggested that "transformation" is a more useful category than "experience" to grasp Ruusbroec's main ideas. A passage from *Vanden XII Beghinen* illustrates the fruitfulness of this perspective. The passage is particularly useful as it reveals quite well what Ruusbroec had in mind when referring to the metaphor of fire.

> When we are lifted up in our pure spirit above all that God has created, then the Holy Spirit gives his eternal shining which is

light and fire into our spirit, and our spirit is like living, boiling oil, that lives and boils in the fire of the love of God; as the oil has scum and crackles and boils, then it is still unlike. But when the fire has consumed and burned up every unlikeness, the oil is pure and hotter than hot. And it is still and immoveable, like the fire. We must feel this in our spirit, which we compare to oil *(die wij der olijen ghelijcken)*. When we are lifted up above disquiet of the desires and practice of virtues in purity of spirit, then we are empty, without activity. And there the Holy Spirit gives his eternal shining into our pure spirit; there we are wrought, and we undergo (God's work). For the Holy Spirit is a consuming fire, which consumes and swallows up in its very self everything that it catches. Where it is hottest, there our spirit burns, and undergoes the love of God; and (when it is) more than hot, it is burned up and undergoes the transformation *(die overforminghe)* by God. But where it is (totally) burned up and one spirit with God, it is inactive, essential love. And that is the highest scale of love that I understand.[22]

This quotation anticipates a number of issues that are developed fully in the following pages. In my view, Ruusbroec, using metaphorical language, describes a transformation of the human person in response to God's grace. Our self-centeredness has to be burned away in order to obtain a perfect theocentric focus, which will keep our actions, desires, and thoughts from being tainted by self-centeredness. The perfect stillness Ruusbroec refers to is a life of pure deiformity; a life that perfectly mirrors the life of the Trinity in its active and enjoyable aspects.

In the first part of Book III of *Die Geestelike Brulocht* Ruusbroec describes this union beyond distinction mainly in terms of vision (*sien:* c 173, 182, 184, 225; *staren:* 190, 198)—which is consistent with the fact that we participate beyond distinction in the generation of God's Light. Thus, Ruusbroec uses "intellectual" or "visual" terminology to describe how we share in the Father's self-understanding from which the Son proceeds. However, we do not only participate in God's knowledge in the Son, but we also love God in his Spirit. In the second part of Book III Ruusbroec explains how we lovingly participate in the Trinity, that is, through the Spirit.[23] In chapter 3 I showed how the Spirit is the bond of Father and Son, not in the sense that he is their *principium diligendi* (the principle by which the Father loves the Son and vice versa), but in the sense that he proceeds as Love from their mutual contemplation.[24] This is what Ruusbroec calls the "active meeting of the Father and Son, in which we are lovingly embraced, through the Holy Spirit, in eternal love."[25] In a second moment, the Spirit is the principle of *regiratio* by which the Persons flow back into their shared or "enjoyable" unity: "This active meeting and this loving embrace are, in their ground, enjoyable and without mode."[26] Through the Spirit the Persons flow back into the unfathomable divine being which is "so modeless that it encompasses within itself all divine modes and activity and property of the Persons in the rich embrace of the essential unity."[27]

However we want to understand this union with God, it is clear that it is shaped by the intra-trinitarian dynamics, namely, (a) the processions of Son and Spirit and (b) their return into the divine unity, where (c) they rest in an enjoyable embrace of loving lostness.[28] Ruusbroec describes our participation in the generation of the Son in terms of vision and contemplation. Our participation in the procession of the Spirit and *regiratio* into "the abyss of namelessness" (c 242) is usually described in more affective language such as *ghebruken* or "enjoying" (c 238, 241, 242, 249, 256), "embracing" (c 230, 235, 237), and tasting (c 201, 223, 225). This confirms my thesis that in the contemplative life *we share in divine knowing and loving—in a finite, opaque, and analogous manner.* We misunderstand Ruusbroec's message if we interpret his description of the contemplative life as a "mystical experience."

Participating in God's Love and Knowledge

It has become clear that the union beyond distinction, or the so-called contemplative life as outlined in Book III of *Die Geestelike Brulocht*, is a participation in the processions of Son and Spirit, that is, in God's knowledge and love. I will now develop this in some more detail, examining the necessity of grace, the continuity of this loving and knowing union, its opaque character, and the relation between the "excess" of love and knowledge.

Although we are already created in God's Image, grace is an essential prerequisite to come to share in this divine knowing and loving. Through grace the faculties become onefold and simple; in this simplicity we encounter God in whose love and knowledge we then share. Ruusbroec says:

> By the created light of God's grace we are elevated and enlightened (so to be able) to contemplate in the uncreated light that God is himself. And thus we are borne within and, through love, mirrored in our eternal Image, which is God. There the Father finds us and loves us in the Son, and the Son finds us and loves us with the selfsame love in the Father. And the Father together with the Son embrace us in the unity of the Holy Spirit in a blessed enjoyment which shall eternally renew itself, ceaselessly, in *knowledge* and in *love*, through the eternal birth of the Son from the Father, and the flowing forth of the Holy Spirit from them both.[29]

Participating in the Trinity, made possible by grace, means to know and love God the way he knows and loves himself. The contemplative life consists in "nothing other than contemplating and gazing and cleaving to God in denuded love, savoring and enjoying and melting in love—and always remaining in this."[30] This contemplation does not refer to a passive, psychological experience but to an active knowing and loving of God. Therefore, when Ruusbroec describes how our faculties stand "empty" in "essential enjoyment" or when he writes that our mind becomes free from images when drawn into unity with God, this should not be interpreted in quietist terms: "When we are united with God in that way, there remains a living knowledge and an active loving in us, for without our knowledge we cannot possess God, and without our practice of loving we cannot be united with God, nor remain united with him. For if we could find bliss without knowing, a stone, which has no knowing, could also find bliss."[31] This quotation not only suggests that union with God is not an unconscious affair, but it also indicates the importance of an active love and knowledge in our union with God. Rather: to love and to know God, however opaquely, *is* to be united with him.[32]

If union with God means to know and to love God, another remarkable feature of contemplation according to Ruusbroec becomes intelligible, namely, its continuity—a feature at odds with the momentariness of mystical "experience" in the Jamesian sense of the word.

Ruusbroec explicitly deals with how contemplation on earth differs from that of the saints in heaven. In answering this question he does not say, as we would expect, that contemplation is only transitory and fleeting, but he only states that it is mediated and imperfect. Whereas the saints enjoy in an unmediated manner the divine sun, "the shadow of God illuminates our inner desert."[33] As long as we walk in the shadow we cannot see the sun itself, but our knowledge is in likenesses and in hidden things, writes Ruusbroec, quoting St. Paul (1 Cor 13:12).[34]

Seeing that we are only finite creatures, this knowledge and love radically exceed our creaturely limitations. Consequently, this union of knowledge and love defies description. Our union with God occurs beyond reason in a state of "unknowing." This unknowing is intrinsically linked to faith. Indeed, we know and love God in the theological virtues of faith, hope, and love. We can only be united to God in faith and love. In *Vanden Blinkenden Steen* Ruusbroec, referring to the metaphors of servants, friends, and sons (see chap. 2), puts it as follows:

> If we have faith, hope, and love we have received God and he dwells in us with grace. And he sends us out as his faithful servants to keep his commandments, and he calls us in again as his secret friends if we follow his counsel, and in so doing he openly reveals us as his sons if we live in opposition to the world. But above all, if we are to taste God or feel the life eternal in ourselves, we must go into God *with our faith, above reason.* And we shall remain there onefold, empty and free from images, *lifted by love* into the open bareness of our mind. For where we pass away from all things in love and die to all consideration in unknowing and darkness, we are wrought and transformed by the Word eternal, which is an Image of the Father.[35]

Through faith and love we are raised in simplicity; that is, our faculties become united in their ground. I explain this in greater detail in the discussion of the link between anthropology and the ideal of the common life: our faculties have to become onefold and focused on God solely, and yet they should be simultaneously engaged in charitable activity. We must look first at the relation between the "excess" of knowledge and love.

Although we cannot understand God we can still love the one we do not comprehend:

> Our *reason* stands open-eyed in the dark, that is in unfathomable unknowing *(in onwetenne sonder gront)*. And in this darkness the unfathomable brightness remains covered and hidden from us, for its overwhelming unfathomableness blinds our reason, but it enfolds us in simplicity and transforms us with its own selfness. And so we are unwrought from ourselves and wrought by God until we are immersed in *love* where we possess bliss and are one with God.[36]

Thus, although our participation in the Trinity refers to both knowing and loving God the way he knows and loves himself, albeit in a finite manner, the will rather than the intellect seems to be the main impetus in our deification. Nevertheless, this difference should not be overemphasized: we cannot comprehend God, but we cannot love him sufficiently either.[37] Just as there is an excess of knowledge—knowledge of God results in an unknowing—there is also an excess of love. This is the "enjoyable" love that always exceeds *(overgheet)*, as distinguished from the "active" love that goes toward God and returns to him.[38] This enjoyable love that is rest in itself does not cancel out the activity of the active love, but it makes it ceaselessly engage in new works so as to perform virtuous deeds. Thus, just as there is an active and enjoyable love in the Trinity (the Spirit who proceeds from Father and Son and the Spirit as principle of the return of the Persons in their enjoyable unity), there is an active and enjoyable dimension in our love of God.[39] We find the same idea expressed in *Vanden Seven Trappen*. God's Spirit is both eternal activity and eternal rest or fruition of Father and Son. We fail *(ghebreken)* in our works—that is, we cannot love God sufficiently—but in fruition we find satiety.[40] We know and love God, and above this activity we are embraced by God's love in fruition.[41] This is how Ruusbroec describes this integration of activity and rest:

> God's Spirit breathes us out to love and perform virtuous works, and he draws us back into him to rest and enjoy: this is an eternal life, just like in our bodily life we breathe air in and out. . . . [T]o

go in in idle enjoyment, and to go out with works, and always remaining united with God's Spirit: that is what I mean. Just like we open and close our bodily eyes, so quick that we do not feel it, likewise we die in God and live from God, and constantly remain one with God. Thus we will go out into our ordinary life and go in with love and cleave to God, and always remain united with God in stillness.[42]

This integration of activity and stillness is Ruusbroec's ideal of the common life. To understand the implications of this ideal, let us return to the crucial notion of the single intention or theocentric focus. To know and to love God, however opaquely, means to be intent on God solely.

A Theocentric Focus, or Being "Intent" on God

Union with God results in a different attitude or *intention (meyninghe)* by which we live in opposition to the world *(dat wij leven contrarie der werelt)*. Only when we transcend ourselves and all things do "we dwell in God."[43] In chapter 2 I indicated that Ruusbroec is at pains to distinguish his ideal from that of the Brethren of the Free Spirit, who turned mystical theology into a technique aimed at undergoing mystical experiences. Now that we have clarified that union with God needs to be understood as a participation in the divine knowing and loving, it is helpful to return to this topic, as it allows us to understand his ideal in more depth.

In the short treatise *Vanden Vier Becoringhen* Ruusbroec identifies four errors, the first being caused by an unrestrained, sensual nature (people who indulge in bodily pleasures, expensive clothing, etc.). This error, he fears, is "extremely common," both within and without the monasteries.[44] The second refers to a hypocritical nature, which exhibits great holiness where there is none. These people perform extravagant, harsh religious practices "so that they may be called holy and rise in people's esteem because of their strange behavior."[45] The third is intellectual pride: those people find self-gratification in their intellectual constructions rather than accept "the things that are beyond reason, the very things that have to be taken on faith and give us eternal bliss."[46] The fourth error, the one of more immediate interest to us, is "the most fearful of all." As indicated, Ruusbroec's comments are particularly relevant as they reveal in a succinct manner what he rejects and the spiritual goal he advances: "These people's way is a quiet sitting down of the body without work, with idle, unimaged sensuality turned inward into themselves. And because they are without practice and do not cling to God in love they do not go beyond themselves but rest idly in their own essence."[47]

Ruusbroec rejects mysticism turned into a technique aimed at undergoing a passive experience of stillness. In the following passage we learn something of Ruusbroec's alternative: we have to "work," love, and know God, just like God himself works.

> They lapse into an idle, blind emptiness of their essential being and they no longer pay attention to any good works, outer or inner. For they spurn all inner works, such as wanting, knowing, loving, desiring and all works that join them with God. But if they had loved God for one hour in all their life and if they had tasted true virtue, they would not have been able to come to this unbelief. For the angels and the saints and Christ himself will work, love and desire, give thanks and praise, want and know for all eternity. And without these works they would not be able to be blessed. And God himself would not be able to be either God or blessed if he did not work. And this is why these wretched people are sorely deceived.[48]

Love and knowledge of God are crucial in our deification. Our love and knowledge have to be solely focused on God: "Whoever is not intent on God and does not love him above himself and all things *(die gode niet en meynt noch mint boven hem selven ende boven alle dinc)* will always be reckless and not heed the honor of God and all true virtue and God himself."[49] Throughout the treatise Ruusbroec stresses the importance of "dying to one's own will," "breaking the bonds of disorderly affections for creatures,"[50] and so forth, so as to be raised above ourselves, "free in mind, unhindered, above all things into the eternal Good that is our inheritance and our bliss."[51] Thus, when Ruusbroec writes that to become deified we have to "turn within and deliver our naked unimaged intelligence *(onze blote onghebeelde verstendicheit)* to God's incomprehensible truth," he does not aim at promoting an

The Common Life 171

experiential state of vacant idleness in which the faculties are unpreoccupied, but he wants to stress the importance of an intention *(meyninghe)* that focuses solely on God and that does not allow for creaturely distractions or disorderly attachments. As explained in chapter 2, this is entirely in line with the Augustinian understanding of solely "enjoying" God.

The concept Ruusbroec uses to describe the freeing of the mind from images *(beelden)* is *onghebeeld* or *onverbeeldet.* Its opposite is being *verbeeldet,* being encumbered by images, that is, being lost in illusory creaturely distractions by not being focused on God.[52] In Ruusbroec's first *Letter,* written to Margareta van Meerbeke, a member of the Poor Clare community in Brussels, we find a convincing application of the concept *verbeelden* in that sense. The *Letter* treats of the problem of factions and particular friendships in the convent. Ruusbroec draws an interesting christological parallel to fight this cause of dissension within the community. He first points out that "whoever looks for gain or pleasure in human beings or anything transient is contrary to the saints."[53] He then refers to St. John the Baptist, "who fled into the desert so that he would not be ensnared by creatures" and who did not join Christ "because he was afraid of his affection and desire, that he might cling too much to the human nature of our Lord with his senses so that he might be hampered by images *(gehyndert ende verbeeldet)* in the free and pure ascent of his spirit into God."[54] Christ's disciples too were prevented from contemplating his divine nature, as his human nature interposed itself, encumbering them with images *(verbeeldet).*[55] After he has quoted Jn 12:32, he goes on to say: "And notice that the holy apostles God had called and chosen from all over the world were unable to receive the Holy Spirit as long as Christ walked with them in his mortal body, because they were impeded and assailed by images *(vermyddelt ende verbeelt)* caused by sensual love for his worthy human nature."[56] Christ's humanity (or anything else that is created) should not be a source of disorderly attachment or distraction *(verbeelden).* This is not to deny the role of Christ's humanity in our redemption, both objective and subjective. On the contrary, we have to follow Christ, imitate his actions and devoutly remember his redemptive work for our sake. Here we find another application of Ruusbroec's idea that we have to unite with God beyond intermediaries or images through those very intermediaries:

They have a heavenly life, for Christ lives in them, God and man. And for this reason they live both with images and without *(hier om sijn si gebeeldet ende ongebeeldet)*. They have the images of the life of our Lord, his suffering and his death and all virtue. And in their spirit they are free and idle and empty of all things *(ledich ende ongebeelt van allen dingen)*. And for this reason they are without images and transformed in divine clarity. And so they can go out with the image of the humanity of our Lord *(gebeelt mitter menscheit ons heren)* in good conduct, holy practice and all virtue. They go in without images *(Si gaen in beeldeloes)* with the Spirit of our Lord where they find and possess eternal clarity, unfathomable wealth, taste and comfort more than they can grasp or comprehend.[57]

The passage above is rich in meaning, for several reasons. First, it hinges on a dialectic of being *ongebeeldet* through being *gebeeldet*. Second, participation in a trinitarian dynamic is suggested (go out, in, and find nourishment and wealth). Third, the "emptiness" or "the being without images" refers, as the context suggests, not to a mystical experience, but to an intention, a way of dealing with God and world that is totally selfless. Indeed, Ruusbroec goes on to clarify how we then should love ourselves and all creatures *in* God, *to* God, and *for* God. People love themselves and creatures in God when they love them with God's love, that is, "in unity of love." They love them to God "where they stand united with God and all the saints before the presence of God, in eternal honor, in eternal praise, with all they are able to achieve." Finally, they love them for God "because they have died to themselves and they have left their own will for the dearest will of God." Thus, "they are of one will with God in doing, leaving undone and enduring and therefore they are free and empty of themselves *(los ende ledich hoer selfs)* and of all that may happen to them in time and eternity."[58]

In summary, the contemplative life as described by Ruusbroec in Book III of *Die Brulocht* and elsewhere sketches a life of indistinct union with the Trinity. This union is founded on the radical transcendence of God in relation to the soul. As the Father knows himself in the Son and as they love each other in the Spirit, so too we have to know and love God the way he knows and loves himself, albeit in a finite, opaque manner. Book III sketches this participation in the generation of the Son and procession of the Spirit. This knowing of God, which is an unknowing, and this love of God, which in its ground is bottomless and enjoyable, imply a radical attitude of selflessness and theocentric intention. Of course, this participation always remains analogous. As creaturely beings we always remain separate from God. These two assertions, our oneness with God beyond distinction and our separation from God, are both essential and complementary to understand Ruusbroec's message. To grasp its implications we need to discuss Ruusbroec's appropriation of the traditional theme of *epektasis*. In chapter 2 I clarified the meaning of this concept by referring to the writings of Gregory of Nyssa, who was one of the first authors in the Christian tradition who propagated the view that we, as finite creatures, have to ceaselessly pursue the inexhaustible, infinite nature of God who inflames our desire even further as it is being fulfilled.

Separation and Union: *Epektasis*

It seems virtually impossible that Ruusbroec was familiar with the writings of Gregory of Nyssa; however, the idea of *epektasis* was widespread among the Cistercians of the twelfth century. St. Bernard too argued that every encounter between God and the human person is always lacking in final satisfaction. Even in heaven, our desire will not cease: God is sought by desire, and therefore that blessed finding will not beat out desire but will extend it.[59]

Ruusbroec has his own version of *epektasis*. As I indicated in chapter 2, Ruusbroec's description of our transformation hinges on the assertion of both our radical difference from God and our union with him.[60] We are one with God beyond distinction through the union of our eternal life in God as idea and our created being (this is the essential unity). But as created beings we also remain "infinitely removed" from God. Recalling a text quoted earlier, this then creates an eternal dynamic of continuing desire and unsatiety:

> And so we live completely in God, where we possess our bliss, and completely in ourselves where we practice our love towards God. And even if we live completely in God and completely in ourselves, yet it is only one life. But it is contrary and twofold accord-

ing to experience, for poor and rich, hungry and replete, working and at rest, those are contraries indeed. Yet in them resides our highest nobility, now and forever. For we cannot become God and lose our createdness: that is impossible. And if we remained in ourselves completely, separated from God, we would be wretched and beyond bliss. And therefore we should feel ourselves completely in God and completely in ourselves. And between those two feelings we find nothing but the grace of God and the practice of our loving.[61]

This quotation needs to be understood in light of our indistinct union with God (based on our eternal life in God as idea), as well as the radical separation of all created beings from God. This tension causes a dynamic similar to the one described by Gregory in his *Life of Moses*: the incomprehensible, infinite divinity can never be grasped by us: the more we "taste" God's grace (and in this grace, God himself), the more we crave for him.

I have pointed out that Ruusbroec suggests that although we cannot fully comprehend God, we can still love the one we do not fully grasp. I also pointed out that this difference should not be overemphasized as love too is "bottomless." Similarly, Ruusbroec explicitly links the incomprehensibility of the divine nature to the role of the will as the dominant force in our spiritual ascent. Talking of the "divine touch," the effect of the bestowal of grace in the ground of the soul, he says:

> But (when) the spirit feels this in its ground, even though reason and intelligence fail in the face of the divine brightness and remain outside, before the door, nevertheless, the faculty of loving wishes to go further; for, like the understanding, it has been compelled and invited, but it is blind and it wants enjoyment; and enjoyment lies more in tasting and in feeling than understanding. This is why love wants to move on, where intelligence remains outside. Here begins an eternal hunger which will never be filled.[62]

This hunger is "an inward avidity and craving on the part of the faculty of loving and of the created spirit for an uncreated good."[63] We cannot comprehend God, but we can love him—yet the more we love God and are loved by him, the more we crave; and still we find bliss. As he states: "A created vessel cannot contain an uncreated good; this is why there is an eternal, hungry avidity here, and God overflows everything, but is always uncontained.... But full satiety in enjoyment is the dish that is missing. This is why the hunger is always renewed. Nevertheless, in this touch flow honey-streams full of all bliss."[64]

Therefore, although a voluntarist bias is unmistakable in Ruusbroec's writings, this voluntarism itself is equally subject to his apophaticism: the faculty of loving cannot "capture" the divine mystery either but is equally subject to a dialectic of hunger and bliss that will never be superseded. As we have seen, the notion of *epektasis* is well embedded in the tradition; Ruusbroec's originality lies mainly in the way he links this theme with his anthropology, as I will now explain.

Anthropology, *Epektasis*, and the Common Life

Under the impulse of grace all our faculties are drawn into the unity of the spirit, which is one with the divine ground. However, as God's nature is fruitful and active our faculties cannot remain in the unity of the spirit either: "For the incomprehensible brightness of God and his fathomless love hover above the spirit and stir the faculty of loving; and the spirit then falls back into its activity with a higher and more inner craving then ever before. And the more inner and nobler it is, the more quickly it must exhaust its activity, being reduced to nothing in love, and then it falls back into new activity. And this is a heavenly life."[65] Thus, the idea of *epektasis* is joined to Ruusbroec's anthropology: under the impulse of grace that is infused into the unity of the spirit our faculties are unified into their ground. And yet they actively flow out into virtuous works, in a rhythm that mirrors the inner Trinity: "The unification of the higher faculties takes place in the unity of the spirit, and here grace and love exist essentially, above activity, for this is the origin of charity and of all virtues. Here there is an eternal out-flowing in charity and virtues, and an eternal return inwards with an inner hunger to savor God, and an eternal indwelling in onefold love."[66]

Ruusbroec's ideal of contemplation in action is developed and underpinned in anthropological terms: the faculties are drawn into their ground and become onefold and are yet engaged in the world. It is therefore wrong to single out one aspect of Ruusbroec's description of deification in isolation from others. His ideal is not a contemplative life (which is only one dimension of his spiritual goal) but the common life. The common life is shaped by but not identical with, the contemplative life, or better, it is shaped by the indistinct union with the Trinity that is characteristic of it.[67] The common man realizes the ideal of a perfect integration of action and contemplation: "Therefore he has a common life, for contemplation and action come just as readily to him and he is perfect in both."[68] He is willing to do all that God commands and to suffer all that God allows to befall him. As explained above, this common life entails a new selfless attitude and theocentric focus or intention towards God and world. The common man "seeks nothing for himself but only the honor of the one who sent him." He is "a living, willing instrument of God with which God does what he wants, the way he wants." Near the end of *Vanden Blinkenden Steen* Ruusbroec once more tries to make clear how this ideal differs from that of those who pursue a quietist state or who have not become selfless yet: "And therefore all men are deceived who think they contemplate while they love, practice, or possess a creature in a disorderly manner, or those who think they can enjoy before they have been cleared of images *(eer sy onghebeelt zijn),* or those who rest before they enjoy: they are all deceived."[69] Being cleared of images does not refer to the results of a practice of introspection in which one sits, without activity, in an empty, imageless vacancy, but to the effects of God's gracing activity, which results in a transformation of the human person who receives "knowledge and discernment" and "power and freedom" that allow him "to work both outwardly and inwardly with all virtues."[70] In short, it refers to a single, theocentric intention.

Thus, Ruusbroec's originality lies not so much in the actual ideal of contemplation in action (although he gives a fairly radical version of it) as in the anthropological underpinning and development of it and, even more important, in the trinitarian foundation of this key idea: the common life is a life of enjoyment and activity, just as the Trinity itself is both activity in the Persons and enjoyment in their mutual interpenetration or *perichoresis.* As explained in chapter 5, it was Christ who objectively and subjectively rendered this participation possible.

Anthropology, Christology, and the Common Life

Ruusbroec's view on the soul as a trinitarian blueprint that results in a going-in and a going-out of the faculties while always remaining united with God underpins his ideal of the common life, which itself is in turn a reflection of the life of the Trinity. Before I discuss how Christ exemplifies the "common" nature of the Trinity it is helpful to discuss a passage in which Ruusbroec links his anthropology to his christology and shows they are, to put it in his terms, "two sides of the same coin." This illustrates once more the integrated character of Ruusbroec's theological synthesis.

In an attractive passage in *Vanden Seven Sloten* Ruusbroec makes clear this connection between anthropology, in particular, the indistinct union between our created life and our life in the Trinity, and christology, using the metaphor of a golden penny with which each person has to purchase the eternal life. This penny is of fine gold, "if we love God for himself and for no other motive"—a clear indication of the importance of the theocentric focus.[71] This penny, which is worth eternal life, has two sides. One side is described thus:

> The blank side of our penny is the essence/being of our soul whereupon God has imprinted his Image. When through faith, hope and love we turn inwards and so love and possess God, then we receive his Image supernaturally on the blank side of our penny. For with the Image of the Holy Trinity, which is God himself, the blank side of our penny, that is our inward-directed life *(onse ingekeerde leven)*, is formed and enriched; for there God lives in us and we in him.[72]

As explained in chapter 4, the soul is a trinitarian blueprint, naturally predisposed to be perfected by grace in order to share in the trinitarian life. This natural predisposition is based on the indwelling of God in the soul. It needs to be perfected by faith, hope, and love if we are to be incorporated in the Son, who mirrors the whole Trinity.

The reverse side—the *cruusside*, or "cross-side," as Ruusbroec calls it with a deliberate wordplay, lost in English translation—represents Christ's virtuous life and merits and our virtues. If we imitate Christ *(Cristume na volgen)*, bear our cross, subdue our nature by penance, and are obedient to the commandments, our reason, and the example of Christ's life, then our penny is "enriched, formed and well minted on the reverse side *(cruusside)*."[73] This passage illustrates how our life of indistinct union with God's Image and our active life of virtue in imitation of Christ are perfectly integrated. In short, our transformation through Christ builds on the natural predisposition of the soul as made in the Image of the Trinity. Crucial in this transformation is being intent on God solely: "If we love, use, and employ all other things in subordination to God, so that the love of God outweighs everything, then our penny is of good and sufficient weight."[74]

We can only participate in the trinitarian life via Christ. He is according to his human and his divine natures the door through which we attain blessedness.[75] Christ exemplified the life of the common person who reflects the common nature of the divinity. In a passage from *Die Brulocht,* Ruusbroec, in the space of seventy lines, uses the term *ghemeyne* twenty-one times. It always refers to the gratuitousness of God's love in Christ, itself a reflection of the "outflowing" nature of the divinity as Christ's human nature was and is shaped by his divine Personhood. Christ exemplified the outgoing, ingoing, and enjoyable dimensions of the divine life: he was always raised with devotion towards his Father and was always turned downward towards the need of his fellow men:[76]

> Now consider how Christ gave himself as common in true fidelity. His inner exalted prayer flowed forth to his Father, and was common for all those who wish to be saved. Christ was common in love, in teaching, in reproving, in consoling with meekness, in giving with generosity, in forgiving with mercifulness and pity. His soul and his service were, and are, common. His sacraments and his gifts are common.[77]

What does "commonness" in this context mean? "Common" can refer to that which is shared by or belongs to a whole community. In that sense Christ is called common, as he "had nothing proper to himself, nothing of his own, but everything (was) common: body and soul, mother and disciples, cloak and tunic."[78] In a more specific sense, the commonness of Christ reflects the common nature of the divinity in its active and fruitive aspects. The common person is somebody

The Common Life 179

who, through her participation in the Trinity, is equally ready for contemplation and virtuous activity and perfect in both.[79] This link with the common nature of the Trinity is explicitly made in a passage in which Ruusbroec describes how the commonness of God causes admiration in the believer:

> And, in particular, the commonness of God and most of all his out-flowing cause the person astonishment. For he sees the incomprehensible essence as a common enjoyment of God and of all the saints, and he sees the divine persons as a common out-flowing and (common) operating in grace and glory, in nature and above nature, in all places and at all times, in saints and in mortals, in heaven and on earth, in all creatures whether rational or irrational or material, according to each one's worthiness and need and receptivity.... God is common with all his gifts.[80]

The divine nature is therefore both flowing out and drawing in and enjoying in the shared unity.[81] Christ exemplified these dimensions in his life and work and so does the person deified in Christ. In chapter 5, I dealt in detail with the ways in which Christ bestows himself, especially in the eucharist.

Summary

The trinitarian dynamics shape our mature spiritual life, that is, the common life, which is characterized by a harmonious integration of activity and fruition, virtuous works and contemplation, mirroring the work and fruition of the Trinity. The contemplative life, as outlined in Book III of *Die Brulocht*, sketches an analogous participation in God's knowing (the generation of the Son) and loving (the procession of the Spirit). This participation is based on an indistinct union with God, a union that has to be understood in light of God's transcendent nature in relation to the soul and God's graceful perfecting of this natural datum (the soul as a "natural" trinitarian blueprint). Our knowledge and love of God exceed the capacities of our faculties: we can only know God in "unknowing" and love him with an active love that is in its ground bottomless and "enjoyable." Ruusbroec explicates this idea of *epektasis*—the infinite nature of the divinity is inexhaustible and has to be pursued eternally in a dialectic of craving and satiety—by developing it anthropologically. Our faculties are drawn inwards and become simplified or imageless, and yet they are actively engaged in the world. To clarify this crucial point, I referred to the single intention: Ruusbroec does not have in mind a psychological state or a mystical experience in which the mind becomes free of images, but he describes the effects of grace that result in a theocentric focus: the person is no longer *verbeeldet,* she no longer loses herself in creaturely distractions but is "intent" on God in whatever she does. This underpins Ruusbroec's ideal of the integration of action and contemplation. An understanding of contemplation in Jamesian terms (as a transitory, passive, and immediate experience of unity with God) is bound to fail to make this connection intelligible. Also, if such an experience of the divinity were actually possible, Ruusbroec's ideas on *epektasis* would become unintelligible. The contemplative life as described in Book III of *Die Brulocht* is not one of higher "experiences" of God. The quality of the relation between God's transcendent nature and the created soul, that is, the union beyond distinction, precludes an understanding of contemplation in experiential terms (especially if one understands "experience" in Jamesian terms, as Ruusbroec scholars have persistently done). It does not make sense to posit a divine essence over against a human essence as God radically transcends our spatiotemporal categories. Likewise, the union of the soul with God (a union of knowing and loving) defies description. This "knowing" is an unknowing, "a knowing beyond knowledge," and this loving an unfathomable "enjoyment."[82] In short, we cannot comprehend the union with God, but we can describe its effects: it results in a radically new attitude towards God and his world. In whatever we do we are intent on God alone. This selflessness and the ideal of contemplation in action were exemplified by Christ in whose redeeming work we can share if we too make ourselves an offering to God in Christ.

The Process of Deification in the Active and Inner Lives

As the contemplative life represents a selfless union beyond distinction with God's knowing and loving, it is only to be expected that both the active and the inner life inchoatively share in the patterns that are characteristic of it. Therefore, we must investigate how the active and interior lives are already shaped by the trinitarian dynamics in which we share in the contemplative life. We must also pay further attention to Ruusbroec's Christocentrism, another element that has been mostly overlooked by commentators who read Ruusbroec's oeuvre as a mere "phenomenology of experience."[83] Because my interpretation runs counter to much of the research on Ruusbroec published in the last decades, I will stick closely to the text itself. This will also allow me to show how Ruusbroec innovates by providing an "experiential feedback"—an approach that was to influence the Spanish mystics in the second half of the sixteenth century.

The Active Life

Ruusbroec divides *Die Brulocht* into three books, corresponding to the three lives, with each book divided into four sections according to the quotation from Mt 25:6: "See-the Bridegroom is coming-Go out-to meet Him!" After he has outlined in the first section of the first book the necessary conditions of conversion,[84] Ruusbroec sketches the triple way in which Christ comes, namely, in the incarnation, daily into the soul with gifts and graces, and finally "at the hour of death or at judgement."

The Christocentric stance is evident from the earliest stages of our transformation: Christ's coming in the *incarnation* offers us a model to be imitated from the active life onwards. Since Christ's humanity reveals to us his (and his Father's) divinity, we ought to imitate Christ in the practice of virtues as best we can and consider his interior life as well as the exterior works that he performed.[85] The mode of Christ's interior life in respect to his divinity, namely, that he is constantly being born of the Father and that Father and Son breathe forth a Spirit, "which is a bond joining them both, and of all the saints and of all the good persons in heaven and on earth," is inaccessible to us in the active life. Therefore, Ruusbroec wants us to focus on Christ's humanity as a revelation of his divine nature.[86] By way of example he considers three virtues characteristic of Christ's life: humility, charity, and patient endurance or suffering.[87]

According to his humanity, both by reason of grace and by reason of divine gifts, Christ wrought all his works for the honor of his

Father; he was submissive to the Old Law and to his parents. He chose poor outcast people for his company and was at the disposal of all just as though he were a servant to the whole world.[88] This humility illustrates and is shaped by the divine nature, which is also humble in character: the Second Person assumed human nature, which was banished to the depths of hell, "so that everyone, bad and good, can say: Christ, the Son of God, is my brother."[89] Thus, Ruusbroec expresses in his own homely way the Augustinian idea that the incarnation is an act of humility that ought to curb man's pride, the cause of the Fall.

Charity—or created love *(ghescapene minne)* (a 200)—held the higher faculties of Christ's soul in stillness and in enjoyment of the same blessedness that he now enjoys. It kept him ceaselessly uplifted to his Father with reverence and love, yet it also made him flow down with fidelity and with benevolence to the bodily and spiritual needs of all, and "therefore, he gave example to all by his life, as to how they should live."[90] Although Ruusbroec does not explicitly say so, it is obvious that Christ's charity reveals the "active" and the "essential" nature of divine Love—Love as the "active" principle of flowing out and flowing in and as the fathomless enjoyment of the Persons in their unity: Christ's charity made him flow out (active aspect) and kept him uplifted to the Father ("essential" aspect). Clearly, the active life represents already an inchoative participation in the trinitarian life.

The third point offers Ruusbroec the opportunity to describe in detail the sufferings of Christ, from early childhood (his birth in poverty and cold, circumcision, etc.) to the death on the cross, with a sense of detail and a zeal that is truly Franciscan in inspiration.[91] Thus, in the active life the individual believer has to incorporate his life into the objective redemption achieved by Christ through a modeling of his own life and works on Christ's.

The *daily* coming of Christ occurs because of God's mercy and generosity and our neediness and desire.[92] It is not insignificant that, according to Ruusbroec, an important form of this coming of Christ occurs when one receives any sacrament with the right intention.[93] The Church and its sacraments occupy a prominent place in Ruusbroec's mystical theology.

Ruusbroec expresses himself in ambivalent terms with regard to the *third* coming, "at the hour of death or at judgement." Ruusbroec's hesitation on this issue reflects his awareness of an important theological controversy of his time on the nature of the beatific vision and the last judgment. Pope John XXII had asserted in a series of sermons preached in 1331 that after death the blessed do not enjoy the *visio Dei*. The access to the vision of the triune God would be available to them only after the resurrection, on the day of judgment. This position seemed to make better sense of the last judgment: after all, what function could the last judgment still have if the blessed immediately after their death already saw God's glory and the wicked were deprived of it? On the other hand, it did not seem right to allocate the blessed to some sort of heavenly waiting room. Benedict XII attempted to settle the issue in his Constitution *Benedictus Deus* (1336), which states that the souls of the blessed do enjoy the vision of God immediately after death. Ruusbroec's hesitation may also confirm that *Die Brulocht* was written before 1336.[94]

Ruusbroec summarizes: we should imitate the first coming of Christ exteriorly through the perfect practice of virtues and interiorly through charity and genuine humility. We should pray and yearn for his coming with grace and await with longing, confidence, and reverence the third coming.[95]

In the third part of Book I Ruusbroec develops what has been called "a genealogy of virtues," which constitutes our response to the coming of Christ in the active life. These pages are better read than summarized. Humility, as the foundation of virtues, gives rise to obedience, this in turn to renunciation of one's own will, to patience, meekness, kindness, compassion, generosity, zeal, moderation and sobriety, and purity. Whereas humility keeps a person facing the *majesty* of God, righteousness keeps a person facing the eternal *truth* of God, and charity keeps one facing the fathomless *goodness* of God. Again one can observe the trinitarian aspect of this life of virtue. The meeting with Christ then consists of being intent on God in every good work. One ought "to rest" in God above all virtues and divine gifts when performing virtuous deeds; that is, activity and rest ought to be perfectly integrated.[96]

Ruusbroec concludes Book I with the observation that "the person who thus lives in this perfection . . . and who offers all his life and works to God's honor and to God's praise and is intent on God and loves him above all things, will frequently be touched in his desire to see, to know, to understand who this Bridegroom, Christ is."[97] This represents the end of the active life and the transition to the inner or God-yearning life: the human person recognizes, in the light of faith, that God is incomprehensible and inclines to God with longing. To illustrate this Ruusbroec refers to the Lucan story of Zachaeus who climbed the tree of faith, which has twelve branches and grows from above downwards, for its roots are in the Godhead.[98] Our intellect fails to comprehend the Godhead, but where intellect fails, longing and love go in.[99] This does not mean that the interior life is beyond reason; its main characteristic is that our faculties become "onefold" and drawn into their unity but not inactive.

The Inner or God-yearning Life

It is in the active unity that we receive the influx of God's grace, which enables us to rest in the simple being of our spirit in which God gives himself with all his richness without intermediary.[100] By the power of grace the higher faculties flow out actively in all virtues and they return in the unity of the spirit in the bond of love in a pattern that mirrors the divine ebbing and flowing.[101] First, however, Ruusbroec discusses the effects of grace on our lower nature, namely, on the unity of the heart.

The coming into the heart
Christ's coming into the heart occurs in four modes: sensible fervor and devotion, a superabundance of consolation and spiritual delight, powerful attraction to God, and a state of abandonment.[102] In these pages Ruusbroec describes in detail "experiences" that are usually associated with "mysticism" in the popular sense, such as rapture, jubilation, spiritual abandonment, and desolation. They all relate to the lower nature of the human person, and we may esteem them only insofar as they conform to Scripture and to the truth—and no more, for attributing too much value to them leads to deception.[103]

The coming into the higher faculties
Grace resides essentially *(weselijcke)* in the unity of the spirit, and it actively *(werkelijcke)* flows into the three faculties,[104] unifying our *memory* by raising it above all multiplicity and busyness and by creating a state

of simplicity;[105] the *understanding* is enlightened by grace, which results in knowledge of many modes of virtues and practice and contemplation of the nature of the Godhead and the attributes of the divine Persons.[106] The enlightened person will examine the attributes of the Father (almighty Power, Creator, Sustainer, etc.), the Word (unfathomable Wisdom and Truth, Exemplar of all creatures and their very Life), and the Spirit (Charity and Generosity, Benevolence, unfathomable Goodness, etc.).[107] By the third stream of grace the *will* is enkindled in a quiet love. The spiritually enlightened person participates already in the intra-trinitarian dynamic, albeit through the intermediary of grace: "The grace of God is present as a fountain in the unity of the spirit. And the streams cause an out-flowing in the faculties, with all virtues. And the fountain of grace always demands a flowing back into the same ground from which that flow issues."[108] Because of the "common" nature of God, our transformation participates in the divine flux and reflux and can only be understood from that perspective.[109] After having warned against those who deviate from this ideal, Ruusbroec once again refers to Christ as the model of "commonness": especially in the sacrament of Communion Christ gives himself as common to all people. Finally, Ruusbroec describes the effects of grace in the topmost of our created being, namely, in the ground of the soul or the active unity of the spirit.

Christ's coming in the unity of the spirit
Ruusbroec likens this coming to a vein in the fountain of God's grace. Here the *gherinen*, or divine touch, takes place. Ruusbroec describes it as "the innermost intermediary between God and ourselves, between rest and activity, between mode and modelessness, between time and eternity."[110] The divine touch is produced in us before all gifts; nevertheless, it is the very last thing to be properly recognized and savored by us, for God's grace works in us from within outwards, and is nearer and more inner to us than our own work.[111] Here, in the unity of the spirit, one is above activity and above reason but not without reason: one feels this touch, but one cannot understand its manner or mode. Above this touch, in the still essence of the spirit, hovers an incomprehensible brightness, the supreme Trinity from whom this touch comes.[112] Ruusbroec describes in colorful language the "inward avidity and craving on the part of the faculty of loving and of the created spirit for an uncreated good" and the "strife of love" that results from

this touch *(epektasis)*.[113] Because only God himself can satisfy the soul, it is permanently dissatisfied and remains "voracious." The more the soul undergoes the divine touch, the more it hungers and craves. The spirit is so possessed by love that it must exhaust its activity and itself become love.[114] Here Ruusbroec metaphorically (storm, fire) describes a process of self-transcendence: the spirit exhausts its activity and becomes love in response to God's gracing activity (cf. *do ut des*). However, because the spirit and God's love are fruitful, the spirit falls back into its activity, in a more sublime and fervent striving than ever before; it again exhausts its activity and then falls back into new activity, and so forth, in a pattern of flux and reflux. In the unity of the spirit, where the unification of the higher faculties takes place and where grace and love exist essentially, above activity, there is "an eternal out-flowing in charity and in virtues, and an eternal return inwards with an inner hunger to savor God, and an eternal in-dwelling in one-fold love."[115] All of this is still in a creaturely fashion and beneath God, in creaturely light: above it there is nothing but a life of contemplating God in divine light after the mode of God.[116] In other words, in receiving God's created grace we receive God himself—another illustration of the dialectic of meeting God without intermediaries through intermediaries.[117] This union with God beyond distinction or intermediaries is the contemplative life.

Observations

The common life, according to Ruusbroec, is a life of virtuous activity and enjoyable contemplation. The contemplative life refers to a participation, however opaquely, in God's knowledge and love. It is a knowledge that is beyond knowledge, or an unknowing: we cannot comprehend God. Likewise, our love always "fails" since we are not able to love God sufficiently. This creates a dialectic in which the faculties are drawn in, find rest and fruition, and go out again in activity, whereby rest/satiety and activity/desire without cease mutually reinforce each other. Ruusbroec puts it this way:

> And we keep the oneness with God above our activity, in bareness of our spirit in divine light, where we possess God above all virtues in rest. For charity in the likeness must be eternally active,

but oneness with God in enjoyable love will be forever at rest. And this is what it is to love. For in one now, in one instant, love acts and rests in its beloved. And the one is reinforced by the other. For the higher the love, the more the rest; and the more the rest, the more inner the love. For the one lives in the other. And he who loves not, rests not; and he who rests not, loves not.[118]

Ruusbroec's ideal of the common life is one in which we actively love and yet enjoyably rest in God; in other words, it is one in which all the activities we engage in are radically focused on God alone. From our eternal life as idea in God originates a dynamic that needs to be perfected by grace by which our faculties become onefold and are being drawn into their essence, which is indistinct from God's essence.[119] As God's being is both movement and rest, so we too need to engage in activity while resting, and vice versa:

> Every lover is one with God and at rest, and Godlike in the activity of love; for God, in his sublime nature of which we bear a likeness, dwells with enjoyment in eternal rest, with respect to the essential oneness, and with working, in eternal activity, with respect to threeness; and each is the perfection of the other, for rest resides in oneness, and activity rests in threeness. And thus, both remain for eternity.[120]

I argued that "resting" in God and becoming "imageless" refer to a state of the deified person in which she has become radically theocentric. Indeed, in the sentence that immediately follows the previous quotation, Ruusbroec states: "And therefore, if a person is to relish God, he must love; and if he is willing to love, then he can taste. But if he allows himself to be satisfied by other things, then he cannot taste what God is."[121] Resting in God in the midst of our activity means being intent on God in whatever one does without being distracted by creaturely attachments. Christ has exemplified this common life in a supreme manner. In a graceful imitation of Christ's life we will be enabled to share in this divine dynamic of rest and activity.

Describing the union with God in terms of a Jamesian notion of mystical experience is inexpedient if the term is used so imprecisely that it simply begs the question: replacing X (i.e., our "union" with

God) with Y (the "experience" of God) is not an illuminating strategy. Those who have tried to give more specific contents to the concept of "experience" are then in danger of committing the opposite error of "appropriating" God's mystery. P. Mommaers, for instance, identified four characteristics of the "mystical experience," immediacy, passivity, annihilation of self, and oneness. Because he assumes that Ruusbroec's descriptions of union of God and soul refer to such a mystical experience—rather than to a specific loving and knowing intention shaped by the practice and doctrine of Christian faith—he takes for granted that it is meaningful to compare them with "similar" descriptions from other "mystical" traditions.[122] It will have become clear how uneasy I am with this approach. Nevertheless, Ruusbroec does inaugurate a new development by providing what D. Turner called "an experiential feedback" in his descriptions of deification, especially in his description of the inner life and the divine touch. In other words, Ruusbroec gives a detailed description of the effects of grace on the human person and the transformation this involves, without wanting to imply that "union with God" itself does not defy conceptualization.

A Jamesian reading of Ruusbroec's description of union with God in terms of immediacy, passivity, annihilation of self, and oneness seems misguided on several accounts. First, it describes union with God in terms of an isolated experience or state of consciousness. However, Ruusbroec's ideal is not an isolated contemplation of God: it is the common life, in which contemplation and action are perfectly integrated. In whichever way we may want to understand "contemplation," it must have a content that accords with this broader ideal of the harmonious integration of action and contemplation. It is also very hard to see how contemplation in Jamesian terms can be harmonized with virtuous activity if one remembers that Ruusbroec's ideal is not one in which momentary contemplation alternates with charitable works but one in which *continuous* contemplation and action are one.[123]

Describing this union in terms of an unmediated experience is therefore highly questionable. As a matter of fact, one of the reasons why Christ has given himself concealed under the form of bread and wine is that "if we were to see our Lord in his glorious resplendence as he is in heaven, we would not be able to bear it, for our eyes are mortal and would lose their power of sight, just as all our senses would fail before the resplendence of our Lord's body."[124] Moreover, the fact that Christ has given himself only in a veiled manner allows us to bear witness in a meritorious way. Ruusbroec adopts the Augustinian theme (again with biblical roots) that we have to bear witness (both in faith and in good works) of Christ so that Christ will bear witness for us.[125]

As we have seen, Ruusbroec's doctrine hinges on the double affirmation of our radical separation from God as creaturely beings *and* our oneness with God beyond distinction, because God completely transcends our spatiotemporal categories. Neither of these assertions can be made in isolation from the other. Indeed, the fact that the soul's ground is one with and indistinct from its life as idea in God is based on the very chasm that separates created beings from God. The contemplative life describes this union beyond distinction. Since the soul is one with and indistinct from God it participates in God's knowing and loving. Yet we remain radically separated from God: this knowing is a "bottomless unknowing" (we cannot comprehend God), and this loving is both "enjoyable" and "fathomless." Thus, our created being is indistinct from and one with our uncreated being which participates in the trinitarian life.[126] Still, we remain creaturely beings. This leads to a dialectic of hunger and satiety. Although this theme—*epektasis*—has traditional roots, Ruusbroec innovates by linking this description of the effects of grace with his anthropology. This approach would be taken up two centuries later by St. John of the Cross, who also gives a detailed description of the effects of grace on the human person. Nevertheless, neither Ruusbroec nor John of the Cross present a description of an immediate, unmediated experience of God. Deification as described by Ruusbroec refers to a transformation (a word he uses regularly) that results in a selfless, single intention. Thus, the will "rests" in God when it is intent on God in whatever one does. The mind is "imageless" when one does not lose oneself in creaturely distractions but is focused on God alone. Union with God always entails an active knowledge and love. For that reason a description of this union in terms of a *passive* experience goes against the very heart of what Ruusbroec says: "Without our own activity, love and knowledge of God, we cannot be blessed."[127] Rest and activity mutually reinforce each other—an affirmation that only makes sense if we understand "rest" as being intent on God.[128]

Similarly, *annihilation of self* should not be understood as referring to a psychological state of a selfless consciousness but needs to be understood in terms of a selfless, detached attitude that focuses on God alone. This too makes clear the relevance of the example of Christ who was supremely selfless: the role of Christ seems to become entirely superfluous in a Jamesian interpretation of mystical "experience" understood as a state of consciousness.[129] Finally, interpreting Ruusbroec's description of union as an *immediate* consciousness of God does not do any justice to the texts, as a union without intermediaries is only possible through intermediaries, such as faith, love, charitable works, and sacraments.[130] A Jamesian reading that concentrates on mystical experiences separate from a wider doctrinal, ethical, and sacramental framework totally overlooks this sort of dialectic.

Ruusbroec's ideal of the common life is a life in which charitable activity and fruition of God are harmoniously integrated. The union beyond distinction, or the contemplative life, is a life of indistinct union with God in the knowledge and love of whom we come to share. This knowledge and love are "bottomless": we can neither know nor love God in any sufficient degree. This is tied in with the traditional theme of *epektasis,* which, in turn, Ruusbroec develops anthropologically. If grace perfects the natural predisposition of the soul as made to the Image of the Trinity, our faculties will be actively engaged with the world and yet be "onefold" and "resting" in God. To understand this ideal we must recognize the importance of the theocentric focus: in whatever activities we engage in, we always need to be intent on God. This theocentric focus implies a radical *self*lessness, first exemplified and made possible by Christ. According to Ruusbroec, both the active and inner lives are already shaped by the indistinct union with God. This understanding of the common life shows why Ruusbroec's ideal should not be understood as a "phenomenological description of a mystical experience."

CONCLUSION

One of the strongest arguments against interpreting Ruusbroec's description of the union between God and soul in terms of a Jamesian, "mystical experience" characterized by immediacy and passivity, separate from a wider theological context, is the argument of inner coherence. Especially in the case of Ruusbroec, who presents a theology in which many traditional themes are adopted in a balanced synthesis, I do not see how such a psychologizing reading can do justice to the complex interrelationships among the different areas of his teaching. In the interpretation put forward in this study all areas of Ruusbroec's theology (trinitarian doctrine, anthropology, christology, spirituality) fit harmoniously. In the briefest possible fashion we can state these interconnections as follows: just as Christ offered up his own will in obedience to the Father, we have to abandon our selfhood in Christ so as to lead the common life, that is, a life of harmonious integration of virtuous activity and theocentric focus ("resting" in God or "enjoying" God) that reflects the intra-trinitarian dynamics to which our created being is already attuned, as we have an eternal life in God's Image with whom we are one beyond distinction.

When one examines Ruusbroec's vehement criticism of the Brethren of the Free Spirit (who sought to undergo idle, mystical experiences without engaging in any charitable activity), it becomes clear that he rejects an experiential understanding of his own project. Ruusbroec advises us to know and to love God the way God knows (in the Son) and loves (in the Spirit) himself. The description of the contemplative life in Book III of *Die Brulocht* aims at making clear how the soul, which is one with God beyond distinction, participates in the divine knowing and loving. Since we are only finite, creaturely beings, this knowing is an "unknowing" and this loving "bottomless": we can neither know nor love God in any sufficient degree. However, Ruusbroec's ideal is not the contemplative life but the common life in which virtuous activity and contemplation are in perfect harmony. His is not an ideal in which contemplation and action alternate but one in which they are fully integrated: throughout our activity we need to be focused on God solely. It is unclear how we are to make sense of Ruusbroec's ideal of the common life if one understands contemplation in terms of an isolated, transient, passive mystical experience.

If the common life is shaped by the indistinct union with God and if God knows and loves himself and yet "rests" in the fruitive unity of the Persons, the common life will be a life of simultaneously knowing and loving God (and creatures in him), on the one hand, and "resting" in him, on the other. Ruusbroec's vocabulary of "enjoying" or "resting" in God has to be understood in light of the Augustinian distinction between *frui* and *uti*. Augustine too had argued that the will should "rest" in God and enjoy God solely, whereas creatures should be loved for God's sake.

Similarly, Ruusbroec's description of the "imageless," deified mind does not refer to a psychological experience in which the mind becomes empty and vacant. Ruusbroec wants to convey that our mind should not lose itself in creaturely distractions or become encumbered with creaturely images but rather that it should be focused on God solely. The same applies to his description of the abandonment of the will: Ruusbroec does not want us to become will-less, but he wants people to renounce their *own* will. Indeed, this radical theocentric focus implies an annihilation of self: we have to die to our self-centeredness so as to be focused on God only. This ties in beautifully with his christology: Christ's sacrificial work is in essence an offering of his own will in obedience to the Father. Likewise we have to make ourselves an offering in Christ to the Father.

Because God radically transcends the soul, he is in the soul and yet we are as created beings infinitely removed from him; that is, we are only made *to* the Image. This view reflects both an Augustinian exemplarism—we have an eternal life in God's Word as idea—and a Pseudo-Dionysian notion of union with God beyond distinction. This observation was confirmed by a closer examination of Ruusbroec's anthropology. Ruusbroec discusses an active unity (the ground of the faculties) and an essential unity. The essential unity refers to the relation between our created being and our eternal life in God as idea, implying that the human person is essentially a relatedness to God. Thus, Ruusbroec adopts the traditional doctrine of exemplarism—we have an eternal life in God as idea and this is the cause of our created being—but transforms it in the light of something that seems more Pseudo-Dionysian in inspiration, namely, that a distinction between our life in God and the soul is impossible.

From the indwelling of God in our soul our created being reflects the trinitarian dynamics: our faculties are not only engaged in external activity, but they also display an inclination towards their ground. If grace perfects this natural disposition, we can attain the common life. Ruusbroec underpins this ideal anthropologically: our faculties are being drawn into their ground in which God dwells, and yet they are involved with the world in a never-ending dynamic of ebbing and flowing.

Ruusbroec's trinitarian theology, more specifically, the notion of *regiratio*, shapes his whole doctrine. Crucial, and unique, in Ruusbroec's trinitarian theology is his assertion that the Spirit is the principle of the return of the Persons into their shared unity, from which they proceed again in an eternal rhythm of going-out, going-in, and fruition. The idea that it belongs to the nature of the Spirit, the Love of Father and Son, to return what he has received has far-reaching ramifications throughout Ruusbroec's doctrine. The theme of *do ut des* shapes his ideas on the relationship between God and humanity, his christology and soteriology, and his sacramental theology.

I hope to have made a convincing case for the status of Ruusbroec as a theologian of considerable stature. It should be noted that on many issues Ruusbroec's theology bears more resemblance to the theology of Bonaventure than to that of Aquinas.[1] These similarities, although significant in themselves, merely *suggest* that Ruusbroec may have undergone a Bonaventurean influence, probably through Hughes Ripelin of Strasbourg. Further research is necessary if one wants to substantiate this suggestion. In any case, it seems to qualify the notion that Ruusbroec belongs to the School of Rhineland Mystics influenced by the writings of Meister Eckhart. As I have shown elsewhere, a thorough comparison illustrates that even a shared vocabulary does not necessarily mean that the German Meister exerted influence on Ruusbroec, or even that they can be legitimately considered representatives of the same theological tradition.[2]

While this study does not claim to give a definitive answer to all the issues emerging from Ruusbroec's thought, I would like to think that I have demonstrated the significance, originality, and attractiveness of Ruusbroec's mystical theology of the Trinity.

NOTES

Introduction

1. For my earlier views on this issue, see "Ruusbroec: Apophatic Theologian or Phenomenologist of the Mystical Experience?" *Journal of Religion* 80 (2000): 83–105. I would like to think that the present study nuances the thesis presented in that article.

2. See, for instance, P. Mommaers and J. Van Bragt, *Mysticism Buddhist and Christian: Encounters with Jan Van Ruusbroec.* (New York: Crossroads, 1995). See also R. Faesen, "Jan van Ruusbroec in Beijing," Part I, *Ons Geestelijk Erf* 72 (1998): 203–16; and Part II, with G. De Baere, *Ons Geestelijk Erf* 73 (1999): 73–91.

3. This trinitarian revival owes much to the work of Karl Rahner who observed that it would not make a major difference to theology textbooks if the dogma were omitted. Interestingly, Rahner mentions Ruusbroec as one of a handful of theologians who are not guilty of this forgetfulness.

4. See L. Ayres, "'Remember that you are Catholic' (*serm.* 52.2): Augustine on the Unity of the Triune God," *Journal of Early Christian Studies* 8 (2000): 39–82.

5. A. Ampe, *Kernproblemen uit de Leer van Ruusbroec,* Vol. I: *De Grondlijnen van Ruusbroec's Drieëenheidsleer als Onderbouw van den Zieleopgang* (Tielt: Lannoo, 1950); Vol. II: *De Geestelijke Grondslagen van den Zieleopgang naar de Leer van Ruusbroec:* A. *Schepping en Christologie* (Tielt: Lannoo, 1951); Vol. III:

B. *Genadeleer* (Tielt: Lannoo, 1952); Vol. IV: *De Mystieke Leer van Ruusbroec over den Zieleopgang* (Tielt: Lanoo, 1957).

6. B. Fraling, *Der Mensch vor dem Geheimnis Gottes: Untersuchungen zur geistlichen Lehre des Jan van Ruusbroec* (Würzburg: Echter-Verlag, 1967).

7. See R. Van Nieuwenhove, "The Franciscan Inspiration of Ruusbroec's Mystical Theology: Ruusbroec in Dialogue with Bonaventure and Thomas Aquinas," *Ons Geestelijk Erf* 75 (2001): 98–111.

8. L. Moereels, *Ruusbreoc en het Religieuze Leven: Kleine Summa van het Geestelijk Leven* (Tielt: Lannoo, 1962). This book was written primarily for those entering religious orders.

Chapter 1. Life and Works

1. Gerard entered the Carthusian order in Herne in 1338 and died in 1377.

2. *Die Prologe van her Gerardus* was published by W. de Vreese in *Het Belfort* 10 (1895): 7–20, and *De Origine Monasterii Viridis Vallis* by Pomerius was published in *Analecta Bollandiana* 4 (1885): 257–334. The two works have been translated by Benedictines in Bonheiden as *Geraert van Saintes & Hendrik Utenbogaerde: De Twee Oudste Bronnen van het Leven van Jan Van Ruusbroec door zijn Getuigenissen Bevestigd*, Mystieke Teksten met Commentaar, no. 4 (Brugge: Uitgeverij Tabor, 1981).

3. This account is entirely consistent with what Ruusbroec says in his introduction to *Boecsken*, 24–33.

4. *Van den Geesteliken Tabernakel*, II, 333.

5. See the contribution by R. Lievens in *Handelingen* 35 (1981): 192–200 and the discussion by K. Ruh in *Geschichte der abendländischen Mystik*, Band IV, *Die Niederländische Mystik des 14. bis 16. Jahrhunderts* (München: C.H. Beck, 1999), 31–33.

6. See G. Warnar, "De Chronologie van Jan van Ruusbroec's Werken," *Ons Geestelijk Erf* 68 (1994): 185–99.

7. Quoted by G. Warnar, "De Chronologie," 187.

8. G. Warnar, "De Chronologie," 194–97.

9. Quoted by D. Nicholas, *The Evolution of the Medieval World: Society, Government and Thought in Europe, 312–1500* (London: Longman, 1992), 403.

10. See B. McGinn, *The Presence of God: A History of Western Christian Mysticism*, Vol. III, *The Flowering of Mysticism: Men and Women in the New Mysticism, 1200–1350* (New York: Crossroads, 1998), 12 ff.

11. See the Introduction by T. Mertens and P. Mommaers to the Letters in *Opera Omnia* 110, 477–83.

12. Van Eyck's painting of the Virgin and Chancellor Nicholas Rolin (Louvre) is a clear illustration of this new secularism. While Rolin sits on the

left side and the Virgin on the right, the center of the painting is occupied by a window, showing a medieval Flemish town, with the typical hustle and bustle of people going about their daily business. Rogier van der Weyden used a similar structure in his painting of St. Luke and the Virgin (Museum of Fine Arts, Boston). This convergence of the religious and secular spheres is a recurring theme throughout the works of other Flemish Primitives as well. (In the case of Rogier Van der Weyden, who donated money and paintings to the Carthusians of Herinnes, near Edingen, where his eldest son, Cornelis, had been residing as a monk since 1448, and who joined the Brethren of the Holy Cross, a lay society, religious in inspiration, for the Brussels elite, the link between the world of art and religion is equally obvious.) Hugo van der Goes joined the monastery of Roodendaele in the Zonien Forest as a lay brother. As these observations suggest, a major study on the connection between the Flemish Primitives and the *Modern Devotion* is long overdue.

13. This surplus resulted from a number of factors, such as the canonical celibacy of the quite numerous clergy, the effects of wars and crusades, and guild regulations related to admission to masterhood. See R. De Ganck's sketch of the historical context in chapter 1 of his work *Beatrice of Nazareth in Her Context* (Kalamazoo: Cistercian Publications, 1991).

14. See De Ganck, *Beatrice*, 7ff.

15. See "Prolegomena" by M.M. Kors, in *Opera Omnia* 7 (ed. G. De Baere), *Vanden XII Beghinen*, CCCM 107 (Turnhout: Brepols, 2000), 74ff.

16. *Tabernakel*, II, 324–25.

17. *Vanden XII Beghinen*, 2b 1379–1423.

18. *Vanden XII Beghinen*, 2b 1441–42.

19. *Vanden XII Beghinen*, 2b 1521–27.

20. *Vanden XII Beghinen*, 2b 1609–36.

21. See, e.g., K. Ruh, *Geschichte der abendländischen Mystik*, Band IV, 37.

22. *Rijcke*, 40.

23. *Rijcke*, 43.

24. *Rijcke*, 50–52.

25. *Rijcke*, 64.

26. *Rijcke*, 70.

27. *Rijcke*, 70.

28. *Rijcke*, 74.

29. *Rijcke*, 78–79.

30. *Rijcke*, 82.

31. *Rijcke*, 86–87.

32. *Rijcke*, 87.

33. *Rijcke*, 100.

34. Bonaventure has the following hierarchy: Angels, Archangels, Principalities; Powers *(Potestates)*, Virtues *(Virtutes)*, Dominions *(Dominationes)*;

Thrones, Cherubim, Seraphim. For the way Bonaventure adopts and "interiorizes" the Pseudo-Dionysian angelic hierarchies, see D. Turner, *The Darkness of God: A Study in the Negativity of Christian Mysticism* (Cambridge: Cambridge University Press, 1995), chap. 5.

35. Gregory (in *Hom. XXIX in Evang.*) has the following hierarchy: Seraphim, Cherubim, Thrones, Dominions, Principalities, Powers, Virtues, Archangels, Angels. Pseudo-Dionysius's order in *The Celestial Hierarchy* is identical, with two exceptions: where Gregory has Principalities, Dionysius has Virtues, and vice versa.

36. This is traditional teaching, although Ruusbroec has some original things to say on the nature of the third one, the "common life," and the way it relates to the previous two.

37. "Of the second book, *Vander chierheit der gheesteliker brulocht*, he [= Ruusbroec] said that he considered it trustworthy and good, and that it had been copied several times, even as far as the mountains."

38. See Mommaers's Introduction to *Opera Omnia* III, *CCCM* 103, 13–14.

39. *Steen*, 139–52.

40. See, e.g., *Steen*, 477–78: "But I would still like to know how we can become hidden sons of God and possess the contemplative life."

41. See Mommaers's Introduction to *Opera Omnia* X, *CCCM* 110, 62–65.

42. See D. A. Stracke's sketch on pp. 88–90 of the first edition of *Van den Geesteliken Taberakel*, *Werken* II (Mechelen: Het Kompas, 1934).

43. See A. Ampe, "De Bestemmelinge van Ruusbroec's *Spieghel* en *Trappen*," *Ons Geestelijk Erf* 45 (1971): 241–89.

44. *Spieghel*, 1840–41.

45. Surius entitles the work *De vera contemplatione opus praeclarum, variis divinis institutionibus, eo quo Spiritussanctus suggessit, ordine descriptis, exuberans.*

46. See A. Ampe, "Orde en wanorde in Ruusbroec's *XII Beghinen*," *Ons Geestelijk Erf* 19 (1945): 55–82.

47. For a more detailed overview of the contents of *Vanden XII Beghinen*, see *Opera Omnia* 107A, 539–47.

48. For these issues, see A. Ampe, *Ruusbroec: Traditie en Werkelijkheid* (Antwerpen: Ruusbroecgenootschap, Studiën en Tekstuitgaven van Ons Geestelijk Erf. Deel xix, 1975).

Chapter 2. Theologian or "Phenomenologist of the Mystical Experience"?

1. See B. McGinn's discussion in *The Presence of God: A History of Western Christian Mysticism*, Vol. I, *The Foundations of Mysticism: Origins to the Fifth Century* (London: SCM Press, 1991), xvii.

2. This view is inspired by U. Schütz, "Experience of God Today?" *Monastic Studies* 9 (1972): 7–22.

3. See, e.g., P. Mommaers and J. Van Bragt, *Mysticism Buddhist and Christian*. See also R. Faesen, "Jan van Ruusbroec in Beijing," Parts I and II. For a good overview of the main presuppositions governing Ruusbroec studies, see A. Deblaere, "Christian Mystic Testimony," *Ons Geestelijk Erf* 72 (1998): 129–53, and all the introductions written by P. Mommaers to the *Opera Omnia*.

4. See B. McGinn, *The Foundations*, 291–93.

5. W. James, *The Varieties of Religious Experience: A Study in Human Nature* (Harmondsworth: Penguin Books, 1985), 68.

6. The following is based on his contribution "God and Religious Experience" in *Philosophy of Religion*, ed. B. Davies (London: Cassell, 1998), 65–69. For a more in-depth study, see his *Perceiving God: The Epistemology of Religious Experience* (Ithaca: Cornell University Press, 1991).

7. "God and Religious Experience," 68.

8. See D. Turner, *The Darkness of God*.

9. Turner, *The Darkness of God*, 26–32.

10. Turner, *The Darkness of God*, 24–26. Basing his reading on chapters 4 and 5 of *The Mystical Theology*, Turner argues that the similar similarities are "conceptual" whereas the dissimilar ones are "perceptual" in nature. For the distinction between dissimilar and similar similarities, see *The Celestial Hierarchy*, 141 A–B, and *The Mystical Theology*, 1033 B.

11. D. Turner, *The Darkness of God*, 20.

12. D. Turner, *The Darkness of God*, 34.

13. D. Turner, *The Darkness of God*, 35.

14. D. Turner, *The Darkness of God*, 38.

15. See B. McGinn's review of Turner's book in *Journal of Religion* 77 (1997): 309–11.

16. D. Turner, *The Darkness of God*, 42.

17. D. Turner, *The Darkness of God*, 43.

18. D. Turner, *The Darkness of God*, 39; my emphasis.

19. In the introduction to *The Foundations*, xiv.

20. See McGinn, *The Foundations*, xix. On p. xvii he defines mystical theology as follows: "Thus we can say that the mystical element in Christianity is that part of its beliefs and practices that concerns the preparation for, the consciousness of, and the reaction to what can be described as the immediate or direct presence of God."

21. Mystical theologians who preoccupy themselves with the nature of negative theology itself usually do so when engaging with the writings of Pseudo-Dionysius in a scholastic setting, such as Albert the Great or Aquinas,

or when writing at a time when "mystical theology" has become a problem area (e.g., Jean Gerson, Denys the Carthusian).

22. See P. Verdeyen, "Un theologien de l'experience," in *SC* no. 380, 557–77.

23. See McGinn, *The Foundations*, 139–42. Before Gregory and the other Cappadocians, "infinity" was generally considered a defect. Infinity was considered "shapeless" or "formless" (characteristics usually attributed to matter). So Gregory was genuinely innovating by emphasizing the intrinsic incomprehensibility and infinity of the divinity. Yet he believed he had some solid biblical support for his innovative views, such as 1 Tm 6:15; Jn 1:18, and Ex 33:20.

24. Turner's views on the nature of apophaticism find a fine illustration in Gregory's works. Examples of his dialectical apophaticism abound throughout *The Life of Moses:* "seeing that consists in not seeing" (no. 163); God "grants what was being requested in what was being denied" (no. 232); "the characteristic of the divine nature is to transcend all characteristics" (no. 234); "what Moses yearned for is satisfied by the very things which leave his desire unsatisfied" (no. 235), etc. For these translations, see Gregory of Nyssa, *The Life of Moses,* translated and introduced by A.J. Malherbe and E. Ferguson, preface by J. Meyendorff, Classics of Western Spirituality (New York: Paulist Press, 1978).

25. See nos. 162–64 and no. 165: "every thought and every defining conception which aims to encompass and grasp the divine nature is only forming an idol of God, without declaring him as he truly is."

26. See nos. 221–22.

27. See nos. 232–33.

28. Moses learns that God's nature is infinite and therefore inexhaustible (no. 236).

29. See nos. 236–38.

30. See nos. 238–39.

31. See nos. 251–52.

32. See nos. 243. The paradox of standing steadfast in Goodness and the progress in the course of virtue suggests that Gregory's talk of "ascent" should be understood in terms of growing in virtue through Christ: our life has to be founded on the rock of Christ who is absolute virtue (see no. 244). Ronald Heine develops this theme in *Perfection in the Virtuous Life: A Study in the Relationship between Edification and Polemical Theology in Gregory of Nyssa's* De Vita Moysis (Philadelphia: Patristic Foundation, 1975).

33. *Sermon 6 on The Beatitudes,* translated by H. Graef in *St. Gregory of Nyssa, The Lord's Prayer, The Beatitudes,* Ancient Christian Writers (New York: Paulist Press, 1954), 149.

34. *Sermon 6 on The Beatitudes,* 148.

35. *Vanden XII Beghinen*, 2a 27–38.
36. *Vanden XII Beghinen*, 2a 224–30.
37. *Boecsken*, 441–51.
38. *Vanden XII Beghinen*, 1, 733–34.
39. *Vanden XII Beghinen*, 1, 744–53.
40. *Spieghel*, 2151–55.
41. *Spieghel*, 918–20 (modified).
42. *Spieghel*, 937–38.
43. See A. Ampe, *Schepping*, 73 ff.
44. *Brulocht*, b 1977–86.
45. *Brulocht*, b 1996 ff.
46. P. Mommaers, Introduction to *Boecsken*, 31.
47. *Steen*, 572–87.
48. D. Turner, *The Darkness of God*, 183.
49. D. Turner, *The Darkness of God*, 183.
50. The essay, entitled "Ignatian Mysticism of Joy in the World," appeared first in 1937 in *Zeitschrift für Aszese und Mystik*. An English translation appears in *Theological Investigations*, Vol. III: *The Theology of the Spiritual Life*, translated by K. Kruger and B. Kruger (London: Darton, Longman and Todd, 1967), 277–93.
51. "Ignatian Mysticism," 283.
52. *Rijcke*, I, 60.
53. For a good introduction to St. Bonaventure's trinitarian thought as a synthesis of Pseudo-Dionysian and Augustinian elements, see the introduction to *St. Bonaventure's Disputed Questions on the Mystery of the Trinity* by Z. Hayes (New York: Franciscan Institute, St. Bonaventure University, 1979), 11–103, from G. Marcil, ed., *Works of St. Bonaventure*.
54. See chapter 3 of this study.
55. *Boecsken*, 378–83.
56. See my article "Ruusbroec: Apophatic Theologian," 90–93.
57. *Vanden VII Trappen*, III, 269.
58. *Vanden Seven Sloten*, 848–58 (trans. slightly modified).
59. J. Alaerts, "La terminologie 'essentielle' dans *Die Gheestelike Brulocht* et *Dat Rijcke der Ghelieven*," *Ons Geestelijk Erf* 49 (1975): 337–65, esp. 360–61: "il s'agit d'un vocabulaire unitif-affectif, indiquant l'aspect d'union de l'expérience amoureuse. De plus, nos recherches semblent montrer que ni les cadres conceptuels de l'Ecole, ni les structures (plus philosophique que mystique) du dionysisme ne suffisent à l'interprétation adéquate de l'ascension mystique de l'âme, telle que Ruusbroec l'a décrite."
60. J. Alaerts, "La terminologie," 350–51: "il nous offre une phénoménologie géniale de la rencontre et de l'union mystique, qui déborde largement les

cadres philosophique et théologiques qui sont pourtant présents. Le vrai Ruusbroec s'intéresse à la vie, et à l'homme spirituellement épanoui qui éprouve d'une façon directe et passive la présence de Dieu." For a similar Jamesian reading, see P. Mommaers and J. Van Bragt, *Mysticism Buddhist and Christian*.

61. P. Mommaers, Introduction to *Boecsken der Verclaringhe*," in CCCM 101, 27.

62. P. Mommaers, Introduction to *Boecsken*. 30.

63. P. Mommaers, Introduction to *Boecsken*. 28.

64. P. Mommaers, Introduction to *Boecsken*. 31.

65. J. Feys, "Ruusbroec and His False Mystics," *Ons Geestelijk Erf* 65 (1991): 108–24.

66. J. Feys, "Ruusbroec and His False Mystics," 114.

67. J. Feys, "Ruusbroec and His False Mystics," 121.

68. This will become clearer in the following pages. For these quotations, see *Brulocht* c 171–72; c 34–37.

69. *Brulocht*, c 67–82.

70. L. Dupré, *The Common Life: The Origins of Trinitarian Mysticism and Its Development by Jan Van Ruusbroec* (New York: Crossroads, 1984), 57 (see also p. 27). According to Dupré, the fact that the Father utters his Word indicates that Ruusbroec is not an apophatic theologian.

71. *Brulocht* c 166–71: "[E]verything that lives in the Father (as) unmanifested in unity lives in the Son (as) having streamed out in revelation. And the simple ground of our eternal Image always remains in obscurity and without mode *(zonder wise)*. But the incommensurable brightness which shines out from this reveals and brings forth the hiddenness of God in modes."

72. *Brulocht*, c 69–70: "For in this darkness there shines and is born an incomprehensible light which is the Son of God, in whom one contemplates eternal life." See also c 169.

73. *Vanden Seven Sloten*, 834–38.

74. *Brulocht*, c 8–9.

75. *Steen*, 115–20; my emphasis. For a more detailed discussion of a similar passage, see chapter 6.

76. *Steen*, 600–607.

77. D. Turner, *The Darkness of God*, 3–5, 171–72, 268–73, and esp. 210, 249, 259.

78. *Boecsken*, 90–100.

79. *Spieghel*, 910–20 (slightly modified).

80. *Brulocht*, b 1629–32 (modified).

81. *Spieghel*, 1849–55: "Want al es dat beelde gods sonder middel in den spieghel onser zielen ende met heme gheëenecht, nochtan en es dat beelde de spieghel niet, want god en wert niet creatuere. Maer de eeninghe des beelds

in den spieghel es soe grooet ende soe edel, dat de ziele ghenoemt es dat beelde gods. Voertmeer, dat selve beelde gods dat wi ontfaen hebben ende draghen in onser zielen, dat es de sone gods, de eeweghe spieghel, de wijsheit gods, daer wi alle in leven ende eewelec in ghebeelt sijn."

82. F. J. van Beeck uses Ruusbroec's writings to illustrate this very point in his magnum opus, *God Encountered: A Contemporary Catholic Systematic Theology*, Vol. II.1: *The Revelation of the Glory, Introduction and Part I: Fundamental Theology* (Minneapolis: Liturgical Press, 1993), chap. 7, "Humanity's Natural Desire for God," esp. 246–57.

83. *Spieghel*, 1711–14 (modified). I discuss the status of the soul as a trinitarian blueprint in chapter 4, dealing with Ruusbroec's anthropology.

84. *Brulocht*, b 1644–50.

85. *The Divine Names*, 5.6 (821A). Translation from *Pseudo-Dionysius the Areopagite: The Complete Works*, translated by C. Luibheid and P. Rorem, Classics of Western Spirituality (New York: Paulist Press, 1987), 99–100.

86. *The Divine Names*, 1.5 (593C), trans., 54.

87. *Brulocht*, b 1637–44. It is worth observing that the addition Alaerts makes in the critical edition is by no means necessary from an apophatic point of view. On the contrary, the dialectical nature of the relation between God and his creation is put forward even stronger when one reads: "For wherever he comes, there he is; and wherever he is, he never comes, for in him there are no chance and changeability" (Want daer hi comt, daer es hi; ende daer hi es, daer en comt hi nummermeer, want in hem es toeval noch wandelbaerheit). Ruusbroec is then stating in paradoxical language that God's transcendent nature implies that he is everywhere and unchangeable.

88. *Brulocht*, b 1655–68.

89. This is discussed in greater detail in chapter 4.

90. It is therefore not without significance that Ruusbroec, when dealing with God's gracing activity in the "three unities," does not mention a supernatural adornment in the third life. See *Brulocht* b 69–72.

91. This argument is developed in chapter 6.

92. *Brulocht*, b 983–1117; b 1121–24 and 1045–63; b 1124–27.

93. *Brulocht* b 2107–20. For a similar discussion, see *Vanden XII Beghinen*, I, 762ff, with the revealing last sentence, "This is what it means to comprehend God in an incomprehensible manner, that is: undergoing and not-comprehending."

94. *Brulocht*, b 2120–22.

95. *Brulocht*, c 76–77; b 1597–98.

96. D. Turner, *The Darkness*, 178–79.

97. *Brulocht*, b 1778–99.

98. *Brulocht*, b 1807–10.

99. *Brulocht,* b 1807–10: "through the ground of a single intention, we go beyond ourselves and meet God without intermediary, and rest with him in the ground of simplicity."

100. *Brulocht,* b 1982–90.

101. *Brulocht,* b 1996–2002.

102. *Brulocht,* b 2002–5.

103. *De Trin.* X. §13, translation from *The Works of St. Augustine: The Trinity,* introduced and translated by E. Hill (New York: New City Press, 1994), 296.

104. *On Christian Doctrine* I. §4: "For to enjoy a thing is to rest with satisfaction in it for its own sake. To use, on the other hand, is to employ whatever means are at one's disposal to obtain what one desires, if it is a proper object of one's desire; for an unlawful use ought rather be called an abuse." See also I. §20. For a classic study of this distinction, see O. O'Donovan, "Usus and fruitio in Augustine, *De Doctrina christiana* I," *Journal of Theological Studies* 33 (1982): 361–97.

105. *Steen,* 952–60.

106. *Tabernakel,* II, 257–58.

107. Throughout Book III of *Die Geestelike Brulocht* Ruusbroec describes the trinitarian dynamics in an almost scholarly manner: *Brulocht,* c 14–17, 119–35, 211–23, 228–53.

108. *Brulocht,* b 2543–44 and 2567–84; *Trappen,* III, 269–70: "Hier sijn wi salegh in bekinnen, in minnen, in ghebruken met gode."

109. *Steen,* 307–8. These metaphors are traditional and have been used from John Cassian to St. Bernard.

110. *Steen,* 271–73.

111. *Steen,* 278–79.

112. *Steen,* 277–78.

113. *Steen,* 279–92.

114. *Steen,* 307–14.

115. *Steen,* 316–27.

116. *Steen,* 327–57.

117. *Steen,* 380–81.

118. *Steen,* 388–89.

119. *Steen,* 391–93.

120. *Steen,* 402.

121. *Steen,* 405. H. Rolfson translates *eyghenheit van gheeste* as "self-consciousness of their spirit." J. Wiseman translates more accurately and with less of a psychological bias as "self-centeredness": *John Ruusbroec: The Spiritual Espousals and Other Works, Classics of Western Spirituality* (New York: Paulist Press, 1985), 167–68.

122. *Steen,* 419–20.

123. *Steen,* 421–22. The same psychological, experiential bias surfaces in Rolfson's translation of *met eyghenscape* as "in a self-conscious way." Surius tranlates "in qua semper perseverare cum proprietate constituunt." I followed Wiseman's translation. "With attachment" would be a free but accurate translation.

124. *Steen,* 422–23.

125. *Steen,* 443–48.

126. *Steen,* 600–603. I adopt the translation by Wiseman, *John Ruusbroec,* 173.

127. This is discussed at greater length below and in chapter 6.

128. This important christological aspect of Ruusbroec's teaching is discussed in more detail in chapter 5. For a beautiful and relevant text on Christ as the example of the common man, see *Brulocht* b 1261–1904.

129. Given the purpose of this chapter I cannot deal with the question of whether Ruusbroec appropriates this Pseudo-Dionysian legacy in a voluntarist or more intellectualist manner. A passage from *Die Brulocht* (a. 1005–6) seems to suggest the latter, although other passages are more nuanced: "Where intellect remains outside, there longing and love go in." However, the point is that the idea that we attain modelessness via modes (the liturgical and sacramental, charitable works, etc.) also has Pseudo-Dionysian roots. See A. Louth, *Denys the Areopagite* (London: Chapman, 1989), 101–9.

130. *Spieghel,* 1354–62 (my trans.).

131. Ampe, *De Grondlijnen,* 42, 40. In the introductory poem to *Vanden XII Beghinen* Ruusbroec offers a helpful explanation of the modelessness of contemplation and its relation to specific "modes": "Aldus selen wij leven in redelijcken wisen, opdat wij, boven redene, een scouwende leven vercrighen."

132. *Spieghel,* 1864–68 (my trans.)

133. *Boecsken,* 103–5.

134. *Brulocht,* b 2311–19.

135. *Brulocht,* b 2303–5.

136. *Brulocht,* b 2308–10.

137. Introduction in J. Wiseman, *John Ruusbroec,* 27.

138. *Boecsken,* 95–100.

139. *Boecsken,* 112.

140. *Boecsken,* 84–86.

141. *Brulocht,* b 2458–60: "Want si segghen dat si leven sonder wille, ende dat si haren gheest gode hebben ghegheven in rasten ende in ledicheiden, ende datsi sijn een met gode, ende te niete worden ane hen selven."

142. *Brulocht,* b 2458.

143. *Brulocht,* b 1782–99. See also *Brulocht* b 1778–1817, 1823, 1826, 1836, 1839, 1845, 1858, 1872, 1878, 1880, 1892, 1904, 1968, 2102, 2392ff., etc. The very

opening lines of *Vanden Seven Sloten*, a treatise written for a member of the Poor Clare community, contain this beautiful counsel: "Dear sister, above all things, May God be your intention and your love (*Lieve suster, boven alle dinc sy god ghemeint ende ghemint*)." (*Sloten*, 1-2.)

144. *Brulocht*, b 2279-80; b 2244-51.
145. *Brulocht*, b 2244-51.
146. *Boecsken*, 514-15.
147. *Brulocht*, b 2148-52.
148. *Brulocht*, b 2421-26.
149. *Brulocht*, b 2428-34.
150. *Brulocht*, b 2477-79.
151. *Brulocht*, b 2528-29.
152. *Brulocht*, b 2535-46.
153. *Steen*, 347-48.
154. *Brulocht*, b 2450-53.
155. *Brulocht*, b 2458-60.
156. *Steen*, 1: "inden volcommensten staet der heiligher kerken."
157. *Brulocht*, b 2374-76.
158. *Brulocht*, b 2357-64.
159. *Brulocht*, b 2407-8.
160. *Brulocht*, b 1147-51.
161. *Brulocht*, b 1788-89.

Chapter 3. "A flowing, ebbing sea": Trinitarian Doctorine and *Regiratio*

1. J.B. Porion, *Hadewijch: Lettres spirituelles,* Traduction du moyen-néerlandais (Geneva: Martingay, 1972), 24-25, cited by C. Hart, *Hadewijch: The Complete Works,* Classics of Western Spirituality (Ramsey, N.J.: Paulist Press, 1980), 10-11.

2. Some of this material appeared in my article "Neoplatonism, *Regiratio* and Trinitarian Theology: A Look at Ruusbroec," *Hermathena* 169 (2001): 169-88.

3. II *Sent.* d. 11, a. 1, arg. 5: "Videtur enim quod sic per Trismegistum qui dicit, quod monas gignit monadem, et in se reflectit ardorem." For a good overview of these issues, see the invaluable book by G. Emery, *La Trinité Créatrice: Trinité et création dans les commentaires aux Sentences de Thomas d'Aquin et de ses précurseurs Albert le Grand et Bonaventure* (Paris: Librairie J. Vrin, 1995). The *Liber Viginti Quattuor Philosophorum* seems a Latin translation of a text written in the Alexandrian tradition. For a recent critical edition, see *CCCM* 143, *Hermes Latinus,* Tomus III, Pars I, ed. F. Hudry (Turn-

hout: Brepols, 1997). The commentary on the work seems to draw on the thought of Plotinus, Proclus, Ps. Dionysius, Macrobius, Boethius, and Eriugena, as well as from the *Liber de Causis*. Apparently Alanus ab Insulis (Alan of Lille) was the first to quote from this enigmatic work. On this, see K. Ruh, *Geschichte der abendländischen Mystik*, Band III, *Die Mystik des deutschen Predigerordens und ihre Grundlegung durch die Hochscholastik* (München: C. H. Beck, 1996), 33–44.

4. The notion of the Spirit as *principium diligendi* was rejected by Albert, Bonaventure (I *Sent.* d. 10; d. 32), and Aquinas (see *ST* I, 37, 2). On these issues, see my article "Meister Eckhart and Jan Van Ruusbroec: A Comparison," *Medieval Philosophy and Theology* 7 (1998): 182–84.

5. See G. Emery, *La Trinité*, 101.

6. I *Sent.* d. 14, q. 2, a. 2: "Respondeo dicendum quod in exitu creaturarum a primo principio attenditur quaedam circulatio vel regiratio, eo quod omnia revertuntur sicut in finem in id a quo sicut principio prodierunt. Et ideo oportet ut per eadem quibus est exitus a prinicipio, et reditus in finem attendatur." The other passages are from his commentaries on *De Anima* (lib. II, lect. 16), where he discusses the phenomenon of "echo," and *De Caelo et Mundo*, where he discusses the circular movement of the stars.

7. Cf. II *Sent.* d. 18, q. 2, a. 2, arg. 4: "Per eadem est reditus in finem ultimum et exitus a primo principio."

8. I *Sent.* d. 14, q. 2, a. 2 sol.

9. See G. Emery, *La Trinité*, 390–402.

10. See *ST* I, 84, 7, and *ST* I, 14, 2 *ad* 1.

11. *Sermon* Q 35. Translation by M. O'C. Walshe, *Meister Eckhart: Sermons and Treatises*, Vol. I (Shaftesbury: Element Books, 1991), 249.

12. *Sermon* XXIX, no. 304.

13. See L. W. IV, 421–28. For a translation of this sermon, see B. McGinn, ed., *Meister Eckhart: Teacher and Preacher*, Classics of Western Spirituality (New York: Paulist Press, 1986), 234–37.

14. *Vanden XII Beghinen*, 2a 568–612 (my trans.). Surius translates the last sentence as follows: "Ex hac autem mutua Patris ac Filii intuitione, sempiterna emanat complacentia, quae est Spiritus sanctus tertia in divinis persona, ex Patre filioque promanans: quippe qui amborum voluntas et amor est, et ex ipsis ambobus aeterno emanat, refluitque intro in divinitatis naturam."

15. Some of the following material has been developed in my articles "Meister Eckhart and Jan Van Ruusbroec: A Comparison"; and "In the Image of God: The Trinitarian Anthropology of St. Bonaventure, St. Thomas Aquinas and the Blessed Jan van Ruusbroec," Parts I and II, *Irish Theological Quarterly* 66 (2001): 109–23, 227–37.

16. *Rijcke*, I, 84; *Brulocht*, a 912–16; *Brulocht*, a 728–30.

17. *Vanden XII Beghinen*, 1, 532–33. Pseudo-Dionysius too calls God "formless" in *The Divine Names* (824B). God "does not possess *this* kind of existence and not *that*" (Pseudo-Dionysius, *The Divine Names*, 5.8, 101). In the introductory poem to *Vanden XII Beghinen*, 1, 260–61, Ruusbroec offers a helpful explanation of the modelessness of contemplation and its relation to specific "modes": "Aldus selen wij leven in redelijcken wisen, opdat wij, boven redene, een scouwende leven vercrighen."

18. *Brulocht*, c 238–46 (slightly modified). Surius translates the last sentence as "Hic vero fruitivus quidam excessus agitur, et defluens in essentialem nuditatem immersio, ubi quaevis Dei nomina, et modi ac vividae rationes omnes in divinae veritatis speculo relucentes, in simplicem illam ac innominabilem decidunt divinitatis essentiam, modi omnis ac rationis expertem." Cf. A. Ampe, *Grondlijnen*, 200. Compare *Rijcke*, I, 73–74: "in the simple unity of the divine being is neither knowledge, yearning nor activity; for this is a modeless abyss which can never be actively understood."

19. *Boecsken*, 438–46.

20. *Boecsken*, 450–53; *Brulocht*, c 242.

21. Pseudo-Dionysius, *The Divine Names*, 1.8 (597C), 58; cf. A. Ampe, *Grondlijnen*, 51.

22. *Brulocht*, c 236–53.

23. *Rijcke*, I, 15: "Hij es wesen der wesenne ende leven ende beghin ende onthout aller creatueren." And: "Ende al dat Hij ghedeylt hevet den creatueren in menichfuldicheyden, dat es in Hem bleven onghemeten in afgrondiger rijcheyt sijnder hogher natueren."

24. *Trappen*, III, 270: "[D]aer de godeleke persone hen-selven ontgheesten in eenheit haers wesens, in dat grondelooese abys eenvuldegher salegheit. Daer en es vader, noch sone, noch heilegh gheest, noch gheene creatuere. Daer en es niet dan eenegh wesen, dat es: de substantie der godleker persone. . . . Daer es god in sinen sempelen wesene sonder werc, eeweghe ledegheit, wiseloese deemsterheit, onghenaemde istegheit, alre creatueren overwesen, ende gods ende alre heileghen eenvuldeghe grondoese salegheit."

25. *Boecsken*, 84–86.

26. *Trappen*, III, 266.

27. *Vanden XII Beghinen*, 1, 663ff.

28. *Vanden XII Beghinen*, 2a 573–75 (my trans.).

29. A. Ampe, *Grondlijnen*, 87.

30. See A. Ampe, *Grondlijnen*, 7; 84–90; 151; B. Fraling, *Der Mensch*, 45–46.

31. See *Vanden XII Beghinen*, 2 a 574–75: "dat selve wesen es natuere ende vruchtbaer."

32. Occasionally, as in his first book, he calls the divine nature "the Oneness of the Persons" *(Eenicheyt der Persone)*. This Oneness is both enjoy-

ing in essence/being and active and fruitful in giving birth to the eternal Wisdom (*Rijcke*, I, 72). Although Ruusbroec's vocabulary sometimes fluctuates, his meaning is usually clear.

33. *Rijcke*, I, 84.

34. *Rijcke*, I, 72.

35. *Boecsken*, 330–36 (my emphasis). Compare *Tabernakel*, II, 34, on the remaining distinction between the Persons.

36. *The Divine Names*, 5.10 (825B), 103.

37. See, for instance, *Rijcke*, I, 72. Without wanting to detract from Ruusbroec's originality: was perhaps *The Divine Names* 2.3–5 a source of influence on this issue?

38. *Brulocht*, b 1996–2002.

39. *ST*, I, 27, 3, 4. This approach can be labeled "psychological" insofar as it has recourse to the created image—the processions of thinking and loving in the human person—to shed some light on the *revealed* mystery of the Trinity.

40. Bonaventure's Pseudo-Dionysian inspiration is evident in the following quotation, despite the appeal to Aristotle who had distinguished three ways of generation, by nature, by art (= by will), and by chance (in *Meta.* 1032a 12–13). Seeing that there is nothing fortuitous in God, Bonaventure argues that there exist only two perfect modes of emanation, *per modum naturae et voluntatis:* "Therefore, since the perfect production, emanation and germination is realized only through two intrinsic modes, namely, by way of nature and by way of will, that is, by way of the word and of love, therefore the highest perfection, fontality and fecundity necessarily demands two kinds of emanation with respect to the two hypostases which are produced and emanate from the first person as from the first producing principle. Therefore, it is necessary to affirm three persons." *Saint Bonaventure's Disputed Questions on the Mystery of the Trinity*, introduced and translated by Z. Hayes (New York: Franciscan Institute, 1979), 263. For Hughes Ripelin's influence on Ruusbroec: see K. Schepers, "Het *Compendium theologicae veritatis* van Hugo Ripelin van Straatsburg als bron voor Ruusbroec," *Ons Geestelijk Erf* 73 (1999): 131–49. For the doctrinal issues on which Ruusbroec seems more indebted to the Franciscan tradition, see my article "The Franciscan Inspiration."

41. Z. Hayes, Introduction to *Saint Bonaventure's Disputed Questions on the Trinity*, 45. Hayes has convincingly argued that the term "natural emanation" expresses an understanding of generation different from that of Augustine and Aquinas, both of whom prefer to speak of this as an emanation of the intellect. Bonaventure also sees the intellect involved, but the intellect precisely as intellect is not fecund; it is so only insofar as it springs from the fecund nature of God. Aquinas, on the other hand, explained the divine processions in terms of the processions within intellect and will. The idea of

the divine nature as the fruitful source of the Godhead, so prominent in the thought of Bonaventure, has disappeared almost entirely from Aquinas's *Summa*. As suggested earlier, the idea of the divine nature as fruitful ground of the Trinity was to reappear in Ruusbroec's doctrine.

42. *Brulocht,* c 127–30.

43. In the major extract quoted in chapter 2, pp. 61–67 Ruusbroec identifies "paternity" with the divine, fruitful nature.

44. See J. Neuner and J. Dupuis, *The Christian Faith in the Doctrinal Documents of the Catholic Church* (Bangalore: Theological Publications in India, 1996), no. 318; Denzinger-Schönmetzer no. 804.

45. *Brulocht,* c 127–30, already quoted; *Brulocht,* b 1410–12; *Vanden XII Beghinen,* 2b 41–44: "The nature of the Persons is fruitful, eternally active according to the mode of the Persons. For the Father generates his Son as another (Person) from his nature; and the Son is born from the Father as the eternal Wisdom of God, a distinct Person yet one in nature with the Father" (my trans.). Also, in *Brulocht* c 164–66, Ruusbroec writes that the Father gives all that he is and all that he has to the Son, with the sole exception of fatherhood, which he alone retains. This implies, of course, that fatherhood and nature are not synonymous.

46. *Brulocht,* b 2067–68.

47. *Tabernakel,* II, 151.

48. *Tabernakel,* II, 34. In *Spieghel,* 922, we read: "Nature is fruitful, paternity and Father" (my trans.). Seeing that the divine nature can only conceptually be distinguished from the divine essence/being in which the Persons flow back, Ruusbroec has no room for a Godhead "beyond" the three Persons, a view that is traditionally attributed to Meister Eckhart.

49. Z. Hayes, Introduction, 39. This position has the advantage that it is not faced with the problem that if the Persons are constituted by relations and if relation arises from procession, the first procession logically presupposes a Person who actively generates (which implies that the first Person is prior to the relation by which he is said to be constituted, etc.). Thomas Aquinas explicitly rejects this approach and holds that the positive reality of the divine Persons is exclusively their co-relations, that is, their personal characteristics. Only fatherhood constitutes the Father as a Person. Therefore, in the view of the angelic doctor, generation is an act of a Person who generates and it is therefore not this act which constitutes him as a Person: *quia Pater est, generat* (*ST,* I, 40, 4 *ad* 1). St. Bonaventure had argued that fatherhood presupposes the act of generation: the one who does not generate is not a Father: *ideo Pater quia generat.* Similarly, Bonaventure argues, if the power to beget does not inchoately constitute the Person of the Father but refers to the divine essence solely, the Father then has something of the divine essence that

the Son does not have. Aquinas, on the other hand, rejects any suggestion that the *potentia generandi* means a relation: if the Father were to beget by fatherhood he would produce another Father (for fatherhood is for the Father what an individual form is for any created individual). Therefore, says Aquinas, the expression "the power to beget" *(potentia generandi)* is comparable to the expression "the essence of the Father": power (and essence) are common to the three Persons, whereas the modifier "begetting" is proper to the Father (*ST,* I, 41, 5). Behind the divergence in these rather technical opinions lies a different understanding of unbegottenness. For Aquinas this concept is largely negative: it does not determine the Father's Personhood, it only means that the Father is not begotten (*ST,* I, 33, 4 *ad* 1). For Bonaventure (and for Ruusbroec) it has also a crucial positive sense: not having an origin means also being primary, it refers to the Father as the fullness of divine fecundity (*Brevil.,* I, 3, 7). The constitution of the Father, therefore, is understood in a less full and in a fuller sense corresponding to the negative pole of innascibility and the positive pole of fecundity and primacy.

50. A. Ampe, *Grondlijnen*, 158–59.

51. *Rijcke,* I, 60: "sien ende wedersien in eender vruchtbarigher natueren." See also the quotation at the beginning of this section.

52. *Brulocht,* b 1076–79.

53. *Vanden Kerstene Ghelove,* 77–91.

54. *Brulocht,* b 213; *Boecsken,* 379–80; *Spieghel,* 2119ff., *Rijcke,* I, 60.

55. Although Augustine never developed the analogy of mutual love between human persons, there are traces in his works that hint at the idea that Richard was to exploit, as Gonzalez has shown (e.g., *De Trin.* VI. §7, where it is said that the Holy Spirit is "something common to Father and Son, whatever it is, or is their very commonness or communion, consubstantial and coeternal. Call this friendship, if it helps, but a better word for it is charity." Further: "Non amplius quam tria sunt, unus diligens eum qui de illo est, unus diligens eum de quo est, et ipsa dilectio": "And therefore there are not more than three; one loving him who is from him, and one loving him from whom he is, and love itself." Translation by E. Hill, *The Works of Saint Augustine: The Trinity* 209–10. In *De Trin.* VIII.14 we find "Ecce tria sunt: amans et quod amatur et amor."

56. *De Trin.* III.19; translation from *Richard of St. Victor: The Twelve Patriarchs, The Mystical Ark, Book Three of the Trinity,* translation and introduction by G.A. Zinn, preface by J. Châtillon, Classics of Western Spirituality (New York: Paulist Press, 1979), 392.

57. *De Trin.* III.19. Latin text and French translation in G. Salet, *Richard de Saint Victor, La Trinité, SC* 63 (Paris, 1969), 210.

58. *De Trin.* V.19; *SC* 63, 350.

59. *De Trin.* V.18; *SC* 63, 348.

60. *De Trin.* V.20; *SC* 63, 352: "Oportet itaque absque dubio ut in summa simplicitate idem ipsum sit esse quod diligere. Erit ergo unicuique trium idem ipsum persona sua quod dilectio sua. . . . Quoniam ergo quaelibet persona, ut diximus, est idem quod amor suus et assignata singularum discretio constat in solis jam dictis tribus, sicut quartam proprietatem sic quartam personam nullatenus ibi invenire poterimus." As this citation makes clear, Richard uses this to argue for the impossibility of the thesis that there are more than three Persons in the divinity.

61. *De Trin.* V.18; *SC* 63, 348: "Quid itaque indebiti amoris possit eis rependere, a quibus constat eam omnem plenitudinem gratis accepisse? Et quoniam proprium est ipsius . . . de se procedentem non habere, non est in divinitate cui possit plenitudinem gratuiti amoris exhibere."

62. *Itiner.* 6.2: "If, therefore, you can behold with your mind's eye the purity of goodness, which is the pure act of a principle loving in charity with a love that is both free and due and a mixture of both, which is the fullest diffusion by way of nature and will, which is a diffusion by way of the Word, in which all things are said, and by way of Gift, in which other gifts are given, then you can see that through the highest communicability of the good, there must be a Trinity of Father and Son and Holy Spirit." Translation from *Bonaventure: The Soul's Journey into God, The Tree of Life, The Life of St. Francis*, translation and introduction by E. Cousins, Classics of Western Spirituality (New York: Paulist Press, 1978), 104.

63. Does this mean that Ruusbroec teaches that the Spirit is the originating principle of the Love between Father and Son? The notion of the Spirit as *principium diligendi* was rejected by Albert, Aquinas, and Bonaventure, and it is illuminating to investigate the latter's position to understand Ruusbroec's teaching, which does not deal with the problem explicitly. In a passage not dissimilar to the extract from Ruusbroec quoted earlier, Bonaventure writes: *Amor qui est Spiritus Sanctus non procedit a Patre in quantum amat se nec a Filio in quantum amat se, sed in quantum unus amat alterum, quia nexus est: ergo Spiritus Sanctus est amor, quo amans tendit in alium: ergo est amor et ab alio et in alium et ista duo complectuntur rationem processionis perfectae* (I *Sent.* d. 13, q. 1). Bonaventure, following Albert, rejects the idea that the Spirit is a bond in the active sense as though he joined Father and Son; rather it ought to be understood in the passive sense, namely, in the sense that he proceeds from each of them. There are therefore three ways to understand love: essential (when it refers to the divine essence, e.g., that love whereby God loves himself or creatures, or whereby one of the divine Persons loves the others); notional (this is the love by which the procession of the third Person becomes known); and personal (the Spirit is the end of a perfectly liberal act

of the will found in Father and Son). From this we can conclude that calling the Spirit the bond of love does not necessarily mean that he is the originating principle by which the Father and Son love each other; on the contrary, the Spirit proceeds from their mutual relation; he does not constitute it. Having said that, "once" the three Persons have been constituted, Ruusbroec (as distinguished from Bonaventure) attributes a special role to the Spirit as an active principle of *regiratio*.

64. *Tabernakel*, II, 98.

65. *Brulocht*, c 218–20, 234–38.

66. *Vanden XII Beghinen*, 2b 39–58.

67. P. Mommaers, "Introduction to *Boecsken der Verclaringhe*," *CCCM* 101, 41–42.

68. *Brulocht* b 2067–68; *Tabernakel*, II, 151; *Vanden XII Beghinen*, 2a 598; *Tabernakel*, II, 151.

69. *Tabernakel*, II, 34.

70. *Brulocht*, c 246–49: "For in this fathomless whirlpool of simplicity, all things are encompassed in enjoyable blessedness, whereas the ground itself remains totally uncomprehended unless it be by essential unity."

71. *Brevil.* I, 3, 8; *ST*, I, 34–35; Z. Hayes, Introduction to *Saint Bonaventure's Disputed Questions*, 51; *ST*, I, 34, 1, Blackfriars edition, vol. 7, edited by T.C. O'Brien, fn. a p. 24.

72. *Brulocht*, b 1069–79. A "personal" property or name is one that can only be applied to one of the three Persons, such as Word (to be applied exclusively to the Second Person). Other names are "appropriated"; that is, they are usually, although not exclusively, said of one Person. The Son is called "Wisdom," although, of course, the whole Trinity is "wise."

73. Compare among many other places *Rijcke*, I, 72; *Brulocht*, c 139–40; *Vanden XII Beghinen*, 2b 43; *Vanden XII Beghinen* 2a 598–99 ("The Father gives birth to his eternal Wisdom, that is his Son") to *Brulocht*, c 127–30 and b 1428–30: "For out of this same unity, the eternal Word is without cease born of the Father, and by means of this birth, the Father knows the Son and all things in the Son."

74. *Brulocht*, b 1049–51.

75. *Rijcke*, I, 60; *Brulocht*, 1076–77; *Vanden XII Beghinen*, 2a 610–12; *Tabernakel*, II, 34.

76. *Brulocht*, b 195–96; *Brulocht*, b 455–56; 942–44.

77. *Brulocht* b 1076–77: "and the Father and Son spirate one Spirit, which is the will, or love, of them both."

78. *Brulocht*, b 297–300.

79. J. Wiseman, "*Minne* in '*Die Gheestelike Brulocht*,'" in P. Mommaers and N. De Paepe, eds., *Jan Van Ruusbroec: The Sources, Content and Sequels of*

His Mysticism, Mediaevalia Lovaniensia, ser. 1, stud. 12 (Leuven: Leuven University Press, 1984), 96.

80. *Vanden Kerstenen Ghelove,* 72–93.
81. *Rijcke,* I, 60.
82. *Vanden XII Beghinen,* 2a 459ff.
83. *Boecsken,* 504–7 (modified trans.).

Chapter 4. "Made to the Image": Anthropology

1. For a helpful introduction to some of the following issues, see P. Verdeyen, "L'Anthropologie de Ruusbroec," *Ons Geestelijk Erf* 67 (1993): 53–56.
2. *Boecsken,* 341–48.
3. See chap. 3, pp. 91–93.
4. *Brulocht,* c 231–34.
5. *Vanden XII Beghinen,* 2a 619–21.
6. *Brulocht,* c 127–37.
7. *Rijcke,* I, 77.
8. *Vanden XII Beghinen,* 2a 45–285.
9. *Vanden XII Beghinen,* 2a 164–68 (my trans.).
10. *De Trin.* VII. §12: "when this image [the human person] is said in the other text [Gen. 1:26] to be "to the image," this is not said as though it meant "to the Son," who is the image equal to the Father; otherwise it would not have said *to our image* (Gn 1:26)." Translation by E. Hill, *St. Augustine: The Trinity,* 231. For a brief overview of the notion of the human person as image of God in the first twelve centuries, see B. McGinn, "The Human Person as Image of God, II, Western Christianity," in *Christian Spirituality: Origins to the Twelfth Century,* edited by B. McGinn, J. Meyendorff, and J. Leclercq (London: SCM Press, 1996), 312–30.
11. *Brulocht,* b 1626ff.
12. *Brulocht,* b 43–49.
13. *Brulocht,* b 50–58.
14. *Brulocht,* b 58–64.
15. *Brulocht,* b 71–78.
16. Ruusbroec only states that the third unity is supernaturally possessed by us, "when we are intent upon the praise of God and his honor in all our virtuous works, and rest in him above intention, and above ourselves, and above all things." This confirms one of the arguments of this study, that "resting" in God is based on our life in the Trinity from which our created life is inseparable and that this rest is essentially about being intent on God. *Brulocht,* b 83–90.
17. *Brulocht,* b 1626–35, translation modified, following Wiseman's translation, *John Ruusbroec,* 117.

18. For the passage referred to, see *Brulocht*, b 1637–40, and chap. 2, pp. 60–61.

19. *Brulocht*, b 1640–42.

20. *Brulocht*, b 1673–77.

21. *Brulocht*, b 1677–81.

22. *Brulocht*, b 1655–65.

23. *Brulocht* c 137–38. In the same context Ruusbroec identifies our ground and the Father's ground (*Brulocht* c 158–62).

24. *Brulocht*, b 48–49.

25. In *Brulocht*, b 53–55, Ruusbroec says that the active unity is "the same unity which is hanging in God, but in the latter instance we understand it as active and in the former as essential. Nevertheless, the spirit is totally within each unity, according to the entirety of its substance."

26. A. Ampe, *Schepping*, 86–104, 121–41; P. Mommaers, Introduction to *Die Geestelike Brulocht*, CCCM 103, 21.

27. P. A. Van de Walle, "Is Ruusbroec a Pantheist?" *Ons Geestelijk Erf* 12 (1938): 385.

28. *Vanden XII Beghinen*, 2a 567–74.

29. Pseudo-Dionysius, *The Divine Names*, 5.4 (817C), 98.

30. Pseudo-Dionysius, *The Divine Names*, 5.8 (824A), 101.

31. Pseudo-Dionysius, *The Divine Names*, 2.10 (648C), 65–66. See also 1.1 (588B), 50 ("the supra-essential being of God") and 1.5 (593C), 54.

32. It is important to note that Ruusbroec treats of this in a christological context.

33. *Spieghel*, 900–912 (my trans.).

34. *Brulocht*, b 1651–68.

35. *Spieghel*, 909–10.

36. *Spieghel*, 1849–51.

37. *Spieghel*, 939–50. Observe that Ruusbroec does not say that we receive the Father: only Son and Spirit are being sent. We can become one with the Father, but we cannot receive him the way we receive Son and Spirit.

38. *Rijcke*, I, 14–15. In chapter 6 I return to the issue of Ruusbroec's voluntarism.

39. *Rijcke*, I, 15, and I, 60.

40. *Brulocht*, b 2337: "Dese raste in haer selven en es gheene sonde, want si es in allen menschen van natueren, waert dat si hem ledighen consten."

41. *Rijcke*, I, 15.

42. *Vanden Vier Becoringhen*, 183–206 (trans. modified).

43. *Boecsken*, 90–96.

44. *Boecsken*, 134–35.

45. *Boecsken*, 92–95.

46. *Boecsken*, 139–43.

47. *Boecsken*, 80–158; *Vanden Vier Becoringhen*, 181–211; *Brulocht*, b 2303ff.
48. *Rijcke*, I, 15.
49. *Boecsken*, 543–49.
50. *Vanden XII Beghinen*, 2a 58–73 (my trans.).
51. *Brulocht*, b 1726–27: "And he receives grace and a likeness to God in the ground of his faculties."
52. *Vanden XII Beghinen*, 2b 2429–32, minor alterations.
53. *Vanden XII Beghinen* 2c 10–13, slight alterations.
54. *Vanden XII Beghinen*, 2a 540–56.
55. *Brulocht*, b 1731–45.
56. *Brulocht* b 1762–63: "God beholds the dwelling and resting-place which he has made with us and in us, that is the unity and the likeness."
57. I have developed this theme in much greater detail elsewhere. See my article "In the Image of God," Parts I and II.
58. *ST*, I, 93, 9.
59. See *Rijcke*, I, 10.
60. *ST*, I, 93, 7 *in corp.* and *ad* 3: "it is clear that memory, understanding and will are not three powers as stated in the *Sentences*."
61. Nevertheless, Bonaventure is also familiar with the more dynamic analogy Augustine proposed in *De Trinitate*, namely, that our act of knowing reflects the generation of the Word and that the procession of love as the mutual bond between memory and understanding reflects the procession of the Holy Spirit, but he could not draw out the full implications of this insight since he regarded the memory as a third faculty. He therefore concluded that the image is only actualized when the three faculties are centered on God. Only after Aquinas had made clear that Augustine did not regard the memory as a third faculty could he shift the perspective from the three supposed "faculties" to the two processions, as the locus of the image of the Trinity within the human person.
62. In *Boecsken*, 419, he calls the soul a "created image." In *Spieghel*, 1852, he calls the soul "image" in a secondary or derived sense. The passages in which he calls the Second Person Image and the soul only "to the Image" defy an attempt at enumeration.
63. *Rijcke*, I, 15.

Chapter 5. "He, remaining God, became man for man to become God": Russbroec's Christology

1. On this notion, see chap. 3, pp. 93–96.
2. *Vanden XII Beghinen*, 2a 321–38 (my trans.).

3. *Vanden XII Beghinen,* English 2a 301.
4. A. Ampe, *Grondlijnen,* 61, fn 24.
5. *Rijcke,* I, 31.
6. *Vanden XII Beghinen,* 2a 11–12.
7. *Vanden XII Beghinen,* 2b 2383ff.
8. *Vanden XII Beghinen:* "Nochtan moechdi merken, dat niet in hem selven en is noch goet noch quaet, noch salich noch onsalich, noch arme noch rike, noch god noch creatuere."
9. *Brulocht,* a 122–25: "Ende oec hevet de mensche een natuerlijc gront neyghen te gode overmids de vonke der zielen ende die overste redene, die altoes begheert dat goede ende haet dat quade."
10. See my article "The Franciscan Inspiration."
11. *Brulocht* a 195–97: "The reason why God became man was his incomprehensible love and the neediness of all men, for they were corrupted by the fall of original sin and they could not repair it."
12. A. Ampe, *Schepping,* 56–62; 248–58; B. Fraling, *Der Mensch,* 126–41.
13. *Vanden XII Beghinen,* 1, 357.
14. *Vanden XII Beghinen,* 1, 733–37 (my trans.).
15. *Vanden XII Beghinen,* 1, 352–54 (my trans.).
16. *Spieghel,* 1930–34, among many other places.
17. A. Ampe, *Schepping,* 253.
18. A. Ampe, *Schepping,* 58.
19. In *Athanasius and the Human Body* (Bristol: Bristol Press, 1990), 41, A. Pettersen develops a similar argument against J. N. D. Kelly: "If the human nature assumed by the Logos is seen as a universal in which all individual men and women participate, when the Logos suffuses the assumed humanity with his divinity, the divinizing force is communicated to all mankind, and the incarnation becomes, in effect, the redemption." As suggested earlier, the interpretation put forward here is far more in line with the tradition. Even the exponents of the so-called theory of physical redemption, such as St. Irenaeus and St. Athanasius, never argued that the incarnation effected a divinization of the human nature as such. Christ's physical body is that through which salvation is perfected and not a collective humanity in which all are saved. The theory of physical redemption does not imply that the incarnation effects a deification of human nature as such but that the union between Christ's flesh and ours makes possible the efficacy of Christ's redeeming work as a whole for our salvation.
20. *Tabernakel,* II, 114–15.
21. *Spieghel,* 1933–34.
22. *Vanden XII Beghinen,* 1, 352–54 (my trans.).
23. *Vanden XII Beghinen,* 1, 364–70 (my trans.).

24. *Spieghel*, 975–90 (my trans.).

25. *Tabernakel*, II, 114–15. In the passage immediately preceding this one Ruusbroec reiterates that in the incarnation "each nature remained in itself all it was, for the divinity could not become humanity, nor humanity divinity, but they were united in the divine Person of the Son"—a clear indication of the point made in the previous section that Ruusbroec does not hold that the incarnation effected an "ontological" or "physical" change in human nature.

26. *Brevil.* IV, 2; *ST*, III, 2. There are some minor divergences, for instance, in *Spieghel*, 1938–41, where Ruusbroec compares the union of two natures in Christ with the union of soul and body in man. This (traditional) comparison had been rejected by Thomas Aquinas because of the lack of perfection of soul and body when taken in separation from each other, whereas the divine and human natures are complete in themselves (*ST*, III, 2, 1).

27. *Spieghel*, 1990–96 (my trans.).

28. A. Ampe, *Schepping*, 224.

29. This is how J. Pelikan defines the orthodox view of "enhypostaton" as an interpretation of the hypostatic union in *The Christian Tradition: A History of the Development of Doctrine*, Vol. II, *The Spirit of Eastern Christendom (600–1700)* (Chicago: University of Chicago Press, 1974), 88–89.

30. *Tabernakel*, II, 110.

31. *Tabernakel*, II, 114.

32. *ST*, III, 2, 6 *ad* 1. Aquinas refers to St. Augustine's *De Diversis Quaestionibus 83*, q. 73.

33. A. Ampe, *Schepping*, 234.

34. *Boecsken*, 497–502.

35. *Brulocht*, b 1372 ff.

36. *Tabernakel*, II, 34.

37. *Vanden XII Beghinen*, 1, 367–70. Christ's habitual grace is the grace whereby he deifies humanity: "His humanity was filled with all God's gifts and with the fullness of sanctity. . . . [O]ur Lord's humanity alone received an undivided fullness of all gifts, with which he has filled all creatures and can fill them still further." (*Spieghel*, 1946–51).

38. *Vanden XII Beghinen*, 1, 350–61 (my trans.), 384–96 (my trans.).

39. *Vanden XII Beghinen*, 1, 384–96 (my trans.).

40. *Tabernakel*, II, 41.

41. *Brulocht*, b 1337–42. Emphasis added.

42. *Brulocht*, b 1377–90.

43. *Brulocht*, b 1353–58.

44. *Brulocht*, b 1394–97.

45. *Brulocht*, b 128–35: "Now the grace of God which flows out of God is an inward impulse or prodding of the Holy Spirit, who impels our spirit

from within and stokes it towards all virtues. This grace flows from within, and not from without. For God is more inwards to us than we are to ourselves, and this inward impulse, or working, within us, naturally or supernaturally, is nearer and more inner to us than our own work. And therefore God works in us from within outwards, and all creatures from without inwards." That the effects are felt from without inwards can be illustrated by the spiritual development of the human person in active, interior, and contemplative lives.

46. *Trappen*, III, 238. Again, this citation makes abundantly clear that man does not become God: only Christ is naturally united with the Word. An individual man can only attain this same union with God through divine grace, which is conferred to him through Christ, via the human nature Christ shares with the rest of humanity.

47. *Vanden Kerstenen Ghelove*, 116–35.
48. *Vanden XII Beghinen*, 2b 674.
49. *Trappen*, III, 259.
50. *Trappen*, III, 245.
51. *Trappen*, III, 246.
52. *Trappen*, III, 259.
53. *Rijcke*, I, 48.
54. *Brulocht*, b 1147–54.
55. See chap. 6, pp. 174–76.
56. *Trappen*, III, 256; and *Spieghel*, 45–50: "You must therefore live for, praise, love, serve, and intend his eternal glory rather than any reward, comfort, savor, consolation, or anything else which would accrue to you from such behavior, for genuine love does not seek its own advantage." Similarly, in *Vanden XII Beghinen*, 2c 698–701: "The one who loves is not a mercenary; he does not look for reward or profit but he loves because he loves. The more he receives, the poorer he is, for all God's gifts have to be returned" (my trans.).
57. See *Spieghel*, 721ff., 853ff.
58. *Spieghel*, 723–30.
59. *Spieghel*, 716–80.
60. *Rijcke*, I, 52.
61. *Rijcke*, I, 51.
62. *Rijcke*, I, 52.
63. *Spieghel*, 70–95 (my trans., following Wiseman).
64. *Spieghel*, 858–63.
65. *Spieghel*, 997–1000 (my trans.).
66. *Cur Deus Homo*, I, 8. The translation is from *Anselm of Canterbury: Trinity, Incarnation and Redemption*, edited and translated by J. Hopkins and H. Richardson (Toronto: Edwin Mellen Press, 1976), 58.

67. *Cur Deus Homo*, I, 15, p. 72.

68. *Cur Deus Homo*, II, 5, pp. 101–2: "He [= God] began this work for our sake and not for his own since he himself needs nothing. When he created man, he was not ignorant of what man was going to do. And, nevertheless, by creating man by his own goodness, he freely bound himself, as it were, to accomplish the good work which he had undertaken. . . . it is necessary that God's goodness—on account of its immutability—accomplish with man what it began, even though the entire good which it does is by grace." The latter remark seriously qualifies the so-called necessity of the incarnation that St. Anselm argues for.

69. Compare *ST,* III, 1, 1 *ad* 1: "The mystery of the incarnation involved no change in God's eternal state, but united him in a new way with what he created, or rather, united what he created with himself."

70. See J. Pelikan, *The Christian Tradition: A History of the Development of Doctrine*, Vol. III, *The Growth of Medieval Theology (600–1300)* (Chicago: University of Chicago Press, 1978), 143–45: "'Satisfaction,' then was another term for 'sacrifice,' and Christ's sacrificial act of penance made even human acts of satisfaction worthy, since of themselves they were not." See in this context Boso's second reply in I, 20, p. 86.

71. *De Civitate Dei*, X, 5, translated as *St. Augustine: The City of God* by H. Bettenson, introduced by J. O'Meara (Harmondsworth: Penguin Books, 1984).

72. *De Civitate Dei*, X, 6.

73. *De Civitate Dei*, X, 19.

74. *De Civitate Dei*, X, 20.

75. One example will suffice: "And it is not fitting that man, who by sinning so stole himself from God that he cannot remove himself to any greater extent, should by making satisfaction so give himself to God that he cannot give himself to any greater extent?" *Cur Deus Homo*, II, 11, pp. 112–13. This quotation suggests that "satisfaction" centers on restoring a relationship with God through the self-gift of Christ.

76. *Cur Deus Homo*, II, 18, p. 133.

77. St. Anselm's metaphor of the pearl (= humanity) illustrates this point (I, 19).

78. He who does not pay to God what he owes will not be able to be happy (I, 24, p. 94). See also I, 19.

79. Of course, there are other reasons why to forgive sin out of mercy alone would be unfitting: for instance, God would be dealing with sinner and nonsinner in the same way, which is unfitting: "this unfittingness is so extensive that it makes injustice resemble God, for as God is subject to no one's law, neither would injustice be" (I, 12, p. 69).

80. See II, 20, which states in a concluding fashion (p. 135): "We have discovered that God's mercy—which, when we were examining God's justice

and man's sin, seemed to you to perish—is so great and so harmonious with this justice that it cannot be conceived to be greater or more just."

81. In *Rijcke*, I, 50, we read that God feels great pity and compassion with poor sinners since he cannot bestow himself and his gifts on them because they do not want them, nor are they intent on them. Then God sends some calamities, grief, and sickness and others bliss, happiness, and recovery, to be recognized by them and make them consider their dependence. From this we learn that a divine fiat would be ineffective, for sin unables people to receive God and his grace. Love can only be freely given, not enforced.

82. *Vanden XII Beghinen*, 1, 374–75.

83. *Spieghel*, 861–63.

84. *Spieghel*, 1001–3.

85. *Brulocht*, a 19–36.

86. *Brulocht*, a 195–203.

87. Some instances illustrate this usage: Christ "wrought all his works for the honor and praise of his Father" (*Brulocht*, a 240–41); "the oblation of all his deeds for the honor of his Father" (*Brulocht*, a 259–60); "to honor God *(gode eere bieden)* with all one's works" (*Brulocht*, a 507–8).

88. *Trappen*, III, 328.

89. J. Pelikan, *The Christian Tradition*, III, 141. See also H. U. von Balthasar, *Theodrama: Theological Dramatic Theory*, Vol. IV, *The Action* (San Francisco: Ignatius Press, 1994), 254–61.

90. *Cur Deus Homo*, II, 14–15.

91. *Cur Deus Homo*, I, 11.

92. *Tabernakel*, II, 34.

93. *Trappen*, III, 256. Compare *Vanden XII Beghinen*, 1, 371–87: "My Father has sent me to live as God and man for everyone who longs for me. My dearest, consider, 'I am yours. I have lived for you, taught you and died for your sake. *With my death I have offered you to my Father and have paid your debt with my holy blood;* I am risen, glorified in soul and body so that you might rise in glory.... Consider what I did further: I have given you my Flesh and living Blood, as food and drink'" (my trans. and italics).

94. In *Vanden Seven Sloten*, 15–33, Ruusbroec admonishes the Poor Clare to consider how Christ, God's Son, humiliated himself and served sinners, and therefore she ought to obey and serve God with her whole heart and remember that it is an honor that God allows her to serve him.

95. *Trappen*, III, 255–56.

96. *Brulocht*, a 225–53.

97. *Brulocht*, a 254–75.

98. *Brulocht*, a 276–330.

99. *Tabernakel*, II, 115.

100. *Vanden XII Beghinen,* 1, 850–53 (my trans.). Compare *Vanden Seven Sloten,* 538–43: "Thus [= by detachment from creatures] we disrobe *(ontcleden)* ourselves, putting off the old man with his works and putting on the new, that is Jesus Christ. He clothes us with himself, with his life, his grace, and his affection. And when he has thus clothed *(gecleet)* us in his habit, with longing and with love, we live in him and he in us."

101. *Vanden XII Beghinen,* 2b, 1807 ff.

102. Especially in those passages where he contrasts the commandments to the counsels in the strict sense, such as *Vanden XII Beghinen,* 2b 1638, and *Tabernakel,* II, 178.

103. *Trappen,* III, 247–49, 249–51.

104. *Vanden XII Beginen,* 2b 2565: "syn leven dat es sine regule."

105. *Vanden XII Beginen,* 2b 1815–30.

106. *Vanden XII Beginen,* 2b 1831–1937.

107. *Vanden XII Beginen,* 2b 1920–24.

108. *Vanden XII Beginen,* 2b 1925–31.

109. *Vanden XII Beginen,* 2b 1938–51.

110. *Tabernakel,* II, 228–30; L. Moereels, *Ruusbroec en het Religieuze Leven,* 282–84.

111. *Vanden XII Beghinen,* 2b 1952 ff.

112. *Vanden XII Beghinen,* 2b 2051–60 (modified).

113. L. Moereels, *Ruusbroec en het Religieuze Leven,* 290. See also *Tabernakel,* II, 251: "the root of sin, namely self-will *(die wortele der sonden, dat es: sinen eighenen wille)."*

114. *Vanden XII Beghinen,* 2b 2115–26 (my trans.).

115. *Vanden XII Beghinen,* 2b 2086–90.

116. *Vanden XII Beghinen,* 1, 624 ff.

117. *Vanden XII Beghinen,* 2b 2132–34 (my trans.).

118. *Vanden Kerstenen Ghelove,* 89–135.

119. *Vanden Kerstenen Ghelove,* 97–99.

120. *Vanden Kerstenen Ghelove,* 103–6.

121. *Vanden Kerstenen Ghelove,* 119–21.

122. *Vanden Kerstenen Ghelove,* 121–25.

123. *Tabernakel,* II, 139.

124. *Brulocht,* a 405–9.

125. Cf. A. Ampe, *Genadeleer,* 30 n. 43, and *ST,* I, II, 114, 3, to which he refers.

126. *Tabernakel,* II, 135, 137.

127. *Tabernakel,* II, 230.

128. *Tabernakel,* II, 276.

129. *Tabernakel,* II, 137–38.

130. *Tabernakel*, II, 138.
131. *Tabernakel*, II, 135.
132. *Tabernakel*, II, 256.
133. *Tabernakel*, II, 299.
134. *Tabernakel*, II, 236.
135. *Tabernakel*, II, 237.
136. *Tabernakel*, II, 263–64.
137. *Tabernakel*, II, 264.
138. *Tabernakel*, II, 248–49.
139. L. Moereels, *Ruusbroec en het Religieuze Leven*, 336.
140. *Tabernakel*, II, 201; *Spieghel*, 69 ff.
141. *Tabernakel*, II, 255–56.
142. H.U. Von Balthasar, "The Mass, a Sacrifice of the Church?" in *Explorations in Theology*, Vol. III, *Creator Spirit* (San Francisco: Ignatius Press, 1993), 185–244; for this quotation, see p. 187.
143. *Vanden XII Beghinen*, 2c 1374–78 (my trans.).
144. *Vanden XII Beghinen*, 2c 1378–79. In *Tabernakel*, II, 253–54, Ruusbroec again refers to Mary in an explicit parallel with the Church (cf. *Tabernakel*, II, 255) as the one who made an exemplary offering to God, namely, by being humble (Lk 1:38) she was being raised by God (Lk 1:46ff.).
145. *Tabernakel*, II, 200–201.

Chapter 6. The Common Life: Deification according to Ruusbroec

1. *Brulocht*, a 83–84: "Want god wilt alle menschen behouden, ende niemenne verliesen."
2. *Brulocht*, a 108–13.
3. *Brulocht*, a 125–28.
4. *Brulocht*, a 141–42.
5. *Brulocht*, a 149–50: "Dese .ij. poente hanghen te gadere also, dat dat een niet volbracht en mach werden zonder dat ander."
6. *Brulocht*, a 155–61.
7. Ruusbroec distinguishes between worthiness and merit: "Then there comes the higher light of God's grace, just like a flash of sunlight, and is poured into the soul unmerited and undesired, according to (its) worthiness. For in this light, out of free goodness and generosity, God gives himself, whom no creature can merit before possessing him." *Brulocht*, a 138–42.
8. U.N.J. Notebaert, "La place du Christ dans le système mystique du Bienheureux Jan Van Ruusbroec l'Admirable" (Ph.D. dissertation, Catholic University of Leuven, 1938): "La conception de Ruusbroec révèle, en effet un

certain semi-pélagianisme courant chez un nombre de théologiens du Moyen-âge et auquel S. Thomas jeune, ne paraît pas avoir échappé" (p. 15).

9. *Boecsken*, 34–36.
10. *Boecsken*, 384–88.
11. *Boecsken*, 339–48.
12. *Boecsken*, 483–85, 70–72.
13. In *Boecsken*, 45ff, Ruusbroec describes the intermediary by which good people are united with God, namely, "the grace of God together with the sacraments of the Holy Church and the divine virtues of faith and hope and love and a virtuous life led according to God's commandments." He then goes on to criticize those who want to be (one with) God, without knowledge or love, disregarding "all the sacraments and all virtues and all practices of the Holy Church, for they think they have no need of them" (*Boecsken*, 103–5).
14. *Boecsken*, 424–25.
15. *Boecsken*, 438–46.
16. *Boecsken*, 446–54.
17. *Brulocht*, c 158–62, 171–73, 182–86.
18. *Brulocht*, c 181–82.
19. See chap. 2, pp. 60–61 and chap. 4, pp. 105–11; *Brulocht*, b 1637–44.
20. *Sloten*, 834–40 (modified).
21. *Sloten*, 840–49.
22. *Vanden XII Beghinen*, 2b 845–63.
23. *Brulocht*, c 197–200: "This is the mode above all modes, in which one goes out into a divine contemplation and into an eternal gazing, and in which one is transformed and transfigured into divine brightness. This going-out on the part of the contemplative person is also a loving one."
24. See chap. 3, II.4.
25. *Brulocht*, c 234–36.
26. *Brulocht*, c 237–38.
27. *Brulocht*, c 237–41.
28. See *Brulocht*, c 250–51.
29. *Sloten*, 690–99.
30. *Sloten*, 680–82.
31. *Steen*, 629–34.
32. Ruusbroec makes the observation that our immersion in God is "essential with habitual love." It continues "whether we are asleep or awake, whether we know it or not." It therefore does not deserve any reward (*Steen*, 603–7). This seems in plain contradiction to what he says in the quotation given in the main body of this text. I take this statement to mean that grace operates continually and habitually, but it requires a conscious response in knowledge and love.

33. *Steen*, 754–59.

34. *Steen*, 759–65.

35. *Steen*, 522–35 (my emphasis). See also *Boecsken*, 517 and 558, for the theme of being united with God in faith.

36. *Steen*, 621–28 (my emphasis).

37. *Tabernakel*, II, 354–55.

38. *Tabernakel*, II, 361; see also chap. 3, II.4.

39. See chap. 3, section II.4.

40. *Trappen*, III, 260–61.

41. *Trappen*, III, 268–69.

42. *Trappen*, III, 269.

43. *Steen*, 521–22.

44. *Vanden Vier Becoringhen*, 60–93.

45. *Vanden Vier Becoringhen*, 94–140.

46. *Vanden Vier Becoringhen*, 141–80.

47. *Vanden Vier Becoringhen*, 204–8.

48. *Vanden Vier Becoringhen*, 188–96. In his little exposition on the Creed we find the same idea. Commenting on the state of eternal bliss, he says: "[L]et no man deceive you with false idleness for our faith bears witness to what I tell you now, as do the holy Scriptures, for it is a truth eternal. We shall love and enjoy, work, and practice and possess rest, all in the same now, with no before or after." (*Vanden Kerstenen Ghelove*, 274–78.)

49. *Vanden Vier Becoringhen*, 51–54.

50. *Vanden Vier Becoringhen*, 292–94, 329–30, 39–40, 302–5.

51. *Vanden Vier Becoringhen*, 340–45.

52. In Modern Dutch the concept of *zich iets verbeelden* still carries connotations of "being under the illusion of" and "getting ideas into your head," etc. "Verbeeld je maar niets !" can be rendered as "Be under no illusion!"

53. *Brief* I, 30–32.

54. *Brief* I, 32–41.

55. *Brief* I, 47–49: "Ende soe worden si vermyddelt ende vergravet ende verbeeldet in sijn edel menschelike natuer, dat si nyet verheven en mochten werden in horen geest te beschouwen sijn hoge godlicke natuer."

56. *Brief* I, 52–56.

57. *Brief* I, 63–72.

58. *Brief* I, 75–86.

59. See *Sermo super Cantica Canticorum*, 84.1 (2:303.10–16), quoted and discussed by B. McGinn, *The Presence of God: A History of Western Christian Mysticism*, Vol. II, *The Growth of Western Mysticism, from Gregory the Great to the Twelfth Century* (London: SCM Press, 1994), 216–17.

60. *Steen*, 641–45.

61. *Steen*, 579–91.
62. *Brulocht*, b 1521–28.
63. *Brulocht*, b 1528–30.
64. *Brulocht*, b 1536–42.
65. *Brulocht*, b 1583–88.
66. *Brulocht*, b 1591–96.
67. *Steen*, 934–35: "And from this wealth derives the common life I promised to tell you about in the beginning."
68. *Steen*, 948–49.
69. *Steen*, 952–54.
70. *Sloten*, 826–30.
71. *Sloten*, 226–28.
72. *Sloten*, 237–44.
73. *Sloten*, 223–57.
74. *Sloten*, 228–30.
75. *Rijcke*, I, 70–71.
76. *Rijcke*, I, 51–52.
77. *Brulocht*, b 1273–80.
78. *Brulocht*, b 1282–84.
79. It is interesting to observe that "common" can also mean "ordinary, without special rank." The heretics claim for instance that the Mother of God was not a Virgin but *eenen ghemeynen wive,* an ordinary woman. *Vanden XII Beghinen,* 2a 271.
80. *Brulocht*, b 1085–95.
81. *Brulocht*, b 1147–51.
82. *Brief* II, *290–91, and *Brief* II, 74: "we neither know nor feel anything but naked love and imageless naked seeing into a divine light" *(bloete mynne ende ongebeelt bloet gesicht in godlicken licht).*
83. In the active life the lower unity is supernaturally enriched "by means of outward practice in perfect conduct after the manner of Christ and his saints, bearing the cross with Christ, subordinating (human) nature to the commandments of the Holy Church and to the teaching of the saints" (*Brulocht,* b 73–77). The second unity is enriched by the influx of grace and our willingness to practice all virtues according to the example of Christ (*Brulocht,* b 78–83), while the third is possessed supernaturally when we are intent on God in all our virtuous works "and rest in him above intention, and above ourselves, and above all things" (*Brulocht,* b 83–87). The third unity is "possessed" and not "enriched" as it is a participation beyond distinction in the divine life via our eternal idea in God.
84. These conditions are God's grace, a will freely turned to God, a conscience unstained by mortal sin (*Brulocht,* a 71–78). See pp. 158–60 above.

85. *Brulocht*, a 206–9.
86. *Brulocht*, a 207–16.
87. *Brulocht*, a 222–24.
88. *Brulocht*, a 235–52.
89. *Brulocht*, a 225–30.
90. *Brulocht*, a 254–63.
91. *Brulocht*, a 276–330.
92. *Brulocht*, a 339–41.
93. *Brulocht*, a 373–85.
94. A.W. D'Aygalliers, *Ruysbroeck the Admirable*, 2d ed. (Washington, D.C.: Kennikat Press, [1923] 1969) shares the widespread misunderstanding that the controversy focused on the question whether or not we can enjoy a face-to-face vision of God in this world (pp. 223–24). This opinion would have been rejected by John XXII and Dominicans alike. The controversy dealt with the time of the beatific vision after this life. He is therefore wrong in assuming that *Vanden Blinkenden Steen* was written as a corrective to *Die Brulocht*. Ruusbroec did not defend the (heretical) view that in this life we can see God face to face in either book. On this controversy, see S. Tugwell, *Human Immortality and the Redemption of Death* (London: Templegate, 1991).
95. *Brulocht*, a 455–66.
96. *Brulocht*, b 848–53 and 889–956.
97. *Brulocht*, a 971–75.
98. Cf. Hadewijch, *Vision* 1, no. 185.
99. *Brulocht*, a 1005–18.
100. *Brulocht*, b 1731–35.
101. *Brulocht*, b 115–18.
102. *Brulocht*, b 212–359; b 360–459; b 460–664; b 665–890.
103. *Brulocht*, b 589–91.
104. *Brulocht*, b 977–80.
105. *Brulocht*, b 983–1007.
106. *Brulocht*, b 1121–24 and b 1034–38.
107. *Brulocht*, b 1045–63. Important for our argument is that Ruusbroec writes: "These people need absolutely no revelations, nor (do they need) to be rapt above their senses, for their life and their dwelling and their converse and their (very) being is in the spirit, above senses and above sensibility, and there God shows these persons what he wishes, what is necessary for them and for others" (*Brulocht*, b 1017–22).
108. *Brulocht*, b 1128–31.
109. *Brulocht*, b 1142–51.
110. *Brulocht*, b 2112–13.
111. *Brulocht*, b 130–35; b 2118–20.

112. *Brulocht*, b 1469–90.

113. *Brulocht*, b 1528–30.

114. *Brulocht*, b 1532–77.

115. *Brulocht*, b 1591–96.

116. *Brulocht*, b 1597–98.

117. *Sloten*, 690–92: "For by the created light of God's grace we are elevated and enlightened (so as to be able) to contemplate in the uncreated light that is God himself." Similarly, in the second *Letter:* "In the created light of my grace I show you my light uncreated which I am myself" (*Brief* II, 54–55).

118. *Brulocht*, b 1982–91.

119. *Brulocht*, b 1969–82: "It has a fundamental natural and supernatural inclination towards the unfathomable being from which it has flowed forth. And the unity of the divine being is eternally drawing all likeness into its unity. And therefore the spirit sinks away from itself in enjoyment and floats away into God as into its eternal rest. . . . Nevertheless, we maintain the likeness eternally in the light of grace or of glory, where we possess ourselves as active in charity and virtues."

120. *Brulocht*, b 1996–2002.

121. *Brulocht*, b 2002–5.

122. See P. Mommaers and J. Van Bragt, *Mysticism Buddhist and Christian*. The authors seem blissfully unaware of the serious hermeneutical difficulties of applying a psychological theory of the twentieth century to medieval texts. I wrote a short review of the book in *Modern Theology* 13, no. 4 (1997): 547–48.

123. *Brulocht*, b 2279–80, b 2244–51. In *Brulocht*, c 98 and c 111, Ruusbroec says that we receive the coming of the Bridegroom without cease. See also *Steen*, 753–73, discussed earlier in this chapter.

124. *Spieghel*, 1062ff. Ruusbroec refers to 1 Cor 13:12 and Jn 1:5. He concludes: "In a special way the Lord of all gifts, Jesus Christ, through the power of his words, concealed and hid his flesh and blood from us in the blessed Sacrament, so that here on earth we would have to live amidst all his gifts with a firm faith rather than with a clear and glorious sight of them, for it is through a complete and integral faith that we will merit this eternal sight" (trans. by J. Wiseman, *John Ruusbroec*, 217–18).

125. See the quotation in the previous note. The theme of mutual witnessing has Augustinian roots. In allowing us to offer testimony or not to God, God allows us to judge ourselves. I am indebted to Lewis Ayres's "Augustine on God as Love and Love as God," *Pro Ecclesia* 6 (1997): 470–87.

126. *Brulocht*, c 135–38: "This eternal going-out, this eternal life which we have and are within God, eternally, without ourselves, is the cause of our created being in time. And our created being is suspended in the eternal

being, and, with respect to (its) essential being, it is one with it." See also *Brulocht*, c 171–77.

127. *Brulocht*, b 2535–46.

128. *Brulocht*, b1780–1817, b 2244–51.

129. Mommaers's reference to a passage from R. Musil clearly indicates that he interprets Ruusbroec's exposition as a psychological state of selfless consciousness in which the person no longer perceives a self (see P. Mommaers and J. Van Bragt, *Mysticism Buddhist and Christian*, chap. 3). Nevertheless, Ruusbroec quite explicitly rejects (*Brulocht*, b 2458–60) this sort of empty, passive states of consciousness.

130. *Brulocht*, b 1758–61: "all men and all spirits need an intermediary, for without the mediation of the grace of God and a loving, free conversion, no creature will be saved."

Conclusion

1. The main issues appear to be the following: the primacy of the Father within the Trinity; the fecundity of the divine nature (a remote Pseudo-Dionysian legacy); a more voluntarist focus than is usual in Thomistic circles; the view that memory, intellect, and will are three faculties; the distinction between vestige, image, and likeness; a distinct Franciscan focus on the humanity and life of Christ; the idea that the nothingness out of which we are made results in a deficiency of the will, a more Bonaventurean understanding of the justification of the sinner, and so forth. For a discussion of these issues, see my article "The Franciscan Inspiration."

2. See my article "Meister Eckhart and Jan van Ruusbroec: A Comparison."

BIBLIOGRAPHY

Editions of Ruusbroec's Works

Werken, Vol. I. Dat Rijcke der Ghelieven. Die Gheestelike Brulocht. Edited by J.B. Pouckens and L. Reypens. Mechelen: Het Kompas, 1932; 2d ed., Tielt: Lannoo, 1944.

Werken, Vol. II. Van den Gheesteliken Tabernakel. Edited by D.A Stracke. Mechelen: Het Kompas, 1934; 2d ed., Tielt, Lannoo, 1948.

Werken, Vol. III. Vanden Blinckenden Steen. Vanden Vier Becoringhen. Vanden Kerstenen Ghelove. Vanden VII Sloten. Een Spieghel der Eeuwigher Salicheit. Vanden VII Trappen. Dat Boecksen der Verclaringhe. Edited by L. Reypens and M. Schurmans. Mechelen: Het Kompas, 1934; 2d ed., Tielt: Lannoo, 1947.

Werken, Vol. IV. Vanden XII Beghinen. Edited by J. Van Mierlo, ed. Mechelen: Het Kompas, 1932; 2d ed., Tielt: Lannoo, 1948.

Boecsken der Verclaringhe. Opera Omnia I, *CCCM* 101. Edited by G. De Baere, translated into English by P. Crowley and H. Rolfson. Tielt: Lannoo-Brill, 1981.

Vanden Seven Sloten. Opera Omnia II, *CCCM* 102. Edited by G. De Baere, translated into English by H. Rolfson. Tielt: Lannoo-Brill, 1981.

Die Geestelike Brulocht. Opera Omnia III, *CCCM* 103. Edited by J. Alaerts, introduction by P. Mommaers, translated by H. Rolfson, directed by G. De Baere. Tielt: Lannoo-Brepols, 1987.

Vanden Blinkenden Steen. Vanden Vier Becoringhen. Vanden Kerstenen Ghelove. Brieven. Opera Omnia X, *CCCM* 110. Edited by G. De Baere, T. Mertens, and H. Noë, introduction by T. Mertens and P. Mommaers, translated into English by A. Lefevere. Tielt: Lannoo-Brepols, 1991.

Vanden XII Beghinen. Opera Omnia VII A, *CCCM* 107. Edited by M. M. Kors, translated into English by H. Rolfson. Tielt: Lannoo-Brepols, 2000.

Een Spieghel der Eeuwigher Salicheit, Opera Omnia, VIII, *CCCM* 108. Edited by G. De Baere, introduction by P. Mommaers, translated into English by A. Lefevere. Tielt: Lannoo-Brepols, 2001.

Translations into English
(apart from the English translation in the Opera Omnia, 6 Vols.)

John Ruusbroec: The Spiritual Espousals and Other Works. Introduced and translated by J. A. Wiseman, preface by L. Dupré. Classics of Western Spirituality. New York: Paulist Press, 1985.

The Spiritual Espousals. Translated by E. Colledge. Christian Classics. London: Faber and Faber, 1952.

Secondary Works Relating to Ruusbroec

Alaerts, J. "La terminologie 'essentielle' dans *Die Gheestelike Brulocht.*" *Ons Geestelijk Erf* 49 (1975): 248–330.

———. "La terminologie 'essentielle' dans *Die Gheestelike Brulocht* et *Dat Rijcke der Ghelieven*," *Ons Geestelijk Erf* 49 (1975): 337–65.

Ampe, A. "Bernardus en Ruusbroec." *Ons Geestelijk Erf* 27 (1953): 143–79.

———. "De Bestemmelinge van Ruusbroec's *Spieghel* en *Trappen.*" *Ons Geestelijk Erf* 45 (1971): 241–89.

———. *Kernproblemen uit de Leer van Ruusbroec.* Vol. I: *De Grondlijnen van Ruusbroec's Drieëenheidsleer als Onderbouw van den Zieleopgang.* Tielt: Lannoo, 1950.

———. Vol. II: *De Geestelijke Grondslagen van den Zieleopgang naar de Leer van Ruusbroec:* A. *Schepping en Christologie.* Tielt: Lannoo, 1951.

———. Vol. III: B. *Genadeleer.* Tielt: Lannoo, 1952.

———. Vol. IV: *De Mystieke Leer van Ruusbroec over den Zieleopgang.* Tielt: Lannoo, 1957.

———. "Orde en wanorde in Ruusbroec's *XII Beghinen.*" *Ons Geestelijk Erf* 19 (1945): 55–82.

———. *Ruusbroec: Traditie en Werkelijkheid.* Antwerpen: Ruusbroecgenootschap, Studiën en Tekstuitgaven van Ons Geestelijk Erf. Deel xix, 1975.

———. "La théologie mystique de l'ascension de l'âme selon le bienheureux Jean de Ruusbroec." *Revue d'Ascétique et de Mystique* 36 (1960): 188–201, 303–22.

Axters, S. *Geschiedenis van de vroomheid in de Nederlanden*. 4 vols. Antwerpen: De Sikkel, 1950–60. See especially Vol. II: *De Eeuw van Ruusbroec*. Antwerpen: De Sikkel, 1953, 213–91.

———. "Hadewijch als voorloopster van de zalige Jan Van Ruusbroec." In *Dr. Reypens Album*, edited by A. Ampe, 57–74. Antwerpen: Ruusbroecgenootschap, 1964.

Beuken, W. H. *Ruusbroec de Wonderbare*. 's Gravenhage: Martinus Nijhoff, 1981.

Bos, E. P., and G. Warnar. *Een claer verlicht man. Over het leven en werk van Jan Van Ruusbroec (1293–1381)*. Middeleeuwse Studies en Bronnen 38. Hilversum: Verloren, 1993.

Bras, K. *Mint de Minne: Eros en Agape bij Jan van Ruusbroec*. Kampen: Kok, 1993.

Colledge, E., and J. C. Marler. "'Poverty of Will': Ruusbroec, Eckhart and 'The Mirror of Simple Souls.'" In *Jan Van Ruusbroec: The Sources, Content, and Sequels of His Mysticism*, edited by P. Mommaers and N. De Paepe, 14–47. Mediaevalia Lovaniensis, ser. 1, stud. 12. Leuven: Leuven University Press, 1984.

D'Asbeck, Melline. *La mystique de Ruysbroeck l'Admirable: Un echo du Neoplatonisme au XIV siècle*. Paris: Librairie E. Leroux, 1930.

D'Aygalliers, A. W. *Ruysbroeck the Admirable*. 2d ed. Washington, D.C.: Kennikat Press, [1923] 1969.

De Baere, G. "De ontplooing van Ruusbroec's mystieke terminologie in de 'Brulocht,'" In *Siet, de brudegom comt: Facetten van Die Geestelike Brulocht van Jan Van Ruusbroec (1293–1381)*, edited by T. Mertens, 21–36. Kampen: Uitgeverij Kok, 1995.

Deblaere, A. "Essentiel (superessentiel, suressentiel)." *Dictionnaire de Spiritualité*, 4 part 2, col. 1346–66.

———. "Témoignage mystique chrétien." In *Mystique dans le Christianisme et les autres réligions. Studia Missionalia* 27 (1977): 117–48. An English translation, "Christian Mystic Testimony," is available in *Ons Geestelijk Erf* 72 (1998): 129–53.

Dupré, L. *The Common Life: The Origins of Trinitarian Mysticism and Its Development by Jan Van Ruusbroec*. New York: Crossroads, 1984.

Epiney-Burgard, G. "L'Influence des béguines sur Ruusbroec." In *Jan Van Ruusbroec: The Sources, Content, and Sequels of His Mysticism*, edited by P. Mommaers and N. De Paepe, 68–85. Mediaevalia Lovaniensis, ser. 1, stud. 12. Leuven: Leuven University Press, 1984.

Faesen, R. "Jan van Ruusbroec in Beijing," Part I. *Ons Geestelijk Erf* 72 (1998): 203–16.

Faesen, R., with G. De Baere. "Jan van Ruusbroec in Beijing," Part II. *Ons Geestelijk Erf* 73 (1999): 73–91.

Feys, J. "Ruusbroec and His False Mystics." *Ons Geestelijk Erf* 65 (1991): 108–24.

Fraling, B. *Der Mensch vor dem Geheimnis Gottes: Untersuchungen zur geistlichen Lehre des Jan van Ruusbroec.* Würzburg: Echter-Verlag, 1967.

Geraert van Saintes & Hendrik Utenbogaerde: De Twee Oudste Bronnen van het Leven van Jan Van Ruusbroec door zijn Getuigenissen Bevestigd. Translated by the Benedictine nuns of Bonheiden. Mystieke Teksten met Commentaar, no. 4. Brugge: Uitgeverij Tabor, 1981.

Gubbels, J. "Dat gevuelt in u, dat ghi in Christo Jhesu gevuelt. Een onderzoek naar de Christusbeleving in 'Die Gheestelike Brulocht' van Jan van Ruusbroec." Doctoral thesis, Tilburg, 1979.

Henry, P. "La mystique trinitaire du bienheureux Jean Ruusbroec." *Recherches de Science Réligieuse* 39–40 (1951–52): 335–68, 41 (1953): 51–75.

Hoenen, J. F. M. "'Een godlec ghevoelen dat boven redene es': Jan Van Ruusbroec en Albertus Magnus: Mystiek en filosofie." In *Een claer verlicht man: Over het leven en werk van Jan Van Ruusbroec (1293–1381)*, edited by E. P. Bos and G. Warnar, 47–58. Middeleeuwse Studies en Bronnen 38. Hilversum: Verloren, 1993.

Moereels, L. *Ruusbroec en het Religieuze Leven: Kleine Summa van het Geestelijk Leven.* Tielt: Lannoo, 1962.

Mommaers, P. *The Land Within: The Process of Possessing and Being Possessed by God according to the Mystic Jan Van Ruysbroeck.* Chicago: Franciscan Herald Press, 1975.

———. "De natuurlijke weg naar binnen." In *Siet, de brudegom comt: Facetten van Die Geestelike Brulocht van Jan Van Ruusbroec (1293–1381)*, edited by T. Mertens, 37–48. Kampen: Uitgeverij Kok, 1995.

———. "Une phrase clef des Noces Spirituelles." In *Jan Van Ruusbroec: The Sources, Content, and Sequels of His Mysticism*, edited by P. Mommaers and N. De Paepe, 100–123. Mediaevalia Lovaniensis, ser. 1, stud. 12. Leuven: Leuven University Press, 1984.

Mommaers, P., and N. De Paepe, eds. *Jan Van Ruusbroec: The Sources, Content, and Sequels of His Mysticism.* Mediaevalia Lovaniensis, ser. 1, stud. 12. Leuven: Leuven University Press, 1984.

Mommaers, P., and J. Van Bragt. *Mysticism Buddhist and Christian: Encounters with Jan Van Ruusbroec.* New York: Crossroads, 1995.

Notebaert, U. N. J. "La place du Christ dans le système mystique du Bienheureux Jan Van Ruusbroec l'Admirable." Ph. D. dissertation, Catholic University of Leuven, 1938.

Reynaert, J. "Ruusbroec en Hadewijch." *Ons Geestelijk Erf* 55 (1981): 193–233.

Reypens, L. "Het toppunt der beschouwing voor Ruusbroec." *Ons Geestelijk Erf* 5 (1931): 429-35.

———. "Ruusbroec en Juan de la Cruz: Hun overeenstemming omtrent het toppunt der beschouwing." *Ons Geestelijk Erf* 5 (1931): 143-85.

———. "Ruusbroec's Mystieke Leer." In *Jan Van Ruusbroec, Leven, Werken*, edited by Ruusbroecgenootschap, 1-25. Mechelen and Amsterdam: Het Kompas and De Spieghel, 1931.

———. "Ruusbroec's mystiel als bekroning der inkeeringstheorie." *Ons Geestelijk Erf* 6 (1932): 257-81.

———. "Ruusbroecstudiën: I, Het mystieke 'gherinen.'" *Ons Geestelijk Erf* 12 (1938): 158-86.

———. "Ruusbroecstudiën: II, Natuurlijke en bovennatuurlijke schouwing." *Ons Geestelijk Erf* 12 (1938): 392-411.

Ruh, K. "Jan van Ruusbroec." In *Geschichte der abendländischen Mystik*, Band IV: *Die niederländische Mystik des 14. bis 16. Jahrhunderts*, 26-82. München: C.H. Beck, 1999.

Schepers, K. "Het *Compendium theologicae veritatis* van Hugo Ripelin van Straatsburg als bron voor Ruusbroec." *Ons Geestelijk Erf* 73 (1999): 131-49.

Underhill, E. *Mysticism: A Study in the Nature and Development of Man's Spiritual Consciousness*. London: Methuen, 1911.

———. *Ruysbroeck*. London: G. Bell, 1915.

Van Cranenburgh, H. "Gerechtigheid in de geschriften van Jan van Ruusbroec." *Ons Geestelijk Erf* 67 (1993): 34-52. Part II appeared in *Ons Geestelijk Erf* 68 (1994): 8-29.

Van de Walle, A. "Is Ruusbroec a Pantheist?" *Ons Geestelijk Erf* 12 (1938): 359-91, 13 (1939): 66-105.

Van Mierlo, J. "Over het onstaan der Germaansche Mystiek." *Ons Geestelijk Erf* 1 (1927): 11-37.

———. "Ruusbroec's bestrijding van de ketterij." *Ons Geestelijk Erf* 6 (1932): 304-46.

Van Nieuwenhove, R. "The Franciscan Inspiration of Ruusbroec's Mystical Theology: Ruusbroec in Dialogue with Bonaventure and Thomas Aquinas." *Ons Geestelijk Erf* 75 (2001): 102-15.

———. "In the Image of God: The Trinitarian Anthropology of St. Bonaventure, St. Thomas Aquinas and the Blessed Jan van Ruusbroec," Parts I and II. *Irish Theological Quarterly* 66 (2001): 109-23, 227-37.

———. "Meister Eckhart and Jan van Ruusbroec: A Comparison." *Medieval Philosophy and Theology* 7 (1998): 157-94.

———. "Neoplatonism, *Regiratio* and Trinitarian Theology: A Look at Ruusbroec." *Hermathena* 169 (2001): 169-88.

———. "Ruusbroec: Apophatic Theologian or Phenomenologist of the Mystical Experience?" *Journal of Religion* 80 (2000): 83–105.

Verdeyen, P. "L'Anthropologie de Ruusbroec." *Ons Geestelijk Erf* 67 (1993): 53–65.

———. "Hoe zijn Bernardus en Willem aanwezig in de 'Brulocht'?" In *Siet, de brudegom comt: Facetten van Die Geestelike Brulocht van Jan Van Ruusbroec (1293–1381)*, edited by T. Mertens, 9–20. Kampen: Uitgeverij Kok, 1995.

———. "De invloed van Willem van St Thierry op Hadewijch en Ruusbroec." *Ons Geestelijk Erf* 51 (1977): 3–19.

———. "Oordeel van Ruusbroec over de rechtgelovigheid van Margaretha Porete." *Ons Geestelijk Erf* 66 (1992): 188–96.

———. *Ruusbroec en zijn mystiek*. Leuven: Davidsfonds, 1981.

Warnar, G. "De chronologie van Jan van Ruusbroec's Werken." *Ons Geestelijk Erf* 68 (1994): 185–99.

———. "Meester Eckhart, Walter van Holland en Jan van Ruusbroec: Historische en literaire betrekkingen in de Middelnederlandse mystiek." *Ons Geestelijk Erf* 69 (1995): 3–25.

Wiseman, J. "Minne in 'Die Gheestelike Brulocht' of Jan Van Ruusbroec." Ph.D. dissertation, Catholic University of America, 1979.

———. "*Minne* in *Die Gheestelike Brulocht*." In *Jan Van Ruusbroec: The Sources, Content, and Sequels of His Mysticism*, edited by P. Mommaers and N. De Paepe, 86–99. Mediaevalia Lovaniensis, ser. 1, stud. 12. Leuven: Leuven University Press, 1984.

Zhang, Xianglong. "The Meeting in Ruusbroec's Spiritual Espousals." *Ons Geestelijk Erf* 72 (1998): 154–63.

Works Relating to Other Authors and to Theology and Spirituality Generally

Alston, W. "God and Religious Experience." In *Philosophy of Religion*, edited by B. Davies, 65–69. London: Cassell, 1998.

———. *Perceiving God: The Epistemology of Religious Experience*. Ithaca: Cornell University Press.

Ayres, L. "Augustine on God as Love and Love as God." *Pro Ecclesia* 6 (1997): 470–87.

———. "'Remember that you are Catholic' (*serm.* 52,2): Augustine on the Unity of the Triune God." *Journal of Early Christian Studies* 8 (2000): 39–82.

Bartelink, G.J.M. "Gregorius over de vita mixta." In *Voordrachten over De Heilige Gregorius de Grote, met een keuze uit zijn werken*, edited by E. Dekkers and

G. Bartelink, 91–102. Monastieke Cahiers 31. Bonheiden, Belgium: Abdij Bethlehem, 1986.
Bell, D.N. *The Image and Likeness: The Augustinian Spirituality of William of St. Thierry.* Kalamazoo: Cistercian Publications, 1984.
Catry, P. "Amour du monde et amour de Dieu chez saint Grégoire le Grand." *Studia Monastica* 15 (1973): 253–75.
———. "L'Amour du prochain chez saint Grégoire le Grand." *Studia Monastica* 20 (1978): 287–344.
———. "Désir et amour de Dieu chez saint Grégoire le Grand." *Recherches Augustiniennes* 10 (1975): 271–303.
Cognet, L. *Introduction aux Mystiques Rhéno-flamands.* Paris: Desclée, 1968.
Davies, O. *God within: The Mystical Tradition of Northern Europe.* Foreword by R. Williams. London: Darton, Longman and Todd, 1988.
———. *Meister Eckhart, Mystical Theologian.* London: SPCK, 1991.
Decorte, J. "De finaliteit van de natuur." In *Thomas over Goed en Kwaad*, edited by R. Re Velde, 90–106. Baarn: Ambo, 1993.
———. *Waarheid als Weg: Beknopte Geschiedenis van de Middeleeuwse Wijsbegeerte.* Kampen and Kapellen: Kok Agora and Pelckmans, 1992.
De Ganck, R. *Beatrice of Nazareth in Her Context.* Kalamazoo: Cistercian Publications, 1991.
Emery, G. *La Trinité Créatrice: Trinité et création dans les commentaires aux Sentences de Thomas d'Aquin et de ses précurseurs Albert le Grand et Bonaventure.* Paris: Librairie J. Vrin, 1995.
Ennis, H.J. "The Place of Love in the Theological System of St. Bonaventure in General." In *S. Bonaventura, 1274–1974*, Vol. IV: *Theologica*, edited by G. Bougerol, 129–45. Grottaferrata: Collegio S. Bonaventura, 1974.
Hart, C. *Hadewijch: The Complete Works.* Classics of Western Spirituality. Ramsey, N.J.: Paulist Press, 1980.
Heine, R. *Perfection in the Virtuous Life: A Study in the Relationship between Edification and Polemical Theology in Gregory of Nyassa's* De Vita Moysis. Philadelphia: Patristic Foundation, 1975.
James, W. *The Varieties of Religious Experience: A Study in Human Nature.* Harmondsworth: Penguin Books, 1985.
Kelly, J.N.D. *Early Christian Doctrines.* London: A. & C. Black, 1989.
Lerner, R.E. *The Heresy of the Free Spirit in the Later Middle Ages.* Berkeley: University of California Press, 1972.
Libera, A. de. *La mystique rhénane d'Albert le Grand à Maître Eckhart.* Paris: Editions du Seuil, 1994.
Lievens, R. "Lezenderwijs." *Handelingen* 35 (1981): 192–200.
Lossky, V. *The Mystical Theology of the Eastern Church.* Cambridge: Clarke & Co., 1991.

Louth, A. *Denys the Areopagite.* London: Chapman, 1989.

———. *The Origins of the Christian Mystical Tradition: From Plato to Denys.* Oxford: Clarendon Press, 1981.

McGinn, B. "The Human Person as Image of God, II: Western Christianity." In *Christian Spirituality: Origins to the Twelfth Century,* edited by B. McGinn, J. Meyendorff, and J. Leclercq, 312–30. London: SCM Press, 1966.

———. *The Mystical Thought of Meister Eckhart: The Man from Whom God Hid Nothing.* New York: Herder and Herder, 2001.

———. *The Presence of God: A History of Western Christian Mysticism.* Vol. I: *The Foundations of Mysticism. Origins to the Fifth Century.* London: SCM Press, 1991.

———. Vol. II: *The Growth of Western Mysticism: From Gregory the Great to the Twelfth Century.* London: SCM Press, 1994.

———. Vol. III: *The Flowering of Mysticism: Men and Women in the New Mysticism, 1200–1350.* New York: Crossroads, 1998.

McGinn, B., with J. Meyendorff and J. Leclercq, eds. *Christian Spirituality: Origins to the Twelfth Century.* London: SCM Press, 1996.

Merriell, D.J. *To the Image of the Trinity: A Study in the Development of Aquinas' Teaching.* Studies and Texts, 96. Toronto: Ponitifical Institute of Mediaeval Studies, 1990.

Mommaers, P. *Hadewijch, Schrijfster, Begijn, Mystica.* Averbode: Altiora, 1989.

Neuner, J., and J. Dupuis. *The Christian Faith in the Doctrinal Documents of the Catholic Church.* Bangalore: Theological Publications in India, 1996.

Nicholas, D. *The Evolution of the Medieval World: Society, Government and Thought in Europe, 312–1500.* London: Longman, 1992.

O'Donovan, O. "Usus and fruitio in Augustine, *De Doctrina christiana* 1." *Journal of Theological Studies* 33 (1982): 361–97.

Orcibal, J. *Saint Jean de la Croix et les mystiques rhéno-flamands.* Paris: Desclée de Brouwer, 1966.

O'Rourke, F. *Pseudo-Dionysius and the Metaphysics of Aquinas.* Leiden: E.J. Brill, 1992.

Palhoriès, F. *Saint Bonaventure.* Paris: Librairie Bloud, 1913.

Pelikan, J. *The Christian Tradition: A History of the Development of Doctrine.* Vol. I: *The Emergence of the Catholic Tradition (100–600).* Chicago: University of Chicago Press, 1971.

———. Vol. II: *The Spirit of Eastern Christendom (600–1700).* Chicago: University of Chicago Press, 1974.

———. Vol. III: *The Growth of Medieval Theology (600–1300).* Chicago: University of Chicago Press, 1978.

———. Vol. IV: *Reformation of Church and Dogma (1300–1700).* Chicago: University of Chicago Press, 1983.

Pettersen, A. *Athanasius and the Human Body.* Bristol: Bristol Press, 1990.
Porion, J. B. *Hadewijch: Lettres spirituelles.* Traduction du moyen-néerlandais. Geneva: Martingay, 1972.
Rahner, K. "Ignatian Mysticism of Joy in the World." In *Theological Investigations,* Vol. III: *The Theology of the Spiritual Life,* edited by K. Kruger and B. Kruger, 277–93. London: Darton, Longman and Todd, 1967.
Raitt, J., with B. McGinn and J. Meyendorff, eds. *Christian Spirituality.* Vol. II: *High Middle Ages and Reformation.* London: SCM Press, 1989.
Ruh, K. *Geschichte der abendländischen Mystik.* Band I: *Die Grundlegung durch die Kirchenväter und die Mönchtheologie des 12. Jahrhunderts.* München: C. H. Beck, 1990.
———. Band II: *Frauenmystik und Franziskanische Mystik der Frühzeit.* München: C. H. Beck, 1993.
———. Band III: *Die Mystik des deutschen Predigerordens und ihre Grundlegung durch die Hochscholastik.* München: C. H. Beck, 1996.
———. Band IV: *Die niederländische Mystik des 14. bis 16. Jahrhunderts.* München: C. H. Beck, 1999.
Schütz, U. "Experience of God Today?" *Monastic Studies* 9 (1972): 7–22.
Steel, C. "Over de oorzaak van het kwaad." In *Thomas over Goed en Kwaad,* edited by R. Te Velde, 123–43. Baarn: Ambo, 1993.
Tobin, P. *Meister Eckhart. Thought and Language.* Philadelphia: University of Pennsylvania Press, 1986.
Tugwell, S. *Human Immortality and the Redemption of Death.* London: Templegate 1991.
Turner, D. *The Darkness of God: A Study in the Negativity of Christian Mysticism.* Cambridge: Cambridge University Press, 1995.
Van Beeck, F. J. *God Encountered: A Contemporary Catholic Systematic Theology,* Vol. II.1: *The Revelation of the Glory, Introduction and Part I: Fundamental Theology.* Minneapolis: Liturgical Press, 1993.
Verdeyen, P. "Un theologien de l'experience." *SC* no. 380. Paris: Editions du Cerf, 1992.
Von Balthasar, H. U. "Action and Contemplation." In *Explorations in Theology,* Vol. I: *The Word Made Flesh,* 227–40. San Francisco: Ignatius Press, 1989.
———. "The Mass, a Sacrifice of the Church?" In *Explorations in Theology,* Vol. III: *Creator Spirit,* 185–244. San Francisco: Ignatius Press, 1993.
———. *Theodrama: Theological Dramatic Theory.* Vol. IV: *The Action.* San Francisco: Ignatius Press, 1994. See especially pp. 231–65.
Wéber, E. H. *Dialogue et Dissensions entre Saint Bonaventure et Saint Thomas d'Aquin à Paris (1252–1273).* Paris: Librairie J. Vrin, 1974.
———. "La Théologie de la grâce chez Eckhart." *Revue des Sciences Réligieuses* 70 (1996): 48–72.

Editions and Translations of Other Authors Referred to in the Text

Anselm of Canterbury: Trinity, Incarnation and Redemption. Edited and translated by J. Hopkins and H. Richardson. Toronto: Edwin Mellen Press, 1976.

Aquinas, Thomas. *Summa Contra Gentiles.* Translated in 4 Vols. by A. Pegis, J. Anderson, V.J. Bourke, and C.J. O'Neill. Notre Dame: University of Notre Dame Press, 1975.

———. *Summa Theologica.* Translated in 5 Vols. by Fathers of the English Dominican Province. Westminster, Md.: Christian Classics, 1981.

Augustine, St. *City of God.* Translated by H. Bettenson, introduction by J. O'Meara. Harmondsworth: Penguin Books, 1984.

———. *Confessiones.* Edited by M. Skutella, revised by L. Verheijen. *CCSL* 27. Turnhout: Brepols, 1981.

———. *Confessions.* Translation and introduction by H. Chadwick. Oxford: Oxford University Press, 1992.

———. *Faith Hope and Charity (Enchiridion de Fide, Spe et Caritate).* Translated and annotated by L.A. Arand. Ancient Christian Writers. The Works of the Fathers in Translation. New York: Newmann Press, 1947.

———. *De Trinitate.* Edited by W.J. Mountain. *CCSL* 50. Turnhout: Brepols, 1968.

———. *The Works of St. Augustine: The Trinity.* Translation and introduction by E. Hill. A Translation for the 21st Century, Part I Books, Vol. 5. New York: New City Press, 1994.

Bonaventure, St. *Bonaventure: The Soul's Journey into God. The Tree of Life. The Life of St. Francis.* Translation and introduction by E. Cousins, preface by I. Brady. Classics of Western Spirituality. New York: Paulist Press, 1978.

———. *Doctoris Seraphici S. Bonaventurae opera omnia.* Edita studio et cura pp. Collegii a S. Bonaventura, ad plurimos codices mss. emendata, anecdotis aucta, prolegomenis scholiis notisque illustrata. X volumina. Quaracchi: Collegium S. Bonaventurae, 1882–1902.

———. *Saint Bonaventure: Breviloquium.* Texte latin de Quaracchi et traduction française. 8 Vols. Bibliothèque Bonaventuriennes, Série Textes. Paris: Editions Franciscaines, 1966–67.

———. *Saint Bonaventure: Le Christ Maître.* Edition, traduction et commentaire du sermon universitaire "Unus est magister noster Christus" par G. Madec. Paris: Bibliothèque des Textes Philosophiques, Librairie J. Vrin, 1990.

———. *St. Bonaventure's Disputed Questions on the Mystery of the Trinity.* Translation and introduction by Z. Hayes. New York: Franciscan Institute, St. Bonaventure University, 1979.

———. *The Works of St. Bonaventure.* 5 vols. Translated by J. De Vinck. Paterson, N.J.: St Anthony Guild Press, 1960–70.

Devotio Moderna. Basic Writings. Translation and introduction by J. Van Engen, preface by H. A. Oberman. Classics of Western Spirituality. New York: Paulist Press, 1988.

Eckhart, Meister. *The Essential Sermons, Commentaries, Treatises, and Defense.* Translation and introduction by E. Colledge and B. McGinn, preface by H. Smith. Classics of Western Spirituality. New York: Paulist Press, 1981.

———. *Master Eckhart: Parisian Questions and Prologues.* Translation and introduction by A. Maurer. Toronto: Pontifical Institute of Medieval Studies, 1974.

———. *Meister Eckhart: Die deutschen und lateinische Werke.* Herausgegeben im Auftrage der Deutschen Forschungsgemeinschaft. Stuttgart: W. Kohlhammer, 1936–.

———. *Meister Eckhart: Sermons and Treatises.* 2 Vols. Translated and edited by M. O.'C. Walshe. Shaftesbury: Element Books, 1991.

———. *Meister Eckhart: Teacher and Preacher.* Edited by B. McGinn, with the collaboration of F. Tobin and E. Borgstadt, preface by K. Northcott. Classics of Western Spirituality. New York: Paulist Press, 1986.

Gregory of Nyssa. *The Life of Moses.* Translation and introduction by A. J. Malherbe and E. Ferguson, preface by J. Meyendorff. Classics of Western Spirituality. New York: Paulist Press, 1978.

Hadewijch. *Brieven.* 2 Vols. Tekst en commentaar. Edited by J. Van Mierlo. Antwerpen: Standaard, 1947.

———. *The Complete Works.* Translation and introduction by Mother Columba Hart, preface by P. Mommaers. Classics of Western Spirituality. New York: Paulist Press, 1980.

———. *Visioenen.* 2 Vols. Edited by J. Van Mierlo. Leuven: Vlaamsch Boekenhalle, 1924–25.

Pseudo-Dionysius. *The Complete Works.* Translation by C. Luibheid and P. Rorem; introduction by J. Pelikan, J. Leclercq, and K. Froelich; preface by R. Roques. Classics of Western Spirituality. New York: Paulist Press, 1987.

Richard of St. Victor. *La Trinité.* Translated into French by G. Salet. *SC* 63.

———. *The Twelve Patriarchs. The Mystical Ark. Book Three of The Trinity.* Translation and introduction by G. A. Zinn, preface by J. Châtillon. Classics of Western Spirituality. New York: Paulist Press, 1979.

William of St. Thierry. *De contemplando Deo.* Critical edition by J. Hourlier, *Guillaume de Saint-Thierry: La contemplation de Dieu. SC* 61.

———. *Expositio super Cantica Canticorum.* Critical edition by J. M. Déchanet, *Exposé sur le Cantiques des Cantiques. SC* 82.

———. *Meditativae Orationes. PL* 180, 205–48.

INDEX

active life, 18, 22, 61, 67, 135, 148, 161, 179, 181–85
Alaerts, J., 4, 52
Albert the Great, 77, 78–79
Alston, W., 32
Ampe, A., 3–4, 87–89, 107–8, 123, 125–26
analogy, 42–44, 163. *See* likeness
angels, 17–22
Anselm, St., 136, 140–42
anthropology, 89, 97, 101–20, 178–81, 195
apophaticism, 29, 34–37, 55, 71, 74, 103, 168–70, 176
appropriation, 215n.72
Aquinas. *See* Thomas Aquinas
attachment, 67–70, 172, 188. *See* detachment; self-transcendence
Augustine, St., 1, 2, 35, 50, 58, 65, 78, 84, 91, 101, 103–4, 135, 141–42, 145, 155, 172, 183, 190, 194, 195
—Rule of, 8, 10
autotheism, 70

Balthasar, H. U. von, 155
beatific vision, 184
Beatrice of Nazareth, 14
beguines, 14, 25
Benedict XII, 184
Bernard of Clairvaux, 1, 34, 37, 174
birth of Son in soul, 37
Boendale, J., 12
Bonaventure, St., 1, 3, 23, 35. 50, 84, 91, 92, 93, 94, 97, 117–18, 129, 195, 231n.1
bonum sui diffusivum, 84, 91
Brabant, 10, 13, 15
Brethren of Free Spirit, 13, 57, 70–76, 87, 122, 124, 170, 193
Brother Gerard, 7–8, 23, 24, 25
Buddhism, 2

Carthusians, 8, 16, 160
cataphaticism, 34
Christ, 15, 19–21, 68–69, 123–36, 139–56, 178–80, 182–85, 189,

Christ (*cont.*)
    194. *See also* Word; Image; Son; sacrifice; God; priesthood
christology, 121–22, 124–55, 178–80
Church, 15, 31, 57, 70, 72, 93, 98, 105, 133, 135, 141, 150, 151, 154–55, 183
circulatio completa, 79
Cistercians, 1, 14, 35, 174
common life, 5, 21, 22, 24, 51, 62, 64–65, 73–75, 99, 120, 158, 160–80, 187–91, 194
common man. *See* common life
condilectio, 94
consciousness, 36–37
contemplative life, 20, 24, 61, 63, 133–35, 148, 160–70, 173, 187–91
Coudenberg, Frank van, 7, 8
Council of Vienne, 13,
creation, 18, 33, 35, 60, 85, 86, 93, 102–3, 162–63
—and evil, 122–24
creed, 127, 129, 151

De Baere, G., 4
Deblaere, A., 4
deification, 55, 56, 72, 74, 75, 98, 116–19, 125–27, 131, 134, 147, 160–70, 171, 177, 188. *See also* union with God; self-transcendence; common life; transformation of the soul
detachment, 46, 65, 66, 76, 149, 191. *See also* self-transcendence; intent on God
Devotio Moderna, 27, 121, 147. *See also* Geert Grote
dilectio, 94
divine being. *See* essence
divine nature. *See* God
divine touch, 19, 62, 164, 175–76, 186–87

Dominicans, 1, 13
Dupré, L., 55

Eckhart, Meister, 1, 32, 34, 35, 37, 71, 77, 196
—on detachment, 46–47
—on *regiratio*, 81–82
—and Ruusbroec, 231n. 2
emanation, 92, 93. *See also* processions
emptiness, 41–42, 72–73
enhypostasization, 121, 24–32
enjoyment, 65–66, 74, 75, 85, 87, 99, 161–62. *See also* rest
epektasis, 39, 160, 174–77, 187, 190
essence, divine, 55, 59–60, 84–91, 95–97, 114–15, 136, 162–63, 166, 188. *See also* modelessness
essence, human, 107–11
essential unity. *See* ground of the soul
eucharist, 25, 84, 124, 125, 133–34, 138–40, 189
Eunomius, 38
evil. *See* sin
excessus, 69, 84, 85, 168–70
exemplarism, 57–61, 75, 101–20, 174, 195
experience, 3, 5, 71–74, 164
—general critique of, 29–38; 48, 187–91
—in Gregory of Nyssa, 38–41
—and passivity, 72–73, 190
—in Ruusbroec, 41–46, 52–57, 112, 161, 166, 170–74, 187–91, 193–95
—*See also* James, W.
exitus, 80

faculties, 17, 20–21, 42, 104–20, 111, 117–19, 161, 167–68, 172, 176, 185–86, 188, 191, 194
faith, 70

Father, 84, 96–97, 131–32, 136, 142–46, 154, 182–83, 186
—fruitfulness of, 84, 87–93
—primacy of, 84
fecunditas naturalis. *See* God, fruitfulness of nature
Feys, J., 53
Flanders, 10, 13
Flemish Primitives, 14, 198n.12
Fraling, B., 3, 125
Frank van Coudenberg. *See* Coudenberg
Franciscans, 4, 13, 183
Free Spirit. *See* Brethren of Free Spirit
frui, 65, 75, 194. *See* enjoyment, intent

Geert Grote, 9, 23, 25, 27, 147,
generation. *See* Son
Geraert van Saintes, 7
Gerson, J., 9
gherinen. *See* divine touch
gifts of the Spirit, 17–23, 84, 95, 98, 137. *See* grace
God.
—fruitfulness of nature, 19, 50, 87–93, 95, 96, 187
—immutability, 140–41
—infinite nature, 38, 84
—*See also* Trinity; Father; Son; Image; Spirit; processions; transcendence
grace, 26, 58, 70, 72, 73, 113–17, 125, 132–39, 143, 153, 158–60, 161, 166, 175, 181–87. *See also* gifts of the Spirit
Gregory of Nyssa, 37–41, 174–75
Groenendaal, 7, 9, 10
Grote. *See* Geert Grote
ground of the soul, 59–61, 104–15.

See also unity of spirit; anthropology

Hadewijch, 77
Hayes, Z., 93
Henricus Pomerius, 7–9, 23, 25
Hinckaert, J., 9
hope, 70
Hughes Ripelin of Strasbourg, 91, 196
hypostatic union, 124–32

idleness. *See* rest
Image (as Word): 20, 23, 25, 44, 57–61, 82, 97, 102–20, 125–27, 132–33, 157, 162, 166, 178–80
image of God (soul), 89, 102–20, 124, 178. *See also* exemplarism; union with God
image as intermediary, 41, 68–70, 149, 167, 171, 174, 177
imageless, 41, 71, 149–50, 163–64, 171–74, 177
incarnation, 47, 84, 125–30, 135, 143, 182, 183
indistinction, 58–61, 105, 117, 160–70, 173, 174–75, 177, 178–80, 188, 190
inner life, 22, 61–62, 133–35, 161, 185–87
intellect, 111, 117–18. *See also* faculties
intent on God, intention, 5, 61, 63–66, 71–72, 134, 151, 157, 170–74, 177, 179, 188, 190

James, W., 30, 75
—problems with Jamesian approach, 2, 29–37; 45–57, 167, 181, 188–91, 193–95
—*See also* experience, union with God
John XXII, 184

Index 247

John of the Cross, 32, 34, 35, 41, 46, 62, 190
Jordaens, W., 23, 24, 25, 27, 136
Julian of Norwich, 34
justification, 158–60

likeness, 43, 44, 115–17, 124, 164
love as *do ut des*, 94, 98–99, 122, 135–38, 145–46, 187, 195
—essential love, 164–65
—as Spirit, 78, 84, 93–96, 97–98, 195
—as virtue, 70, 150–51

Mary, 18, 74, 155
McGinn, B.
—critique of Turner, 34–35
—on experience, 36
memory, 71, 111–12, 117–18. *See also* faculties
merit, 151–52, 158–60, 225n.7
Mertens, T., 4
meyninghe. *See* intent
Minne. *See* love
mirror, of the soul, 109–11, 163
modelessness, 55, 69, 85–92, 163–66
modes, 69, 76. *See also* modelessness
Moereels, L., 4, 150
Mommaers, P., 4, 45, 53, 57, 189–91
Moses, 24, 38–40, 153
motus circularis. *See regiratio*
mystical theology, 1, 2
—and experience, 3
—nature of, 3, 33–48
—*See also* apophaticism; indistinction; self-transcendence

natural way, 17, 19, 31, 41–42, 59, 70–76, 102, 111–20
nature, divine. *See* God

negative theology. *See* apophaticism
Neoplatonism, 3–4, 78, 84, 86, 90, 101
—and hierarchy of being, 33–34
—and mystical language, 33
—and vocabulary in Ruusbroec, 51–53, 59–60
—*See also* Pseudo-Dionysius; apophaticism; *regiratio*; indistinction; modelessness

oxymoron, 103

per modum natura. *See* God, fruitfulness of nature
per modum voluntatis. *See* Spirit, spiration of
perichoresis, 5, 83
plague, 12–13
Plotinus, 88
Pomerius. *See* Henricus Pomerius
Porion, J., 77
prayer, 72
priesthood
—of believers, 153
—of Christ, 152–55
processions, 84, 88–96, 102, 137
Pseudo-Dionysius, 1, 3, 23, 25, 33, 35, 37, 50, 58, 59, 79, 84, 85, 86, 90, 101, 108, 195

quaternity, 88
quietism, 65, 67, 70, 87, 111–15, 124, 167, 170–72, 177

Rahner, K. 47
redemption, 124–28, 133, 135–56, 219n.19
regiratio, 20; 50ff., 77, 98, 111, 118, 136–38, 161, 166, 195
—in Albert the Great, 78–79

—in Eckhart, 81–82
—*motus circularis,* 91
—in Ruusbroec, 82–86, 90, 95
—in Thomas Aquinas, 80–81
Régnon, T. de, 3
renunciation. *See* self-transcendence
rest, 64, 66, 72, 74, 84, 85, 87–91, 95, 138, 187–91
Richard of St. Victor, 50, 51, 77, 78, 92, 94

sacraments, 17, 57, 70, 76, 133, 138–39, 151, 158, 183
sacrifice, 139–46
—participation in Christ's, 147–56, 157
satisfaction, theory of, 139–46
Schepers, K., 26
Schillebeeckx, E., 140
self, 67–74, 190–91. *See also* self-transcendence
self-abnegation. *See* self-transcendence
self-centeredness, 56, 67–70, 194. *See also* self-transcendence
self-transcendence, 56, 61, 67–70, 128–29, 140, 147–56, 164–65, 171, 177, 187, 194
similitude. *See* likeness
sin, 115–20, 122–24, 144, 150, 153, 154, 155, 158–60
Son, 78
—generation of, 20, 84, 86, 91–93, 97, 163, 165, 174, 212n. 49
—*See also* Word; Christ; Image
soul, 17–23, 102–20. *See also* union with God; mirror of the soul; faculties; natural way; deification; ground of the soul
spark of the soul, 159

Spirit, 26, 78, 84, 93–99, 114–15, 132, 146, 151, 155, 186, 214n.63
—spiration of, 86–96, 165–66, 174
—*See also* love; gifts of
stillness. *See* love, essential
supernatural way, 17, 18
Surius, 26, 27, 50, 51, 123, 130, 136

Tertullian, 141
theocentric focus. *See* intent
Thomas Aquinas, St., 4, 56, 63, 66, 77, 80–81, 91, 97, 117–18, 129, 195
transcendence of God, 33–34, 38, 42, 43–44, 47, 58–61
transformation of the soul, 5, 18, 19, 22, 23, 24, 40, 41, 42, 46–48, 131, 147, 150–53, 157, 161, 164–65, 174, 177, 182, 186. *See also* natural way; supernatural way; experience; union with God; deification; self-transcendence
Trinity, 21, 22, 49–51, 63–66, 71, 102–20, 143, 151, 161, 165, 186
—activity, 5, 64, 85, 95, 157, 165, 169, 177
—in Albert the Great, 78–79
—enjoyment, 5, 85, 95, 157, 165, 169, 177
—in Gregory of Nyssa, 38
—participation in, 17, 44, 68–69, 86, 157, 165–70, 177, 180, 194, 195
—three moments in Ruusbroec, 84, 90, 95, 112, 169, 178–80, 195
—*See also* Father; Image; Word; Spirit; God; divine nature; essence; love
Turner, D. 33–37, 46–47, 49, 55, 57, 63, 71, 189

union with God, 2, 4, 18–22, 24, 25, 33, 42, 43, 44, 54–57, 60, 160–70, 177, 187–91
—and experience, 56, 71, 166–67
—*See also* Trinity, participation in
unity of the spirit, 102–20, 161, 176, 185–87
usus. See uti
uti, 65, 75, 194

Van de Walle, P., 108
Van Eyck, Jan, 14, 198n.12
Van Mierlo, J., 123
Van Schoohoven, Jan, 8
Victorines, 1
virtues, 17, 22, 111, 133, 168, 178, 182, 185

vis spiralis, 78
voluntarism, 176

Warnar, G., 9
ways. *See* modes
wesen. See essence
will, 111, 117–18, 124, 158–60. *See also* faculties
Willaert, F., 4
Wisdom. *See* Word
Wiseman, J., 130
Word, 20, 97, 102–11, 129–32, 135, 142, 146, 156, 186. *See also* incarnation; Son; Christ; Image
works, 73

Zonien Forest, 7

ABOUT THE AUTHOR

RIK VAN NIEUWENHOVE is a lecturer in theology at the School of Hebrew, Biblical, and Theological Studies, Trinity College, Dublin, Ireland.

www.ingramcontent.com/pod-product-compliance
Lightning Source LLC
Chambersburg PA
CBHW060115170426
43198CB00010B/907